AF291807

THE BIRTH OF BRITISH SPECIAL FORCES

THE BIRTH OF BRITISH SPECIAL FORCES:
HOW THE GUARDS REGIMENTS HELPED FORGE THE SAS, COMMANDOS AND PARAS

Charles Richard Trumpess

FONTHILL

First published in Great Britain in 2026 by
Fonthill
An imprint of
Pen & Sword Books Ltd
Yorkshire – Philadelphia

Typeset by Simon and Sons ITES Services Pvt. Ltd., Chennai, India.
Printed and bound in the UK by CPI Group (UK) Ltd, Croydon, CR0 4YY

The Publisher's authorised representative in the EU for product
safety isAuthorised Rep Compliance Ltd., Ground Floor,
71 Lower Baggot Street, Dublin D02 P593, Ireland.
www.arccompliance.com

For a complete list of Pen & Sword titles please contact

PEN & SWORD BOOKS LIMITED
47 Church Street, Barnsley, South Yorkshire, S70 2AS, England
E-mail: enquiries@pen-and-sword.co.uk
Website: www.pen-and-sword.co.uk
or
PEN AND SWORD BOOKS
1950 Lawrence Road, Havertown, PA 19083, USA
E-mail: uspen-and-sword@casematepublishers.com
Website: www.penandswordbooks.com

Foreword:
The Genesis of
the Commando Idea

The roots of the British Army commandos stretch back to earlier conflicts, notably the Boer War of 1899–1902. During this South African conflict, the British faced Boer commandos, highly mobile and skilled irregular units, who were adept at hit-and-run tactics. Their ability to strike swiftly, often behind enemy lines, left a deep impression on British military thought. This Boer War experience influenced the development of small, elite forces capable of unconventional warfare. However, it was not until the start of the Second World War that elements within the British Army started to develop ideas of 'irregular' warfare.

Formation of the Independent Companies

In April 1940, eleven independent companies were formed, mainly from volunteers from the Territorial Army. Initially raised by the War Office and commanded by Brigadier C. Gubbins for guerrilla warfare operations in Norway, these companies were the nascent seeds from which the now-famous British Army commandos would spring.[1]

Birth of the Commando Units

Under the guidance of forward-thinking officers like Lieutenant Colonel Dudley Clarke, General John Dill and Major (later Major General) Robert Laycock, the independent companies began evolving into more structured and purposeful commando units. As Chief of the Imperial General Staff (CIGS), General Dill provided crucial support for developing these specialised forces, recognising their potential for disruption and innovation.

Robert Laycock, an astute and experienced officer with a keen understanding of unconventional warfare, played a pivotal role in shaping the commandos. His leadership and strategic acumen contributed significantly to the organisation and training of these elite troops.[2]

Training and Reorganisation

Among other key figures, Bill Stirling emerged as a driving force behind the rigorous training programs that honed the commandos' skills. Stirling and his cohorts prepared these soldiers for the high-stakes operations that lay ahead through demanding physical conditioning, weapons training and specialised tactics.

The formation and reorganisation of commando units demanded a meticulous approach. Their training encompassed various terrains and exercises, ensuring soldiers were physically fit and capable of adapting to changing circumstances while on operations, a hallmark of the commando ethos.[3]

Early Operations and Layforce

Remarkably, just nineteen days after the unit's formation, the commandos launched their first operation against the coast of enemy-occupied Europe. Unsurprisingly, these early operations were small-scale and amateurish affairs. Nevertheless, the commandos were gaining valuable experience.[4]

In 1941, Layforce, an ad hoc unit comprising commandos and other specialists under Robert Laycock's command, was dispatched to the Middle East. Initially, Layforce was tasked with carrying out raids against German lines of communication along the North African coast. However, the commandos soon found themselves diverted to support the evacuation of Crete and the defence of Tobruk.

Disbandment and Evolution

By August 1941, having been misused by the Desert Army, Layforce was disbanded. Yet, from the ashes of Layforce, a new unit emerged. Fired by a belief in the possibilities of unconventional warfare, former commandos like David Stirling coalesced to form L Detachment, Special Air Service (SAS) Brigade.

The political context surrounding the formation of army commandos involved debates over resource allocation and the role of specialised forces vis-à-vis traditional infantry units. Some opposed diverting resources to elite forces, arguing for a focus on bolstering conventional army formations.

Legacy and Opposition

Political and military opposition to the formation of special forces persisted, echoing concerns over resource allocation and the potential dilution of regular army units. However, the successes and prowess demonstrated by the commandos in their early operations gradually diminished such opposition, solidifying their place in Britain's military strategy.

The birth and evolution of the British Army commandos from 1940 to 1942 was marked by visionary leadership, strategic insight, and the relentless determination of key personalities. Their innovative spirit laid the groundwork for future special forces and underscored the crucial role of elite units in modern warfare.

Acknowledgements

This work would not have been possible without the assistance and resources provided by numerous institutions and individuals who maintain vital historical records and preserve our military heritage.

The Imperial War Museum provided access to personal papers and firsthand accounts that illustrated individual experiences of military service. The National Archives supplied war diaries and official reports that documented training, operational planning and execution. The Churchill Archives Centre granted access to the personal papers of Ralph Bagnold, founder of the Long Range Desert Group. The Liddell Hart Centre for Military Archives at King's College London provided access to Robert Laycock's personal papers, offering insight into commando recruitment, operations and leadership.

Peter Connelly of the East Surrey Museum sourced images of the Guards Depot in Caterham, offering a glimpse of 'Little Sparta' during the war years. Airborne Assault Ltd sourced photographs of various aspects of the start of the Parachute Regiment.

The ParaData website and archive proved an excellent resource for finding information on recruitment, training and early airborne operations. Both the Imperial War Museum and ParaData provided access to recordings of interviews with veterans, offering firsthand accounts that proved invaluable for understanding the lived experience of special-forces personnel. The British Newspaper Archive provided access to contemporary press reports that documented public reaction and media coverage of military operations.

Grateful acknowledgement must be made to the numerous authors, historians and memoirists whose published works informed this study. Their detailed research and personal accounts, listed in the bibliography, provided essential context and analysis. The cumulative scholarship of military historians and the candid memoirs of veterans created the foundation upon which this research was built.

Finally, this book is dedicated to my partner, Amanda Campbell, whose unwavering love and support sustained this project through countless weekends spent in archives and museums, as well as the many evenings devoted to writing. Her understanding, patience and encouragement were essential in ensuring the completion of this book.

Contents

Abbreviations

BEF	British Expeditionary Force
CIGS	Chief of the Imperial General Staff
C-in-C	Commander-in-Chief
CTC	combined training centre
DCO	Director of Combined Operations
DSO	distinguished service order
GHQ	general headquarters
GOC	general officer commanding
GSC	general service corps
IWM	Imperial War Museum
LCA	landing craft, assault
LRDG	Long Range Desert Group
NCO	non-commissioned officer
OCTU	officer cadet training unit
RAF	Royal Air Force
RSM	regimental sergeant major
SAS	Special Air Service
SS	Special Service
WOSB	War Office Selection Board

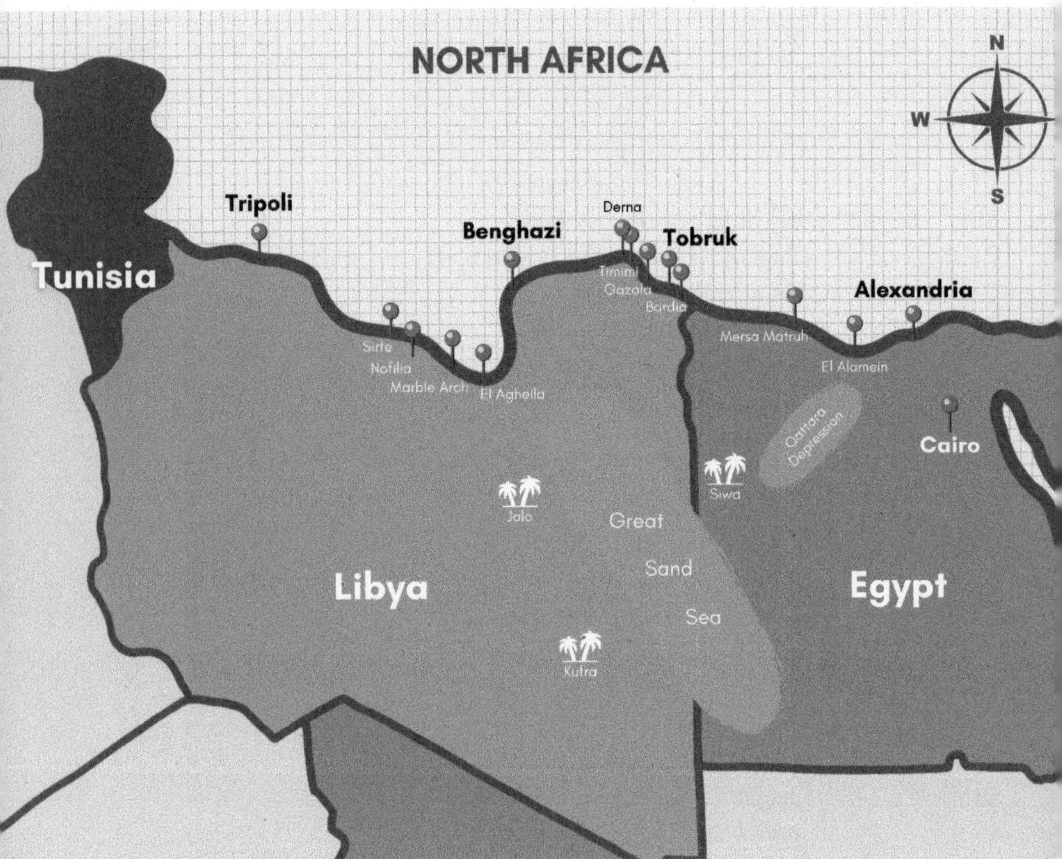
NORTH AFRICA
N
W
S
Tunisia
Tripoli
Benghazi
Derna
Tobruk
Trmimi
Gazala
Bardia
Alexandria
Sirte
Mersa Matruh
Nofilia
El Alamein
Marble Arch
El Agheila
Qattara Depression
Cairo
Siwa
Jalo
Great
Sand
Sea
Libya
Egypt
Kufra

Introduction

On 5 May 1980 one of Britain's most secretive military units, the Special Air Service (SAS), burst into public awareness. On 30 April six Iranian terrorists took control of the Iranian embassy at Prince's Gate in London's Knightsbridge. For six days, the world watched as members of the Metropolitan Police successfully negotiated the release of three hostages. It appeared that a peaceful resolution to the 'Iranian Embassy Siege' might be possible. On the sixth day of the siege, at around 19.00hrs, shots were fired inside the embassy, and the body of cultural attaché Abbas Lavasani was dumped outside. What happened next astonished the watching world.

In the preceding days, the counter-terrorism wing of the SAS had carefully prepared and rehearsed its strike plan: Operation Nimrod. At 19.07hrs, Deputy Assistant Commissioner John Dallow, Metropolitan Police, handed over control of the siege to the SAS. Fifteen minutes later, and broadcast live on television, the heavily armed assault teams launched their carefully coordinated attack. Abseiling down the rear of the building and clambering across balconies at the front, shaped explosive charges blew out doors and windows to accelerate ingress into the embassy at multiple points.

Next, as the SAS teams swept into the building, stun grenades were used to confuse and immobilise the occupants temporarily. Floor by floor, the SAS troops systematically cleared the building, killing the gunmen and releasing the hostages. By 19.40hrs, it was all over. Five terrorists were dead, and one was in custody. Regrettably, one hostage was killed and two were wounded during the assault, but nineteen people were rescued. The SAS, almost unheard of before the siege, was now famous.

In 1991 an SAS team was inserted deep behind enemy lines during Operation Desert Storm (17 January–28 February 1991). On 2 August 1990 Iraq, governed by the dictator Saddam Hussein, invaded and occupied neighbouring Kuwait. When Iraq failed to comply with a UN resolution demanding that it withdraw its forces from Kuwait, an international coalition of forty-two countries led by the United States commenced military action against it.

The SAS mission harked back to their origins of long-range reconnaissance and raiding operations in the deserts of North Africa. The SAS team, call sign Bravo Two Zero, was tasked with monitoring enemy movements, gathering intelligence, and locating and, if possible, destroying Iraqi mobile Scud missile launchers. However, the mission went badly wrong for the eight-man team.

After insertion by helicopter into the Iraqi interior, two members of Bravo Two Zero died of hypothermia, another was killed during a firefight with a local militia, and four members of the team were captured. After making an epic 190-mile trek to the Syrian border, Corporal Colin Armstrong was the only member of the team to evade capture. Later, two team members published their personal accounts of the disastrous patrol under the pen names of Chris Ryan (Corporal Colin Armstrong) and Andy McNab (Sergeant Steve Mitchell). McNab's book *Bravo Two Zero* (1993) and Chris Ryan's *The One That Got Away* (1995) became international bestsellers.

Fast-forward to 2025 and the SAS has become a brand in its own right, with its instantly recognisable winged dagger logo and marketing strapline, Who Dares Wins. The Goodreads book-review website lists over 170 SAS-related titles. There have been seven series of Channel 4's so-called 'reality TV' game show *SAS: Who Dares Wins*. At the time of writing, the BBC has just finished airing the second season of its historical drama *SAS: Rogue Heroes*, with a third series in the pipeline. Former SAS trooper Phil Campion is an author, public speaker and television personality with his own collection of merchandise sold on the UK veteran-owned and -operated Forces Wear website.

Not to be outdone, the film industry has also cashed in on the public's insatiable appetite for anything SAS-related, from big-budget Hollywood movies like *Patriot Games* (1992) and the British-New Zealand production *6 Days* (2017) to the low-budget comedy-horror flick *Dog Soldiers* (2002). Although hard to quantify, the SAS's reputation as one of the world's best special forces units means it has media and merchandise appeal to a broad audience, generating several significant income streams.

Ever since the SAS went crashing through the windows of the Iranian embassy, books about the 'original' founding members of the regiment have been published with a predictable regularity. The long shadows of David Stirling and Robert Blair 'Paddy' Mayne have left much of the true story of the formation of Britain's special forces hidden in the shade. Readers of this book might be surprised to learn that the common ancestor of the army commandos, the Special Air Service, the Special Boat Service and the Parachute Regiment was that bastion of tradition and ceremony, the Household Division. Britain's special forces also had two fathers who nursed them into the world and guided their growth and development. Unlike David Stirling and Paddy Mayne, their stars have faded from the firmament of public interest and imagination.

Major General Sir Robert 'Bob' Laycock was born into a life of wealth and privilege. In 1925, he was admitted to the Royal Military College, starting his military career. The adjutant at Sandhurst when Bob arrived was Captain Frederick 'Boy' Browning of the Grenadier Guards. In 1941, Bob commanded the Middle East Commando, and by 1943, he was promoted to Chief of Combined Operations. In May 1941, it was Bob Laycock's idea to drop by parachute a small raiding party to attack an airfield at Derna. Laycock also sanctioned Jock Lewes, co-founder of the SAS, to experiment with the use of parachutes as a means to deploy small raiding parties behind enemy lines. In November 1941, Boy Browning was appointed Paratroops and Airborne Division commander. According to Browning's biographer, 'Boy has often been called 'the father of the airborne forces'. It is certainly true that he took this important new branch of Britain's armed services from infancy to maturity in three short years, but he was not present at the conception.'

Laycock and Browning both enjoyed the advantages of a privileged upbringing and education before being commissioned into elite regiments of the Household Division. Their careers also benefited from the patronage of senior politicians, military commanders and members of the Royal Family. Nevertheless, both men would find themselves the subject of controversy. Never seriously questioned at the time, Laycock's leadership and behaviour during the Allied evacuation of Crete have since been criticised by historian Antony Beevor. Browning's career was smashed on the rocks of Operation Market Garden. After the debacle, Boy was quietly sidelined, packed off to the Far East and never held a field command again.

An old adage, sometimes attributed to the American author and humourist Mark Twain, says, 'Never let the truth get in the way of a good story'. But sometimes the truth is stranger than fiction and needs no embellishment.

For instance, in 1946, after the war with Japan, Bob Laycock's Combined Operations Command was scaled down, and his headquarters were relocated to a block of flats in Prince's Gate, Knightsbridge. In 1960, Bob was appointed Colonel Commandant of the Special Air Service, the unit he had helped conceive. Five years later, he would accompany the Shah of Iran during a state visit to the UK. The Shah would be overthrown during the Iranian Revolution of 1979. A year later, the SAS lost their anonymity forever when they stormed the Iranian embassy.

This book explains how Britain's special forces were created and the essential role that members of the Household Division played in that process. It is also the story of an interconnected web of privilege and patronage that enabled a small cohort of arrogant, ambitious young men to bypass military bureaucracy and opposition to forge new ways of waging war against a seemingly unbeatable enemy.

This book begins with a summary of how the commandos came into being during the dark days of 1940, when Britain stood alone against the might of the German war machine. The subsequent chapters examine the integral role members of the Brigade of Guards played in the establishment of the army commandos, the Long Range Desert Group (LRDG), and the Special Air Service, revealing the intimate relationship between the Household Division and these elite units. For those who wish to know more about the broader history of the commandos throughout the Second World War, there is plenty of reading material to choose from, such as *The Green Beret* by Hilary St George Saunders (1949), Robin Neillands' *The Raiders* (1989) or Charles Messenger's *Commandos* (2015).

The Formation of the British Army Commandos (1940–42)

The Second World War was a time of unprecedented challenges and opportunities for Britain's armed forces. Facing a formidable enemy that had conquered most of Europe, Britain needed to find new ways to strike back and undermine the Nazi war machine. One of the most innovative and daring responses to this situation was the creation of the British Army commandos, a special force of highly trained and motivated volunteers who could carry out raids on the enemy-occupied coastline of Europe, sabotage vital installations, gather intelligence and sow fear and confusion among the German forces.

In this chapter, my intention is to provide you, the reader, with a brief overview of the formation of the army commandos and some of the early challenges they faced within the British military and political establishment and operationally, as they launched raids against enemy-held territory.

Prior to the outbreak of the war in September 1939, Britain's armed forces were incapable of launching any type of amphibious operation to strike at an enemy. According to the *History of the Combined Operations Organisation 1940–1945*:

> Britain lacked suitable landing craft, landing ships, transport vessels, armaments, equipment, and the specially trained troops required to embark on any type of offensive seaborne operation. The collapse of British and French forces in the summer of 1940 would demand rapid and unconventional solutions to the challenges of continuing the war against Nazi Germany.[1]

On the evening of 4 June 1940, Lieutenant Colonel Dudley Clarke, a general staff officer of the Royal Artillery, was walking home from the War Office to his flat in London's Mayfair. At the time, Clarke was military assistant to the Chief of the Imperial General Staff, Sir John Dill. Operation Dynamo, the evacuation of over 300,000 British soldiers of the British Expeditionary Force (BEF) and remnants of the French land army from the beaches of Dunkirk, had just been completed.

British propaganda would spin the evacuation story into a tale of ingenuity, determination and heroism in the face of a seemingly unstoppable German war machine. Nevertheless, Dunkirk was a defeat.

The BEF might have gotten away by the skin of its teeth, but the Allies had been forced to abandon most of their heavy equipment, vehicles and supplies. Britain stood alone, the military cupboard was bare, and a German invasion appeared inevitable. Britain had limited options for mounting offensive action against the Germans. The Royal Air Force (RAF) could launch bombing raids against German targets in occupied Europe, but losses would likely be heavy and unsustainable. Dudley Clarke thought there was a better alternative to using conventional forces to strike back at the Germans.

As a professional soldier, Clarke had seen a thing or two in his military career. In 1936, he had served in Palestine when 'The Great Revolt' broke out against British rule of the mandated territory and Jewish immigration. Clarke had been struck by the ability of a handful of determined Arab nationalists to resist British authority and military power. Ultimately, the revolt failed to secure a Palestinian homeland, but it did leave an impression. Clarke was also familiar with the concept of commando units from his studies of military history. During the Boer War, Dutch settlers in South Africa used small units of mounted riflemen called 'commandos' to harass and ambush British troops, often with devastating results.

Clarke thought it possible to create a force that could conduct hit-and-run attacks on the German-occupied coasts of Norway, France, Belgium, and Holland, destroying enemy installations, capturing prisoners, and collecting information. He also hoped that these raids would divert German resources, hamper invasion plans, and demonstrate Britain's determination to fight on.[2]

Before retiring for the evening, Clarke wrote down his ideas for a special raiding force on a single sheet of paper. The next day, Sir John Dill approved the plan to raise a force of commandos. However, the plan still needed the authorisation of the prime minister, Winston Churchill. The timing seems to have been fortunate. On 3 June 1940, the Prime Minister wrote a minute to General Ismay, his chief military assistant, about offensive operations that contained the following passage:

> The completely defensive habit of mind, which has ruined the French, must not be allowed to ruin all our initiative. It is of the highest consequence to keep the largest number of German forces all along the coasts of the countries they have conquered, and we should immediately set to work to organise raiding forces on these coasts where the populations are friendly. Such forces might be composed of the self-contained, thoroughly equipped units of 1,000 up to not less than 10,000 when combined.

Two days later, the prime minister went on to clarify some of his thinking on raiding operations when he wrote:

> Enterprises must be prepared with specially trained troops of the HUNTER class, who can develop a reign of terror down his coasts first of all on the "butcher and bolt" policy.
>
> I look to the Chiefs of Staff to propose to me measures for a vigorous, enterprising and ceaseless offensive against the whole German occupied coastline.[3]

Two days after Dudley Clarke had conceived the idea of raising a special raiding force to attack the coast of occupied Europe, the prime minister enthusiastically approved the plan. Traditionally, amphibious warfare was the realm of the Royal Marines. However, in the dark days of 1940, the marines lacked everything from ships and landing craft to men and equipment. All available landing craft had been used as part of the Dunkirk evacuation, and nearly all had been lost. Only four LCAs (Landing Craft, Assault) and one LCM (Landing Craft, Mechanised) survived.

New landing craft and support ships were ordered, but no arrangements were made for the naval personnel required to crew the vessels when they arrived. At the time, the Admiralty had to prioritise building destroyers and convoy escort ships rather than landing craft. The lack of landing craft and specialised support vessels remained a problem for the commandos until the United States of America entered the war in December 1941, and its enormous industrial resources became fully available to the British. In the early days of Combined Operations, civilian boats and crews were often pressed into service with mixed results.[4]

As the Royal Marines could not provide sufficient manpower or the ships to start conducting raiding operations, it was decided to use the army's independent companies, initially raised for the Norwegian campaign, and raise new commando units.

On 9 April 1940, the Germans invaded Norway. In response, ten independent companies of volunteers were raised mainly from the Territorial Army. The initial intention was for the independent companies to raid the enemy's lines of communication, although no raiding was ever carried out. Each independent company would be a self-contained unit operating from a mother ship that performed the dual role of both a floating base of operations and transport. In early May 1940, half the independent companies arrived in Norway while the remainder stayed home. By early June, although British forces had achieved some tactical successes, such as the capture of Navik, the Norwegian campaign ended in defeat and the German occupation of the country.[5]

On 9 June 1940, the War Office sent out a letter to the Northern and Southern Commands, Home Forces, calling for the names of forty officers and a thousand other ranks to join a special force for mobile operations. A couple of days later, a similar letter was sent to the other commands. The ultimate aim was to raise an initial force of around 5,000 troops.[6] From its small beginnings, the nuisance raiders of 1940 would eventually grow into the Commando Group, composed of four Special Service Brigades, each comprising four commandos, and a small number of independent units for special purposes.[7]

On 14 June 1940, Lieutenant General Sir Alan Bourne, Adjutant General, Royal Marines, was appointed as the first commander of raiding operations. He was also an adviser to the chiefs of staff on Combined Operations. General Bourne set up his headquarters in the Admiralty, and an RAF officer was attached to help form a fledgling parachute unit. By October 1940, around 100 paratroopers were undergoing training. Later, when the number of parachute troops had increased, they were removed from Bourne's command and would later help form the First Airborne Division.[8]

On 17 June 1940, the War Cabinet and Chiefs of Staff Committee issued the following directive (C.O.S. (40) 468) about raiding operations to General Bourne:

DIRECTIVE

To: Lieut.-General A. G. B. Bourne, C.B., D.S.O., M.V.O., Royal Marines.

1. You are appointed Commander of Raiding Operations on coasts in enemy occupation and Adviser to the Chiefs of Staff on Combined Operations.

Raiding Operation

2. The object of raiding operations will be to harass the enemy and cause him to disperse his forces, and to create material damage, particularly on the coastline from Northern Norway to the western limit of German-occupied France.

3. We propose to give you within the limits of the forces and equipment available and subject to directions which you receive from time to time from the Chiefs of Staff, complete discretion in the choice of objectives and the scale of operation undertaken. The Joint Intelligence Sub-Committee have been instructed to help you in the choice of suitable objectives. You are to keep the Chiefs of Staff informed of the operations you propose to carry out.

4. Six Independent Companies and a School of Training in Irregular Operations have already been raised by the War Office. These and the irregular Commandos now being raised will come under your operational command and any administrative suggestions you may wish to make, e.g., for the organization of units, their location in the United Kingdom, etc., will be met.

In addition, the War Office have taken preliminary steps to raise parachutist volunteers of whom a number will be placed under your command. When raised, they will be trained by the Air Ministry and the War Office according to your requirements and advice.

5. Should you want further independent units, over and above those already raised, you should discuss your requirements with Service Departments and advise us accordingly.

6. Certain raids by the independent companies have already been planned by the General Staff Office—You should make yourself acquainted with such projects at once and take over control of any planned raids when you deem it advisable.

7. Irregular actions of various types are undertaken from time to time by the Service Intelligence Departments. There must therefore be close touch between your staff and these departments in order that your several activities shall not interfere with each other and that, on occasions, co-operation that may be possible.

Combined Operations

8. Your second role will be to take over command of the Inter-Services Training and Development Centres and to act as our adviser on the organisation required for opposed landings.

9. Three brigade groups are being detailed for special training in combined operations as soon as they can be equipped. Of these, one may be made available at your request for purely raiding operations, in which case it would, of course, be placed under your command. You will, however, be responsible for supervising the technical training of all troops earmarked for combined operations.

In addition, we wish you to press on the development and production of special landing craft and equipment and to advise us, when the occasion arises, as to its allotment.

10. If it is desired to undertake a combined operation, detailed plans will be worked out by the Service Departments (through the medium of the Inter-Service Planning Staff) and the commander designate. Both will require your technical advice and help.

Relations with other Staffs

11. We are directing the Inter-Service Planning Staff to consult you whenever they receive a combined operational project for examination which implies a landing on a hostile shore.

You should maintain close liaison with this staff and also with the operational and intelligence staffs of the Service Departments and with the Inter-Service Project Board. At the same time, you will have direct access to the Chiefs of Staff Committee who will also advise you of any combined operations which are envisaged.

Headquarters and Staff

12. Your headquarters will be at the Admiralty. You should let us know as soon as possible what staff you need.

13. An officer of the Royal Air Force will be attached to your staff who will also be responsible, under the Air Ministry, for the development as far as the Air Force are concerned, of parachute troops other air requirements for raiding and irregular operations.

Secrecy

14. You will appreciate the paramount need for secrecy.[9]

Incredibly, on 24 June 1940, just eighteen days after the new formation's inception, the first commando raid was launched. The attack was hastily organised, small in scale, and limited in its ambitions. The raid's objective was to reconnoitre the enemy defences of the port area of Boulogne. The only casualty was Dudley Clarke, who accompanied the raiding party as an observer. Clarke suffered a superficial head wound. He later described the raid as being a muddle from start to finish. Nevertheless, overall, the raid was considered a minor success, and showed the promise of things to come.[10]

On 17 July 1940, Admiral of the Fleet, Sir Roger Keyes was appointed director of combined operations (DCO) replacing General Bourne. According to the prime minister, the new role of DCO required an officer of higher rank and authority. Apparently, the sidelining of General Bourne was no reflection on his abilities, which was probably of little comfort to him. Keyes was a veteran of the Gallipoli campaign and had been the architect of the famous Zeebrugge raid against German U-boat pens during the First World War.

Between July and September 1940, the first inter-service Combined Training Centre (CTC) was established at Inveraray, Scotland under the command of Vice-Admiral T. J. Hallett. The centre trained both army and naval personnel in amphibious warfare techniques. At about the same time, a similar training centre was established in the Middle East. The DCO had a force of about 500 commandos, 750 men from the independent companies and around twenty assorted vessels available to him.

Several operations were considered and then abandoned at this time. In early August 1940, the Chiefs of Staff decided to combine the independent companies and commandos. However, in September, all available commando units and independent companies were placed under the Commander-in-Chief, Home Forces, as a response to the threat of a German invasion. This prevented the commandos from conducting any operations for the remainder of the year.[11]

In early October 1940, a reorganisation of Special Service troops got underway. The independent companies, together with 5, 6 and 11 commandos, would be formed into three Special Service (SS) Battalions. The abbreviation of Special Service Battalion to SS Battalions did not pass without comment and proved an unpopular acronym. A battalion would have two 500-man companies, each formed from an existing commando. Two more battalions would then be raised from 3, 4, 7 and 8 commandos. They would make up a 'Special Brigade' and reorganisation would be completed by November.

The reorganisation took place as follows:

1. Special Service Battalion formed from 1, 2, 3, 4, 5, 8 and 9 independent companies
2. Special Service Battalion formed from 6 and 7 independent companies and 9 and 11 commandos
3. Special Service Battalion formed from 4 and 7 commandos
4. Special Service Battalion formed from 3 and 8 commandos
5. Special Service Battalion formed from 5 and 6 commandos.

No. 2 Commando became the 11th Special Air Service Battalion. It would eventually become the 1st Parachute Battalion, the Parachute Regiment. On its formation in July 1940, 6 Commando raised a special boat troop using 'folboat' canoes. No. 8 Commando also formed a folboat troop under the peacetime adventurer and long-distance canoeist Lieutenant Roger Courtney. On 9 October 1940, Brigadier J. C. Haydon, Irish Guards, was appointed to command the Special Service Brigade. By March 1941, the brigade consisted of eleven commandos, each consisting of six troops of three officers and sixty-two other ranks, which fitted neatly into two LCAs.[12]

While Vice Admiral Hallett was assuming command of the CTC, cracks started appearing in the Combined Operations administration. The DCO, Admiral Sir Roger Keyes, advocated using all available irregular forces to attack the enemy at its most vulnerable points. However, the chiefs of staff held a very different strategic view. They saw little value in expending scarce resources on 'pinprick' nuisance raids against the occupied coast of Europe. Instead, as the threat of German invasion receded during 1941, the chiefs of staff wanted to build up an amphibious strike force for deployment in the Mediterranean. They also wanted to gradually build up Combined Operations to a size when it could launch the large-scale amphibious operations required to invade western Europe.[13] Perhaps unsurprisingly, the chiefs of staff resolved this disagreement between themselves and Admiral Keyes by replacing him as DCO.

In October 1941, they appointed the newly promoted Commodore, Lord Louis Mountbatten, to the post of director of combined operations. Alongside Mountbatten's appointment came a new directive that clarified the strategic direction and purpose of Combined Operations for the remainder of the war.[14] It began by restating the principles that governed the conduct of Combined Operations, including the unalienable responsibility of the chiefs of staff to advise the War Cabinet and of the chosen service Commanders to plan and train the forces allotted to them for a specific operation. It went on:

The above principles must govern Combined Operations, which are a specialised form of warfare, and for which special technique and training are needed. But over and above the responsibilities which devolve upon the Chiefs of Staff on the one hand and on the Commanders on the other hand, as set out in paragraph 2 above, we see that there is a definite need for a special Inter-Service Organisation which can give its full time to studying the special requirements of Combined Operations and to assisting in the training of the forces required for them.

To win the war it will be necessary, eventually to undertake a large-scale operation across the seas. The time has come when the Army at home has progressed far in the training for its primary role of the defence of this country, and we consider that we should begin now to train a large part of our Home Forces for amphibious operations. This will be a big task and will require the help of a large and well-developed organisation.

The actual training of troops is, of course, the responsibility of their Commanders. But skilled advice in training for special operations must be available to the Commanders and to their staffs. Furthermore, schools of instruction on a large scale will be required both for officers and for senior N.C.O.s. One of the functions therefore of the Inter-Service Organisation, which we have in mind, will be to organise and provide the teaching at these schools and to provide officers skilled in this form of operation at the big training camps which will be necessary. This system would be analogous to that existing in the Royal Artillery, which has proved most satisfactory.

There is much specialised equipment which is peculiar to Combined Operations and it is essential that research, design, and development of this equipment should be furthered. This then would be a second function of our Combined Operations organisation.

A third function would be the study and development of the tactics and technique to be used in all forms of Combined Operations, varying from raiding patrols up to the full-scale invasion of the Continent. Close liaison should be maintained with the organisation for the development of airborne forces.[15]

Layforce

In July 1940, General Wavell asked for a Combined Operations Training Centre to be established in the Middle East. On 15 January 1941, the training centre was opened at Kabrit. One of the centre's first tasks was to prepare the Desert Army's 6th Division for an attack on the island of Rhodes, codenamed Operation

Cordite. The Division was short a brigade. Consequently, in February 1941, 7, 8 and 11 commandos under the command of Colonel Robert Laycock sailed for the Middle East onboard three infantry assault ships named HMS *Glenearn*, *Glenroy* and *Glengyle*, collectively known as the Glen ships.

In early March, the commandos arrived in Egypt and were joined by two locally raised commando units, 50 and 52. This composite formation became known as Layforce. The commandos were brigaded and joined the 6th Division, although Operation Cordite was cancelled. The commandos were recategorised as Battalions: No. 7 became A Battalion, No. 8 B Battalion, No. 11 C Battalion, Nos. 50 and 52 D Battalion. However, the new brigade lacked the usual support echelons of transport, signals and engineers.[16]

Layforce's arrival in Africa was not propitious. The newly arrived German General Erwin Rommel and his *Deutsches Afrikakorps* (DAK) quickly took the initiative and won several victories against the British. In March 1941, the prime minister diverted troops from Egypt and sent them to Greece. On 6 April 1941, German forces invaded Greece and Yugoslavia. As a result of the Greek misadventure, the Desert Army was severely weakened as thousands of British and Commonwealth troops were taken prisoner and materiel squandered. In April, Layforce launched a disappointing raid against the enemy-held port of Bardia, which achieved little.

On 20 May 1941, the Germans launched Operation Mercury, a major airborne and amphibious assault on the island of Crete. Toward the end of May, most of Layforce was sent to reinforce the garrison on Crete and then cover its evacuation of the island. The commandos had no artillery or mortars to forestall the German advance. Laycock lost around two-thirds of his force, killed, wounded or captured, as many of the commandos found themselves hopelessly stranded.

In June, 11 Commando (C Battalion) was involved in Operation Exporter, the invasion of Vichy French-controlled Syria and Lebanon, before being returned to garrison duties in Cyprus. In July, during the siege of Tobruk, a detachment from 8 Commando (B Battalion) executed a daring raid on an Italian position known as the Twin Pimples, aiming to relieve pressure on the besieged garrison. Although the raid was successful, the commandos were gradually bled of men, who were syphoned off to help with the defence of the port.[17]

In late July 1941, having faced various operational difficulties and being reduced in strength due to previous operations, Layforce was disbanded. The remnants of Layforce either returned to their parent regiments or joined other special forces units. Winston Churchill, a proponent of the commandos, immediately ordered the formation of a new Middle East Commando. On 23 July 1941, in a Prime Minister's Personal Minute (Serial No. D222/1), Churchill wrote to General Ismay:

> I wish the Commandos in the Middle East to be reconstituted as soon as possible. Instead of being governed by a committee of officers without much

authority General Laycock should be appointed D.C.O. The three Glen ships and the D.C.O. with his forces should be placed directly under Admiral Cunningham, who should be charged with all combined Operations involving Sea transport and not exceeding one Brigade. The Middle East Command have indeed maltreated and thrown away this invaluable force.

On 16 August 1941, Churchill wrote again to General Ismay (Prime Minister's Personal Minute Serial No. D231/1), to clarify how he wanted the new Middle East Commando to be constituted:

COMMANDOS.

I settled with General Auchinleck that the three Glen ships were all to remain in the Middle East and be refitted for amphibious operations as soon as possible. That the Commandos should be re-constituted, so far as possible, by volunteers by restoring to them any of their former members who may wish to return from the units in which they have been dispersed, and that Brigadier Laycock should have the command and should be appointed Director of Combined Operations. The D.C.O. and the Commandos will be under the direct command of General Auchinleck. This cancels the former arrangement, which I proposed of their being under the Naval C-in-C.[18]

In mid-November 1941, elements of Laycock's newly constituted Middle East Commando undertook its most audacious raid, codenamed Operation Flipper. The operation was intended to capture or kill Erwin Rommel. With Laycock in overall command, the operation involved a small party landing from submarines and targeting various enemy positions, including what was believed to be Rommel's Headquarters. However, adverse weather conditions and limited forces hindered their efforts.

Lieutenant Colonel Geoffrey Keyes, the son of Admiral Roger Keyes, led the daring assault on Rommel's presumed location. Keyes was killed during the attack on the building and was awarded the commandos' first Victoria Cross posthumously for his bravery. Overall, the operation was something of a fiasco with few objectives accomplished and most of the commandos either killed, captured or missing. Colonel Laycock and Sergeant Terry managed to escape German encirclement and capture, spending the next forty-one days in the desert. On Christmas Day 1941, the two men finally contacted British forces. They were the only two to make it back from the raid. Following Operation Flipper, Laycock returned to Britain. He was promoted to Brigadier and took command of the Special Service Brigade when Brigadier Haydon became military adviser to Mountbatten.

Meanwhile, in March 1941, Brigadier Haydon commanded a successful raid on the Lofoten Islands, northwest of the Norwegian mainland. The intention of the operation, codenamed Claymore, was to disrupt valuable fish oil production, kill German troops, arrest Norwegian collaborators and transport any Norwegian volunteers who wanted to return to Britain. On 26 December 1941, the commandos struck again. This time, they launched a major raid against the Norwegian port of Vaagso, codenamed Operation Archery. This raid was noteworthy for being the first genuine example of a combined operation with air and naval forces supporting an amphibious landing of ground forces.[19]

The Scots Guards

In August 1939, Nazi Germany and the Soviet Union signed a non-aggression pact known as the Molotov-Ribbentrop Pact. This alliance, born out of necessity between two ideologically opposed regimes, paved the way for the invasion and partition of Poland between September and October. Despite this agreement, the Soviet Union remained wary of its new ally. Consequently, Russia sought to expand its western border and protect Leningrad from potential future German attacks. In December 1939, the Soviets invaded their neighbour, Finland. However, the Soviet Red Army significantly miscalculated the military forces needed for a swift victory and gravely underestimated the Finns' ability to resist. As a result, Britain and other Western nations felt compelled to offer aid to Finland, if possible.

5th (Special Reserve) Battalion, Scots Guards

France was the prime mover behind an effort to send a relief force to buttress Finland's defences. As part of the British contingent, it was decided that a small force capable of skiing and trained in winter warfare techniques should be formed. This new unit was the 5th (Special Reserve) Battalion, Scots Guards.

The recruitment, organisation and training of this new battalion was a rushed and improvised affair as no one could predict how long Finland would be able to resist Soviet aggression. The British Army lacked the time, expertise, and infrastructure to raise and train a battalion of novice skiers. Instead, the War Office decided to recruit the troops required for this new battalion from the army's existing manpower pool. In January 1940, the War Office sent a telegram to every corner of the British Empire asking for volunteers to report for duty at Quebec Barracks, Bordon, Hampshire, at the start of February.

Lieutenant Colonel Jimmy Coats, Coldstream Guards, was selected to command the new battalion, nicknamed 'The Snowballers'. Coats was one of the leading bobsledders of his day, winning numerous major trophies. During the First World War, Coats was mentioned in dispatches and awarded the Military Cross. At the start of the Second World War, he led a special unit to act as a personal bodyguard to the Royal Family in the event of a German invasion of the British Isles. Colonel Coats was told to have his battalion assembled, equipped and ready for overseas service by 1 March 1940. This gave him just twenty-three days to organise and train a unit collected from every branch of the army.

On 6 February 1940, around a thousand volunteers started to arrive at Quebec Barracks. The recruits were interviewed and closely questioned about their qualifications to join a ski battalion. Over six hundred officers of varying ranks came forward as volunteers. The result was that the new battalion found it had a surplus of qualified officers and a deficit of non-commissioned officers (NCOs) and guardsmen. However, many of the officers agreed to temporarily relinquish their rank, while retaining their pay, and serve in the battalion as NCOs or guardsmen.

Another 180 guardsmen came directly into the unit from civilian life, although some had previous military experience. Amongst the motley crew of volunteers were Arctic explorers, mountaineers, and winter sports personalities. The volunteers were organised into a headquarters and four ski companies. The unit was then reinforced by a company of newly qualified Scots Guardsmen who came straight from the Training Battalion at Pirbright. But none of these men had ever seen a set of skis before.[1]

Many of the Guards officers who would be so instrumental in the forging of British special forces joined the ranks of the 5th Battalion, Scots Guards including David Stirling, George Jellicoe and Carol Mather.

Like many Guards officers, Archibald David Stirling came from a privileged and aristocratic background. His ancestral home was Keir House, Perthshire, Scotland. Named after his father, Brigadier General Archibald Stirling, the family took to calling him David. As a boy, David, along with his five siblings, often spent their summers hunting, fishing and riding with their cousins, the Lovats of Morar. The Stirling brothers along with their cousin, the Honourable Simon Fraser, the Master of Lovat, attended Ampleforth prep school, known as the Catholic Eton.

Unlike his brothers and cousin, David's school days appear to have been quite unremarkable, although he would embellish and occasionally lie about his past in later life. On the death of their father, David's brother Bill inherited the title of Laird of Keir. In 1932, Bill and Simon Fraser were commissioned into the Scots Guards. Five months later, Simon became the 15th Lord Lovat.

In 1935, David went up to Cambridge University to study architecture. Instead of studying, he spent most of his time partying and attending the Newmarket races. Eventually, David abandoned university for the bohemian life of an artist in Paris. In 1936, Bill Stirling felt compelled to resign his commission so that he could focus all his time and attention on his duties as Laird.

In 1937, the tall, lumbering and feckless David Stirling was also commissioned into the Scots Guards. Predictably, David showed little enthusiasm for life in the regiment and soon quit.

Next, he travelled to America to reinvent himself once again. At the outbreak of the war, David returned to Britain and the Guards training battalion. As a young officer in the Scots Guards, Willie Whitelaw, who would later become home secretary in Margaret Thatcher's first government, recalled how David Stirling frequently ignored his military duties to attend parties in London. David appears to have relied on his family name, aristocratic connections and privileged status, frequently avoiding his military responsibilities. On 25 February 1940, probably to avoid the tedium of regimental life at Pirbright, David Stirling joined the ranks of the Snowballers. He could barely ski, having spent just one winter in Switzerland during the late 1930s.[2]

George Jellicoe was the son of John Jellicoe, 1st Earl Jellicoe, the First World War naval commander at the Battle of Jutland, and admiral of the fleet. George was educated at Winchester College and then Trinity College, Cambridge. He went to the Royal Military Academy, Sandhurst for just two months but did not think he was much good as an officer cadet. He joined the Coldstream Guards but got very bored with regimental life. While convalescing from a bout of pneumonia, he heard that volunteers were needed for the 5th (Special Reserve) Ski Battalion of the Scots Guards for intended operations in Northern Scandinavia in support of the Finns. The new battalion wanted experienced skiers, and so on 16 February Jellicoe transferred to the Ski Battalion. On arrival at Bordon, Jellicoe found many familiar faces such as David Stirling and Carol Mather.

The volunteers were immediately subjected to a program of intense physical fitness training and a series of lectures on winter survival techniques. The guardsmen were taught everything from how to load a sledge to frostbite prevention methods. The Battalion's lack of readiness for deployment was made manifest when a shipment of new No. 4 Lee-Enfield rifles arrived at the camp, as many of the volunteers had never handled or fired a service rifle before.

Nevertheless, on 2 March 1940, the Battalion set sail for France, and then onward by train to Chamonix. Although the Battalion's movements were supposed to be a military secret, they were reported in the French and British press and broadcast on German radio. On arrival at Chamonix, a French Chasseurs Alpins (mountain infantry) battalion provided much-needed equipment and instruction to the novice guardsmen. On 11 March, the battalion was suddenly ordered back to Britain. After recrossing the Channel, the battalion moved north to Scotland and the Glasgow docks. Then, on 14 March, the Finnish Prime Minister Risto Ryti went to Moscow to seek the terms of an armistice with Russia. With the Winter War over, the 5th Battalion returned to Bordon, where it was immediately disbanded.

Carol Mather attended Harrow School and then Trinity College, Cambridge. General (later Field Marshal) Montgomery was a family friend Mather had known since he was a boy. In 1999, Mather was interviewed by the Imperial War Museum (IWM) for its oral history project. According to Mather, he wanted to join the Royal Air Force but ended up in the Welsh Guards instead. In the autumn of 1939, he attended the Royal Military College, Sandhurst, where he claimed to have received only rudimentary training. In 1940, Mather volunteered for the 5th Battalion, Scots Guards. Mather recalled that at the time, the newspapers had been full of stories and photographs of Finland's Winter War. As an experienced skier and someone who had visited Finland as a child, Mather felt compelled to volunteer for the special duty.[3]

In his book, *With Stirling's SAS in the Desert*, Carol Mather writes that he believed the members of the 5th Battalion, Scots Guards had a lucky reprieve when Finland sued for peace. In Mather's opinion, there was no way the Snowballers could have survived the rigours of the campaign:

> The conclusion reached from the experience of the British Ski-Battalion is how unfit this battalion was to fight under the special conditions for which it was formed.
>
> No study had been made of this type of warfare, and therefore no tactics or proper equipment had been evolved. Having been formed in such a hurry, the Battalion was quite untrained in the tactics of arctic warfare. Only 25 percent of its potential efficiency could be expected in the early stages of a campaign! About one fifth had only 3 days on skis, and therefore could not ski. About one sixth had no military experience or were specialists, and therefore could not shoot. Only about one in five knew how to use a primus stove or how to fit skins on skis. Only one man in fifty had used snowshoes or knew how to haul a sledge. A high degree of frostbite and snow blindness was expected.[4]

It seems evident that, had the Scots Guards been deployed in the dense forests of Finland, the battalion's principal challenge would have been to survive the harsh, unforgiving climate and rugged terrain. In his book, *The Scots Guards 1919–1955*, David Erskine described the history of the Battalion as an example of the amateurish improvisation to which the British Government was forced to resort at the outbreak of the war. He also points out the folly of concentrating so many leaders and potential leaders into one poorly equipped and untrained unit. He concludes that it was fortunate indeed that these men were not flung away in an altruistic and ill-prepared side-show. Instead, a new phoenix would arise from the ashes of the defunct 5th (Special Reserve) Battalion, Scots Guards.[5]

Operation Knife and the School of Irregular Warfare

In April 1940, shortly after the German invasion of Norway, the British military planned a special operation, codenamed Knife. The objective was to land a party of six officers by submarine on the southern shore of the Sogne Fjord in Norway. They were to link up with Norwegian army officers and local guides and then make their way south across the country on skis to sabotage the Bergen-Oslo railway. The special unit was also to deliver a shipment of arms, ammunition and explosives to Norwegian partisans. Subsequent plans for the unit would depend on circumstances: they might remain in Norway to help organise the partisans or escape across the Swedish frontier if necessary.

The six officers were to be led by Lieutenant Colonel Brian Mayfield of the Scots Guards. Mayfield was an experienced skier and had recently been second-in-command to Colonel Jimmy Coats in the short-lived 5th Scots Guards ski battalion. The other members were Captain Bill Stirling of the Scots Guards, Major Jim Gavin, Royal Engineers, Captain Ralph Farrant and Captain David Stacey.

Major Gavin was the team's explosives expert and an experienced mountaineer. The most junior team member was the recently promoted Captain Peter Kemp. Educated at Wellington College and Trinity College in Cambridge, Kemp was preparing for a career as a lawyer before he volunteered to fight for the Nationalists during the Spanish Civil War. According to Kemp, he had the least skiing experience of the group, apart from Bill Stirling, who had never been on skis in his life. They were briefed and prepared for the mission at the War Office in London.

The party embarked on the submarine HMS *Truant*, commanded by Lieutenant Commander Hutcheson. However, not long after leaving Rosyth on route to Norway, *Truant* struck a magnetic mine laid by a German U-boat, causing significant damage and flooding. With the batteries leaking chlorine gas and the submarine's machinery compromised, Hutcheson had no choice but to abort the mission and return to port.

On arrival at Rosyth, Bill Stirling arranged for the party to stay at his ancestral home of Keir, near Dunblane, while a replacement submarine was found. However, after the decision to withdraw Allied troops from Norway, Operation Knife was cancelled. In his book, *No Colours or Crest*, Peter Kemp recalled that it was thanks to Bill Stirling's imagination and initiative that the special unit was not immediately disbanded. In the later stages of the Norwegian campaign, the independent companies demonstrated the potential of using partisan or guerrilla warfare against targets under German occupation. There was, however, no organised instruction in this type of warfare.

It was Bill Stirling's idea that the six officers from the aborted Operation Knife, reinforced by a few selected officers and NCOs, should form the nucleus of the new irregular warfare training school. The remote, rugged and inclement Scottish Highlands provided the perfect location for such an institution. In May 1940, as Germany invaded France, Brian Mayfield and Bill Stirling secured War Office approval to establish a special training centre at Inverailort House, a large square building of plain grey stone situated at the head of Lochailort.[6]

With the help of the War Office, Stirling was able to recruit a cadre of outstanding officers and NCOs to bring the staff of instructors up to full strength. Training in amphibious operations formed an important part of each course and was supervised by a naval commander. The senior instructor in fieldcraft was Stirling's cousin, Lord Lovat, with Peter Kemp as his assistant. Kemp described Lovat as a brilliant instructor and a superb fighting soldier. In his memoir, Lord Lovat remembers how Peter Kemp and Brian Mayfield recruited him to the Special Training Centre staff while enjoying drinks at White's, an exclusive gentlemen's club in London. According to Lovat, White's was a second home to Guards officers and a place where military horse-trading at the bar was a common practice.

By June 1940, Lord Lovat and his fellow instructors were ready to welcome the first group of students to the newly established irregular warfare training centre:

The midges were bad, there were insufficient tents, and we were short of cooks, rations and transport; but every instructor was determined to succeed in this new venture. Our first students arrived at the beginning of June: twenty-five puzzled subalterns, some of them volunteers, others arbitrarily dispatched by their commanding officers. They were supplemented by an equal number of NCOs. Among the new boys was Second Lieutenant David Stirling. Hard work was the order of the day and night. Each course was to last a fortnight, with a few days' break before the arrival of the next intake. From this small beginning, Special Training Schools developed apace, which were later established throughout Great Britain, in the Middle and Far East, Australia and on the North American continent. The work was interesting, and I think our efforts were appreciated. We settled down to a strenuous and busy summer.[7]

According to Peter Kemp, Bill Stirling assured his team that there was no danger of their having to remain instructors for the rest of the war. Instead, after the first few cadres of students were trained, there would be a plentiful supply of officers to fill the posts of those who wished to be released for operational duties.

As the summer turned to bleak winter in the highlands of Scotland, the Nazis held sway across western Europe, and Britain stood alone, the establishment of new Special Service formations was already underway elsewhere.

No. 8 (Guards) Commando

On 11 July 1940, the war diary of the newly formed 8 Commando records the unit's inception:

> A/Lt. Col. R.E. Laycock appointed to raise and command no: 8 Commando. He visited the Eastern Command H.Q. and was issued with W.O. Letter 20/Misc 1786 (A.G. 17A) dated June 26th. 1940., and W.O. Letter 20 Gen 5876 (SDIB). He was also given a list of Eastern Command volunteers.

No. 8 Commando, known informally as 8 (Guards) Commando, was primarily raised from the London District and Household Division. Therefore, the troops were formed by regimental affiliation to the Foot Guards or Household Cavalry. In the days immediately following the unit's formation, acting Lieutenant Colonel Robert Laycock of the Royal Horse Guards interviewed prospective troop commanders. Those officers selected as troop leaders interviewed and selected other ranks to join the commando. Laycock preferred to select his headquarters staff from a group of friends and acquaintances, except for Major Walter Curtis, his second-in-command.[1]

Robert 'Bob' Laycock was born into a military family. His father was Brigadier General Sir Joseph Laycock, a famous figure from the Boer War and the First World War. He was brought up in affluent circumstances, attending the prestigious Eton College. As a youth, Laycock showed promise as a cricketer, but contrary to expectations, he abandoned the game when his housemaster suggested he could excel at it. Instead, he took up rowing, which he pursued in a deliberately mediocre manner. This contrary behaviour stemmed from his belief that cricket should be enjoyed for its own sake rather than to advance one's career. Laycock's apparent lack of ambition did little to impede his later military career.

In 1927, Laycock received his commission and joined the Royal Horse Guards, known as the 'Blues'. Finding peacetime soldiering dull, he and his friend Anthony Head, who would later become a Brigadier General and win the Military Cross, engaged in an unusual pastime— recreational burglary. The two friends would steal items from their circle of wealthy friends and acquaintances, only to return them to their owners the next day. Maybe the pair's most daring caper was to successfully steal and later return Auguste Rodin's famous sculpture *The Kiss* (*Le Baiser*) from a house in Beaulieu, Hampshire. The owner of the house immediately hired additional security after discovering the theft. Nonetheless, Laycock and Head managed to successfully replace the statue without being detected. When interviewed for the commandos, Laycock's skill as a housebreaker was considered a virtue.

Laycock was a thick-set, dark, and rather quiet young man who developed a wide range of interests, including poetry, gardening, science, and mathematics, amassing an extensive library. He was described as a first-rate boxer and a good horseman, spending his winter holidays hunting and riding. Laycock was noted for being imaginative yet realistic in planning military operations. He was also a stern disciplinarian, which he believed ensured orders were executed quickly and intelligently under the most difficult circumstances.

Bob's path to the command of 8 Commando was not straightforward. While stationed at the Household Cavalry Training Regiment in Windsor and awaiting his movement orders to India, Laycock heard about the War Office letter that called for volunteers for a special raiding force. He read a copy of the letter in the orderly room and liked what he saw.

Bob asked his commanding officer, Lieutenant Colonel Lord Forrester, to recommend him for a special service appointment. Forrester nominated Bob to the general officer commanding (GOC) London District, Lieutenant General Sir Bertram Sergison-Brooke. Although Brooke said he disapproved of losing good officers like Laycock to special service units, he nevertheless agreed to endorse the transfer. In fact, Brooke recommended Laycock not only for a troop commander role, but as the overall commander of the new 8 Commando, promoting him from captain to lieutenant colonel. Bob's initial joy quickly turned to disappointment when Brooke informed Laycock that he was quite certain it would be impossible for him to be relieved of his staff position in India. Nevertheless, Brooke's recommendation was forwarded to Section MO9 of the War Office.[2]

At the War Office, the actor David Niven, who had served in the army in the 1930s and rejoined when war was declared, was working as a staff officer for Lieutenant Colonel Dudley Clarke in setting up the new commando units. In his memoir, *The Moon's a Balloon*, Niven claimed credit for suggesting Laycock join the commandos and facilitating his appointment, which was stretching the truth almost to breaking:

The Commandos were being prepared for offensive operations but these were held up while landing craft were designed and built. In the meanwhile, the danger of our own invasion by the German Army, poised across the Channel, was very real.
A new and highly secret outfit within the Special Services was formed to

help deal with this possibility and I was ordered to join it in Richmond Park. Before I went, I did something for which, in my opinion, the military has never adequately rewarded me. I suggested to my new uncle by marriage, Robert Laycock, that he should join the Commandos. He was then a captain in the Royal Horse Guards and had just received a posting to India to become gas officer of a division and was due to embark in a few days' time. He came to the War Office and I introduced him to Dudley Clarke who immediately decided that this was just the man he wanted. Bob and I paced the stone corridors of that dreary old building while Clarke dashed about, pulling strings as a result of which somebody else went to India and Bob formed No. 8 Commando, embarking on a career of legendary gallantry which included his famous efforts to blow up Field Marshal Rommel in the desert some 200 miles behind the German lines in Libya. It culminated, five years later, in his becoming Chief of Combined Operations with the rank of major-general.[3]

Laycock, who, among his many other talents, was a qualified seaman, attended an interview at the War Office. It seems that his seafaring skills were the deciding factor in Clarke's eyes, leading to his selection for a commando leadership role. Clarke duly recommended that Laycock be posted to the commandos, but the Military Secretary turned down the transfer on the grounds that Bob was an expensively trained staff officer and must fulfil the role already assigned to him. Shortly afterwards, Bob received his movement orders and was advised by the War Office that his passage had been fixed on a ship leaving for Egypt in three days' time. Following an interview with CIGS Sir John Dill, it was agreed that Laycock could only transfer to the commandos subject to a suitably qualified replacement officer being found for the post in India. Bob managed to find a qualified replacement, Captain Geoffrey Marnham of the Royal Artillery, who was delighted to take the posting, overcoming the final obstacle to the transfer. So, while David Niven did help facilitate Laycock's appointment, it was Brooke's surprising recommendation and Bob's own persistent efforts that secured his command of 8 Commando.

In early August, the unit dispatched its first cadre of officers and NCOs to the Special Training Centre at Lochailort. No. 8 Commando set up camp at Burnham on Crouch, Essex, just north of the Thames Estuary. On 8 August, 1 Troop under the command of Captain the Lord Sudeley, Scots Guards arrived at Burnham. The next day, 2 Troop formed under the authority of Captain Kenneth Tufnell, Grenadier Guards. Captain Tufnell also assumed temporary operational command until Laycock's second-in-command, Major Walter Curtis, of the Somerset Light Infantry (SLI), arrived.[4]

On 28 June 1940, Major Curtis submitted his application to join the commandos. He was 40 years old. Between 1918 and 1919, Curtis had seen active service in France, Belgium, and North Russia, where he was wounded and later awarded the Military Cross. He had also helped to pacify 'civil disturbances' in Ireland, India, and the West Indies. With over twenty-two years of military experience, Curtis had held a wide variety of posts and travelled extensively. In his application letter to join the commandos, Curtis mentions five days drifting in the North Sea as part of his sailing qualifications. Among his list of sporting accomplishments, he records the shooting of two tigers, two panthers and one bear.

Since the 1960s, there has been a steady social shift in attitudes away from the glorification of big game hunters and towards the compassionate conservation of endangered species. Today, it might seem abhorrent that anyone would consider a man who had suppressed the rights of indigenous people and killed wild animals for sport as suitable for a senior military appointment, but back in 1940, Major Walter Curtis was considered an ideal candidate.[5]

Another 8 Commando recruit was George Jellicoe. After the 5th Battalion, Scots Guards had been disbanded, he had been sent to a holding battalion and then back to his parent regiment, the Coldstream Guards. Interviewed in 1993, Jellicoe recalled that he felt very frustrated that he did not get an opportunity to fight in France and was bored sitting on his 'arse' waiting for an assignment. Then he saw a notice asking for volunteers for the commandos and applied. He was interviewed by Colonel Laycock. He confessed to Laycock that he was bored, sitting on his backside, and kept being confined to barracks for staying out late and drinking too much.

Jellicoe joined 3 Troop commanded by Mervyn Griffith-Jones, Coldstream Guards, who would become a famous barrister. Griffith-Jones had two subalterns under him; one of them was Ian Collins of the Coldstream Guards. Collins had been a professional tennis player before the war and represented Great Britain in the 1929 and 1930 Davis Cups. Collins would go on to serve with the Special Air Service and later run Collins Publishers. Jellicoe was the other subaltern. He recalled that 8 Commando had more than a sprinkling of aristocracy, including Gavin Astor (later 2nd Baron Astor of Hever), Life Guards, Randolph Churchill (member of Parliament and the prime minister's son), 4th Hussars, Lord Fitzwilliam, Royal Scots Greys, and Philip Dunne (member of Parliament), Royal Horse Guards, who would later become Lord Jellicoe's father-in-law. To Jellicoe and his fellow officers, 8 Commando was like an extension of the exclusive White's Club.[6] The preponderance of aristocrats led to 8 Commando being christened 'The House of Lords' by rival units.[7]

Like George Jellicoe, Carol Mather was bitterly disappointed when the 5th Battalion, Scots Guards was disbanded. He believed the battalion might have been used in the Norwegian campaign. Instead, Mather returned to training with the Welsh Guards and was commissioned in March 1940. Mather was sent to the Guards training battalion, where he found regimental life boring and full of petty rules and regulations. Boredom led to rule-breaking. Due to his unruly behaviour, Mather lost his name several times and was punished for failing to meet the Guards standards of good order and military discipline. The term 'losing one's name' dates to a time when guardsmen in training were issued brass name plates bearing their regimental details, which would hang above their bedspace in barracks. If a guardsman was found to have committed some infraction of the rules and regulations and was subject to punishment, the brass plate was removed, and his name was taken down for disciplinary action. Eventually, Mather escaped the boredom of barrack room life and was accepted into the commandos.[8]

As a unit of volunteers, Mather recalled that the petty rules and regulations of army life were forgotten in the commandos. He joined 8 Commando and was assigned to the Scots Guards troop, where he found that the guardsmen seemed to relish the tough physical training and were self-disciplined. The greatest punishment any volunteer could face was the shame of being summarily kicked out of the commandos and returned to their original unit (RTU). Mather's initial commando training included boating, hill climbing and various amphibious landing exercises. Mather believed that his childhood experiences in the Boy Scouts, where he had learned fieldcraft, helped to prepare him for some of the challenges of the training regime.[9]

Jock Lewes, a fellow Welsh Guards officer and acquaintance of Carol Mather, joined 8 Commando at Burnham-on-Crouch. Mather recalled that the Welsh Guards contingent was too small to form its own troop, so Jock was posted to the Irish Guards (5 Troop) and Mather was assigned to the Scots Guards troop. Mather's fellow subaltern in 4 Troop was David Stirling. Mather described Stirling as a tall, gangling fellow who was charming, manipulative and generally considered rather an idle officer.

In contrast to Stirling, Jock Lewes was a somewhat puritanical and zealous young officer. Born in India to Anglo-Australian parents, Lewes attended Christ Church college, Oxford, and worked for a spell at the British Council in Berlin. In late 1938, with war imminent, Lewes joined the First Battalion of the Tower Hamlet Rifles as an Ensign. After the outbreak of the war, he was posted to the Welsh Guards Training Battalion at Colchester. Excelling in weapons training, he became the weapons training officer and prepared detailed manuals that reflected his exacting standards and single-minded focus on combat-readiness. Lewes maintained a sharply critical eye towards many of his fellow commando officers during the unit's training.

Lewes railed against what he perceived as a 'workless tradition' and decadent aversion to physical exertion among certain officers more interested in leading a charmed life than a life of self-sacrifice and service to the nation. His letters expressed a clear contempt for 'decadence' as he believed the commandos should be comprised of men willing to endure hardship and focused solely on their military purpose without distractions. Lewes held himself to the highest of standards, which, in his eyes, many of his colleagues failed to meet. In the late summer of 1940, Jock Lewes and David Stirling must have appeared the most unlikely pair of junior officers to form an elite fighting force.[10]

On 12 August, training instructions were issued to the troop leaders (See Appendix A). The training instructions issued by Colonel Laycock outline the essential elements required for the men of 8 Commando to accomplish their tasks successfully. The document emphasises the importance of rigid discipline, achieved through regular drill parades and the development of specialised commando techniques.

At first glance, an emphasis on parade-ground drill might seem counterintuitive to training independently minded volunteers. However, Laycock understood that parade-ground drill could be used as a tool to enforce strict discipline among the commandos, which was vital for their success. The drill itself was irrelevant and quite separate from the specialised field tactics the commandos intended to use on operations. Discipline was the end goal, not the drill formations themselves (something we will examine in the next chapter, alongside the role of the barracks square).

The desired characteristics for individual commandos included physical fitness, mental alertness, an offensive spirit, courage, predatory instincts, self-reliance, subterfuge, thuggery and the ability to operate confidently at night, considering the cover of darkness as a friend and ally. The training was divided into individual (Appendix A) and collective training (Appendix B).

Individual training covered a wide range of subjects, including weapons proficiency (i.e. rifles, pistols, machine guns, grenades and mortars), physical training (i.e. physical training, boxing, jiu-jitsu, swimming, marching and running), boat work, climbing, map reading, field sketching, camouflage, scouting, sniping, signals, self-defence, wire-cutting, demolitions, incendiarism, sabotage, knots and lashings, prisoner handling, intelligence gathering, foreign languages and first aid. Many of these subjects were to be practised at night.

Collective training of the unit involved progressive stages from sub-section, section, troop and commando levels. It included night operations, urban warfare, fighting in woodland and forests, patrolling, prisoner capture and document seizure. The commandos would also have to learn how to cooperate with the Royal Navy and Royal Air Force. Sabotage training ensured that the commandos were skilled at disabling or destroying a variety of targets such as vehicles, ammunition dumps, docks, factories, communication lines, railways, airfields, canal locks and dams.

The training instructions also emphasised the importance of maintaining esprit de corps among the volunteers from various regiments, encouraging healthy competition between troops but discouraging 'scrapping' when off duty.

The document also stressed the need for the strictest secrecy regarding commando operations.

To promote an ethos of inter-troop rivalry, 8 Commando was organised into ten troops along regimental lines:

No. 1 Troop (Household Cavalry) was under the command of Captain the Lord Sudeley, Scots Guards.

No. 2 Troop (Grenadier Guards) was under the command of Captain Kenneth Tufnell, Grenadier Guards.

No. 3 Troop (Coldstream Guards) was under the command of acting Captain Mervyn Griffith-Jones, Coldstream Guards.

No. 4 Troop (Scots Guards) was under the command of Captain Dermot Daly, Scots Guards.

No. 5 Troop (Irish and Welsh Guards) was under the command of Captain Edward Fitzclarence, Irish Guards.

No. 6 Troop (units in London District and Eastern Command, and known as 'the Buffaloes') was under the command of acting Captain Toby Milbanke.

No. 7 Troop (Somerset Light Infantry) was under the command of Captain Geoffrey Lance.

No. 8 Troop (Line Cavalry) was under the command of acting Captain Sir Godfrey Nicholson.

No. 9 Troop (Composite) was formed later under the command of Captain Pat Ness.

No. 10 Troop (Specialists such as Royal Engineers, Royal Artillery, and Royal Marines) was under the command of Captain Smyth Osbourne.

Training continued throughout September, which included an exercise where 8 Commando was pitted against the 46th Brigade. In October, the commando moved north to Inveraray, Scotland, where all hands carried out amphibious landing practice from LCAs on the shores of Loch Fyne. Next, the commando moved to Largs, a town on the Firth of Clyde in North Ayrshire.

Towards mid-November, Colonel Laycock was informed that his commando was to be combined with 3 Commando to form 4 Special Service Battalion. According to the unit's war diary, all the volunteers were given the choice to return to their original regiments instead of joining the new formation, but very few left of their own volition. However, the reorganisation provided an opportunity to return a few unsuitable men to their parent units.

One new arrival amongst a small contingent of Royal Marines seconded to the commandos was Lieutenant Evelyn Waugh, who had already established himself as a successful novelist. Waugh would pour his wartime experiences into a series of satirical novels, *Men at Arms* (1952), *Officers and Gentlemen* (1955) and *Unconditional Surrender* (1961). On 28 November, 3 and 8 commandos received orders to mobilise as 4 Special Service Battalion, and by mid-December, the process was complete.

Recruitment and Training

On 15 August 1940, the War Office published a slim pamphlet titled 'Commando Training Instruction No. 1'. Its objective was to create a guerrilla force organised into independent units of approximately 500 men—roughly equivalent to an understrength infantry battalion. These units would operate independently, conducting 'smash-and-grab' raiding operations into enemy territory, typically lasting less than twenty-four hours. The commando organisation was intended to be as decentralised as possible, with each troop and individual soldier trained to work independently, relying on their own operational and administrative resources under any circumstances.

The commandos were expected to operate over wide areas in small groups, relying on speed and cunning to avoid detection by enemy forces. Their tasks involved striking suddenly, inflicting damage on the enemy, and swiftly withdrawing before engaging in combat. This required the highest standards of training, personal and collective discipline, courage, skill, determination and imagination from all ranks, backed by inspired leadership and organisational ability from the commanders.

The training aimed to produce a highly developed team spirit and esprit de corps while also fostering self-reliance and resourcefulness in everyone. It differed from regular army training by emphasising each man's ability to decide his own course of action without being told what to do. Individual training focused on instilling qualities such as offensive spirit, silence and secrecy, inquisitiveness, opportunism, open-mindedness, physical fitness and intelligence.

Collective training involved instruction in various stages of raiding operations, including embarkation, disembarkation, movement and withdrawal, attacks on enemy targets like aerodromes and power stations, capturing prisoners and documents, creating diversions, street fighting, terror tactics, amphibious assault and air transportation.

In July 1940, the commanding officer of Left Flank, 1st Battalion, Scots Guards submitted a list of twenty-eight names of NCOs and other ranks who volunteered for special service. The commander of B Company, 1st Battalion, Scots Guards returned a similar list of eighteen candidates who wished to transfer to 8 Commando. Eight names on the list of volunteers have a red pencil line running through them, identifying them as unsuitable for special service. The reasons for rejecting these guardsmen vary from being too old to withstand the demands of commando training to lacking intelligence. Some volunteers are simply described as 'unsuitable'. The returns from the Scots Guards illustrate that many guardsmen were keen to take a more active role in the war.

We can only speculate how many commanding officers might have deliberately kept back the names of capable men they wanted to retain or put forward the names of troublesome soldiers they were eager to remove from the battalion or company. On 23 April 1941, Colonel E. R. H. Herbert, director of organisation, sent a War Office directive about the poor quality of candidates recommended for special service units. The directive was distributed to all district commanders across the UK, the Special Service Brigade commander, the Special Training Centre commandant in Lochailort, the Guards Depot, and all infantry and Guards training centres and holding battalions. The directive begins:

> Sir,
> I am directed to inform you that the selection of volunteers for Special Service Units has not been found to be satisfactory.
>
> The following are among the chief difficulties which have been brought to notice:
> Many cases have occurred of men being selected by Training Units and sent to the Special Training Centre who, according to their own Statement, had no idea for what they were volunteering. On arriving at the Special Training Centre and having the facts explained to them, they have been found unwilling to volunteer and have asked to be returned to their Units. Out of a recent intake of some 250 men as many as 82 had to be sent back for this reason.
> Many volunteers have been found either physically or mentally unsuitable.
> Volunteers have been sent of ranks for which no vacancy exists. It should be noted that there are at present no vacancies for Non-Commissioned Officers.[11]

During the Battle of France, Guardsman Cyril Feebery had been wounded in action while the 3rd Battalion, Grenadier Guards retreated to the beaches of Dunkirk. After being evacuated by ship, Feebery spent a couple of weeks in hospital. Once considered fit for light duties, he was sent to the holding battalion at Wellington Barracks in London. After a drunken night on the town, Feebery was arrested by the military police and faced disciplinary punishment when he read a notice about volunteering for special service. He described the notice as being his salvation. In 1993, Feebery recounted his wartime exploits to his nephew for posterity:

> They were looking for volunteers from men returning to the Holding Battalion and from young soldiers who had just finished their training to form a 'special unit'. They particularly wanted men who could drive, swim and ride a bike

or a horse—just up my alley, so I put my name down. A few days later I was summoned before the Commanding Officer, who went through the details on the notice.

'How many of these things can you do, Feebery?'

'I can drive, swim and ride a bike, sir.'

'I see. Are you fit?'

'Graded B1, sir.'

'Very well. See the Medical Officer this afternoon. If he gives you A1, I'll consider you as a possible candidate.'

My injuries had healed and there was nothing showing from the dislocated ankle. The doctor was happy to grade me A1 and pass the news on to the CO, and two days later I was summoned for the last time. Four other men had been accepted as well and the CO gave us some more details. We would be paid six shillings and nine pence a day (a small fortune for a Private), allowed to wear civilian clothes and be billeted in civilian houses during training. If we still fancied the idea we were to report at the Guard Room at seven next morning, kit packed and ready to move.[12]

James Sherwood joined the Royal Army Service Corps (RASC) at the start of the war. However, he quickly found that conducting numerous seemingly pointless map-reading exercises was extremely boring. Then, Sherwood heard about the formation of commando units, which sounded exciting to him. He applied to join the commandos and was interviewed by an officer named Roger Courtney of 8 Commando.

Courtney would go on to establish the Special Boat Section (SBS). The SBS operated using small, collapsible canvas folboat canoes to conduct reconnaissance and sabotage missions. Courtney recognised that canoes offered great advantages in stealth and secrecy. They were silent, had a low silhouette and were highly portable. Later, the unit would be renamed the Special Boat Service. Today, the SBS is the Royal Navy's elite maritime counter-terrorism force, like the British Army's SAS.

During his interview for the commandos, Sherwood said that Courtney asked him if he could swim, had any sailing experience or knowledge of demolition. Sherwood misunderstood the question about demolition, taking it to mean knocking walls down with a sledgehammer rather than explosives. As he had worked as a manual labourer, Sherwood told Courtney that he did have demolition experience; however, he knew nothing about the use of explosives. He also told Courtney that he could swim when he could not. Nonetheless, Courtney accepted Sherwood's answers at face value and did not probe any deeper.

Months elapsed before Sherwood heard anything about his application to join the commandos. He recalled that his regiment was unhappy about losing a constant trickle of men who volunteered for special duties elsewhere. Nevertheless, his commanding officer did not prevent his transfer. In September 1940, Sherwood was suddenly told to report to the Horse Guards barracks at Windsor for commando training.[13]

The conditions of service for those who joined the commandos differed from the rest of the British Army. Being volunteers, the commandos had the freedom to withdraw their service and be sent back to their parent units after any operation. Similarly, any volunteer who failed to make the grade could be summarily returned to their unit. The conditions of service stated that volunteers would undertake a form of service which demanded self-reliance. A War Office memorandum set out what was expected of the volunteers:

> From the day they are accepted, they will become irregular soldiers, i.e. one who is subject to Military discipline, but who looks after himself completely, and expects no "nursing".
>
> They will be responsible for their own food and lodging and should be in possession of a suit of plain clothes. They will be required to pay their own daily travelling expenses, if any, between their lodging and place of duty. (Travelling Warrants will be issued only on change of station.)[14]

Special Service volunteers were already trained soldiers and, in some cases, combat veterans. Therefore, commando training had different objectives from the army's basic and trade training. The purposes of commando training were fourfold. First, it aimed to instil a sense of discipline and esprit de corps. Second, it sought to equip volunteers with the necessary skills and resilience to overcome whatever challenges they might face on operations. Officers, NCOs and other ranks endured the same physical challenges during training, such as timed marches that steadily increased in distance and difficulty, with the recruits carrying heavier packs. The training was also designed to quickly identify those individuals who were not suitable for the commandos. Third, volunteers needed to understand that darkness was their friend and learn how to use it to their advantage. Lastly, the commandos had to be proficient in the use of every type of infantry weapon, from a knife to a mortar. The training was also meant to encourage aggressiveness and foster an offensive spirit in the troops.

In October 1940, James Sherwood was sent from Windsor to Scotland to start his commando training in earnest. The day after his arrival, the new recruits were sent on a 7-mile speed march. The exercise aimed to weed out those candidates who were not physically fit enough to keep pace with the arduous training course. Anyone who fell out of the march was returned to their unit the next day. For the next few weeks, the recruits were taught fieldcraft, weapons training, the basic principles of demolition and the use of explosives. Sherwood's group then moved to the small seaside town of Largs, on the coast of Ayrshire, and finally to the Isle of Arran.

Having endured everything the commando instructors had thrown at him, Sherwood was shocked and outraged when he was informed that 8 Troop had failed to meet the 'commando standard'. Therefore, the entire troop was to be disbanded, and the men returned to their parent units. However, before being sent back to his regiment, Sherwood learned that Roger Courtney was raising a special folboat troop. Although Sherwood could not swim, he had purchased a canoe at his own expense and practised with it on the open ocean. He also had some rock-climbing experience and was used to sleeping outdoors in all weathers. Determined not to be returned to his units, Sherwood applied to join Courtney's folboat troop and was immediately accepted.[15]

Bill Stirling and Brian Mayfield assembled a diverse group of instructors at Inverailort House, including experienced soldiers, former explorers, policemen and an Olympian, all contributing their skills to the commando training program. As senior fieldcraft instructor, Lord Lovat was assisted by Peter Kemp. Major John Munn of the Royal Artillery taught map reading. Jim Gavin and Mike Calvert, Royal Engineers, were recruited as demolition instructors. Together, they would co-author the 'Offensive Demolitions' handbook. Two former Shanghai policemen, William Fairbairn and Eric Sykes, taught the art of unarmed combat and dirty-tricks fighting. In 1942, William Fairbairn published a manual on hand-to-hand combat, entitled *All-In Fighting*, which remains in print. Fairbairn and Sykes are probably best known for developing the iconic double-edged commando fighting knife. Today, the Fairbairn-Sykes dagger patch of 3 Commando Brigade remains part of the Royal Marines uniform. Bill Stirling recruited Cyril Mackworth-Praed, Scots Guards, to improve the commandos' shooting. Mackworth-Praed was Britain's most successful marksman at the 1924 Olympic Games, winning one gold and two silver medals. Other instructors included the pre-war mountaineers and explorers, Freddie Spencer Chapman and Jimmy Scott.

The training syllabus alternated between theory classes that lasted from forty minutes to an hour and practical field exercises that ran for two to three days. The subjects taught included demolition and the use of explosives, fieldcraft, sniping, intelligence gathering, camouflage and concealment, boat training and weapons proficiency. The commandos had to be excellent shots, competent with a fighting knife and skilled in unarmed combat. They also had to be able to climb, with and without the assistance of ropes, ford rivers and march, carrying a pack and personal weapon, 15 miles in two hours and fifteen minutes.

Field exercises required the recruits to live off the land and learn how to prepare meals. George Jellicoe recalled being sent out into the Scottish wilderness for two or three days at a time and having to poach deer for food. Tactical training exercises were often conducted using live ammunition and flash bombs to help prepare the commandos for combat. Unsurprisingly, battle inoculation training resulted in some volunteers becoming casualties. Of the 25,000 commandos who passed through the training depot at Achnacarry, around forty were killed in training exercises.[16]

Volunteers were expected always to keep themselves and their equipment clean and in good order, no matter how exhausted they might be. To the guardsmen who joined 8 Commando, this would have been a familiar element of their training. For centuries, the Guards Depot had used 'cleanliness' as a brutally simple training method that eventually engendered a sense of pride, attention to detail and self-reliance in its new recruits. In his book, *Fighting with the Guards*, Keith Briant explains the training technique:

> The Guardsman's training in cleanliness in all its aspects, personally, in equipment, in weapons, and in barrack-rooms, is one of the first painful, laborious lessons inflicted on the recruit. The standards required seem quite impossible, quite unnecessary and quite stupid. Life is a daily misery filled with endless pitfalls and traps which seem cold-bloodedly arranged solely to ensure that a new Guardsman is always on a charge.

Briant writes that although a guardsman's initial training might have seemed childish and pointless, it had a clear purpose:

> It is the beginning of the evolution of the Guardsman who in different circumstances of fighting will consider no trifle too unimportant, no trouble too great, however tired he may be. If he is in the desert, he will have the habit of mind which will ensure that every part of his rifle is clear of specks of sand, and this may save his life and others.[17]

Grenadier Guardsman Cyril Feebery described his commando training as a gruelling mix of route marches and tactical exercises regularly punctuated by seemingly petty sock inspections. The method in the training madness was to ensure that the commandos could overcome their own exhaustion and discomfort and continue to perform at a high level of efficiency.

> I became a member of 2 Troop, 8 Commando, who were all Grenadier Guards. Commando training can best be described as intensive. Our days were spent going up the mountain and down the mountain, then up the mountain and down the mountain again. There was field craft training, map and compass reading, night marching, unarmed combat, weapons training with pistols and light automatics, then up the bloody mountain yet again. There were a few huts

but we ordinary soldiers and most of the NCOs and officers lived in two-man tents. The only water was what splashed and trickled past in the burns around the camp. Shaving was a daily ordeal, and I still cannot stomach porridge. One of the few things I can clearly remember about this time is the CO's passion for socks. Every man was ordered to parade with a dry pair of socks, to be presented for inspection on demand. This was not an easy order to obey because it rained most of the time, but woe betide the man whose dry socks turned out to be even slightly damp. Take it from me there are far worse ways to pass a wet and windy night in Scotland than lying in your blankets in your tent listening to the rain hissing down outside while drying a sock over a candle ready for next morning's parade.[18]

Besides the endless route marches, mountain climbing, field exercises and sock parades, much of the commandos' training was conducted at night. The recruits often worked in pairs or small groups, which helped foster strong bonds of comradeship and trust in one another's abilities. The commandos also trained with the naval personnel who crewed the ships and landing craft that would convey them to their target destinations. Amphibious training taught the naval personnel practical lessons such as approaching a hostile shore, landing troops, remaining on station without being detected, and recovering a landing party. However, for Bob Laycock and the volunteers of 8 Commando, the frenetic pace of training was not being translated into the 'smash-and-grab' raiding operations promised.

When the promise of training does not translate into meaningful action, then unit morale and military discipline can suffer. On the morale front, frustration can arise due to the lack of tangible results or the feeling of being underutilised. A sense of purpose is crucial for maintaining high morale, and soldiers who do not see their training translate into meaningful action may struggle. Furthermore, camaraderie within the unit, often forged during operations, can be missed by those who remain in training mode.

As for discipline, soldiers who see their peers deployed while they remain in training can feel disillusioned. This can have an impact on their overall discipline and commitment. Soldiers may struggle to maintain the same level of discipline when faced with repetitive training routines combined with the disappointment of cancelled operations. Maintaining discipline without the external pressure of combat requires strong self-discipline and effective leadership. While some soldiers might adapt well, others may struggle, gradually eroding unit cohesion.

The commandos started to face several challenges that stemmed from their rushed formation and a lack of direction from higher military authorities. Early commando operations had all been failures, and the promise of raiding the occupied coasts of Europe had already started to fade. Commanding officers were often reluctant to provide their best men for special service, knowing it would strip their own units of talented soldiers and NCOs. For 8 Commando specifically, Laycock took an unorthodox approach to recruitment. Rather than relying on the provided volunteer lists, he preferred to use the exclusive White's club in London as an impromptu recruitment centre and tap into his socially elite circle of friends and acquaintances, such as Lords Jellicoe, Sudeley and Stavordale.[19]

Laycock's unconventional method of recruitment had its advantages. He was able to quickly staff 8 Commando with men he personally knew and trusted, rather than interview and evaluate strangers. Many of his aristocratic recruits were accomplished sportsmen and adventurers who knew how to ride, hunt, shoot, box, climb, sail, ski and drive a motorcar. Most of these activities were popular pastimes of the upper classes, which now became qualifying skills for fledgling commandos.

Upper-class officers came from privileged backgrounds, receiving the best educations and attending elite schools and universities such as Eton, Oxford, and Cambridge. However, academic achievement was no guarantee of military competence. Unfortunately, Laycock's decision to recruit his officers mainly based on social class significantly reduced his talent pool. Furthermore, some of Laycock's officers seemed more interested in drinking, gambling, and flouting military discipline than in doing their jobs. According to Evelyn Waugh, 8 Commando was in a shambolic state when he started his secondment from the Royal Marines:

When formed they had been exceptionally zealous; discipline was already deteriorating when I joined. After RM Brigade the indolence and ignorance of the officers seemed remarkable, but I have since realized they were slightly above normal army standards. Great freedom was allowed in costume; no one even pretended to work outside working hours. Troop leaders never sent in returns required by the orderly room at the proper time or in the proper form. Officers took leave when their troops were not allowed it. The special lodging allowance did little to cover the very high standard of expenditure in No. 8. Two night operations in which I acted as umpire showed great incapacity in the simplest tactical ideas. One troop leader was unable to read a compass. The troops, however, had a smart appearance on inspection parades, arms drill was good, the officers were clearly greatly liked and respected. The men had no guard duties. After parade they were free from all restraint and were often disorderly. There was already a slight undercurrent of impatience that they had not yet been put into action (No. 3 Commando had done one ineffectual excursion to the Channel Islands).[20]

Overall, Waugh's disparaging assessment of 8 Commando seems justified—though Waugh, a celebrated misanthrope known for his snobbery, cynicism and biting wit, was hardly a reliable witness.

The selection process did little to ensure quality. During interviews, recruits were asked if they had specific skills, such as swimming, sailing, boxing, and driving, but candidates were only required to answer with a simple 'yes' or 'no' without further explanation. James Sherwood's interview revealed a concerning lack of critical evaluation by Roger Courtney, who accepted Sherwood's answers at face value. As noted, Sherwood lied about being able to swim. A breakdown in communication also led Sherwood to tell Courtney that he had prior demolition experience—factually correct, as he had worked as a manual labourer. Still, Courtney's real question was whether Sherwood had any expertise in handling explosives. Throughout the interview, Courtney failed to clarify his questions or make any attempt to verify Sherwood's responses.[21]

Although the call for special service volunteers might have stripped regular army battalions of some of their best men, it also appears to have created an opportunity for some units to rid themselves of indolent and troublesome individuals. The Scots Guards were glad to see the back of David Stirling when he was posted to 8 Commando in November 1940, for example.[22]

There is an old English proverb, *The Devil finds work for idle hands*. The proverb's meaning is simple: unoccupied people tend to fill their time with mischief. As time passed, Bob Laycock recognised that a lack of operational activity and having his men billeted in lodgings rather than barracks was leading to discipline issues. The arrogance of youth, military inexperience and an overweening sense of entitlement brought out the worst tendencies in some of 8 Commando's young officers. Between brief periods of extreme activity, military life often consists of long periods of intense boredom that, when left unchecked, can negatively affect morale and unit cohesion. Undoubtedly, constantly preparing for operations only to see them cancelled must have been frustrating and demoralising for the men of 8 Commando. However, Bob Laycock's discipline and morale issues within 8 Commando were symptomatic of wider organisational difficulties across the newly formed Special Service Brigade.

On 9 October 1940, Brigadier Joseph Charles Haydon was appointed as the commander of the Special Service Brigade, and he promptly reorganised the commandos into battalions. In December 1917, Haydon received a commission into the Irish Guards and served on the Western Front. At the outbreak of the Second World War, he was Commanding Officer, 2nd Battalion, Irish Guards, during which time he was involved with the operations at the Hook of Holland and Boulogne in May 1940.

On 12 November 1940, the Special Service Brigade moved its Headquarters from London to Theale near Reading in Berkshire. Throughout November and

December, the Brigade prepared for Operation Workshop, intending to capture the Italian island of Pantelleria in the Mediterranean Sea between Sicily and North Africa. On 28 January 1941, it was decided to cancel Operation Workshop. Instead, a force of three commandos (7, 8 and 11) were dispatched to the Middle East by ship.

During February 1941, Brigadier Haydon was involved in a series of meetings to discuss the reorganisation of the Special Service Battalions. On 5 March, it was decided to abandon the battalion as the preferred operational unit and revert to commandos. In a memorandum on the reorganisation of special service units, Haydon conceded that after three and a half months' experience, it was clear that the battalion system was not working, and it was time to make changes. In the memorandum, Haydon set out the reasons why the battalion was not the ideal formation for commando operations:

> There is no doubt whatsoever that the Commandos, each raised by an individual officer and each filled with his individual enthusiasm, had a most marked spirit and pride of their own.
>
> This characteristic was to some extent drowned and lost when the Commandos were amalgamated into Special Service Battalions. It was, however, my hope that it would be replaced by an equally beneficial Battalion spirit. I do not think that I can truthfully say that this has proven to be the case. It is my view that this should in no way be attributed either to the Battalion Commanders themselves, or to the personnel who went to make up the Commandos.
>
> It was the fault, if fault there be, of the changed organisation under which they worked, and of the conditions and surroundings under which they originally volunteered for Special Service.
>
> In short – Special Service Battalions started their careers under distinctly unfavourable psychological conditions. They were resented perhaps consciously but certainly unwillingly both by those who had raised the Commandos and by those who had joined them, though this did not, and does not, prevent a real and honest endeavour to make the new organisation a success.[23]

When it comes to the effectiveness of combat units, size and force composition matter. A Special Service Battalion consisted of seventy-seven officers and 1,055 men of other ranks. The size of a Special Service Battalion and the fact that its personnel were billeted in private lodging rather than being housed together in barracks created administrative and discipline problems. A typical infantry battalion, for example, would consist of officers and men from the same regiment, housed together in barracks for training and administration purposes. This was not the case for commando units. Furthermore, the battalions lacked enough experienced administrative officers and adequate motor transport for their needs.

The principal role of the commandos was to conduct raiding operations against enemy occupied coastlines. However, Haydon quickly discovered that the size of the Special Service Battalions made the units too large for most ships being used by the commandos for amphibious landings. As a result, battalions would have to be split between two or more vessels, making operations more complicated, time-consuming, difficult to control, and hazardous. It was also recognised that many operations would not require a force the size of a battalion, but a smaller and more flexible formation instead.

At a meeting held in the DCO's office on 3 February 1941, Brigadier Haydon proposed a new force structure for special service units that consisted of a commando headquarters and six fighting troops, each of around sixty-five men of all ranks. This new formation would better suit the capacity of LCAs and large infantry landing ships like HMS *Glengyle*, *Glenroy* and *Glenearn*. A month later, the Special Service volunteers were officially re-organised into commando units once again.

Brigadier Haydon recognised that one of the biggest challenges and threats to the commandos was a lack of employment, as operations were planned only to be cancelled. Haydon repeatedly wrote to his officers offering a mixture of practical advice on military training and pastoral care:

> It is fully realised how extremely hard it is to keep a Battalion on the alert and ready for operations at short notice over a long period of time. Delays are very apt to cause enthusiasm to flag and to raise doubts that active employment will ever come about. It is not possible to make promises and it would be unwise to do so.
>
> The true solution to the problem lies in the following direction:
>
> It must be explained to all ranks that patience is a necessity and not to put too fine a point on it, that those who do not possess it have no place in a Special Service Battalion.[24]

In December 1940, Haydon prepared a lecture on points of discipline and training to be given to the officers of each battalion. In his lecture notes, Haydon acknowledged the difficulties faced by Special Service units, which he diagnosed as being primarily organisational in origin. The commandos were made up of troops from numerous different regiments, each with their own customs. When off-duty, the volunteers were geographically dispersed, billeted in private accommodations rather than barracks. There was a lack of organised recreational activities and a shortage of administrative staff. As a result, the commandos lacked unit cohesion and esprit de corps. Haydon also understood the damaging psychological effects of repeatedly bringing troops to a high state of readiness only to 'prick the bubble' by cancelling operations. Nevertheless, the volunteers did enjoy some benefits and privileges that were denied others. For example, they did not have to endure the daily fatigues and petty restrictions of barrack life.

In a stern rebuke to his officers, Haydon made it clear that he expected better from the commandos, acknowledging the difficulties they faced but refusing to accept any excuses for the widespread indiscipline and drunkenness he had seen within the battalions. He also had to deal with local police reports about soldiers' disorderly conduct. He told his officers that they needed to improve discipline and stamp out alcohol abuse as a matter of urgency. Haydon recognised that many of the young inexperienced officers required more training on managing the welfare of their men and the basic skills of soldiering. He suggested that senior officers make every effort to fill the gaps in the knowledge of their subordinates.

Similarly, the battalions lacked experienced NCOs. However, Haydon cautioned his officers to only promote those men who had shown initiative and understood that rank meant work and responsibility, not just wearing stripes and drawing extra pay. As a fillip to his audience, Haydon suggested that new operations were in the pipeline and that the commando experiment still had good prospects for success. Nonetheless, if volunteers decided they wanted to return to their parent units, they should be permitted to do so without hindrance. Haydon suggested that his officers should prioritise training and encourage soldiers to share their ideas for making improvements. Haydon gave his officers and troop leaders the following advice:

> Each man must be studied as an individual so that he is so placed where he gives the best that is in him. Look after your people in every way—Take hold of them and lead them.
>
> If Troop Leaders and their Officers will realise their full responsibilities, then they will do great things.
>
> Please neglect nothing—please think and act in urgent terms.
>
> Leave nothing to chance and let no trouble be too much.[25]

It takes a true leader to recognize when a new system or approach is not working as intended, despite the best efforts and resources invested in implementing it. Haydon's willingness to admit that the battalion system was ineffective for the Special Service Brigade, after only three and a half months, shows his ability to critically evaluate the situation objectively, without letting pride or stubbornness cloud his judgment. More importantly, Haydon displayed the courage and humility to approach his superiors and propose abandoning the battalion system to return to the original commando unit structure, albeit with improvements based on lessons learned. This decision could not have been easy, as it meant admitting that his initial plan had failed.

However, Haydon's primary concern was clearly his brigade's effectiveness and operational readiness, rather than saving face or perpetuating a flawed system out of misguided pride. By proposing to revert to the proven commando-unit structure, while incorporating enhancements based on the experience gained, Haydon demonstrated a willingness to learn from his mistakes and adapt quickly to changing circumstances. Such flexibility, coupled with the humility to acknowledge shortcomings and the courage to make tough decisions, even if it means reversing course, are hallmarks of an exceptional military leader. Haydon's actions exemplify the kind of decisive and principled command essential in ensuring any military force's combat-effectiveness.

Haydon understood that effective leadership extended far beyond just tactical and operational matters. He took great pains to offer guidance and support on a wide range of issues, from his soldiers' pastoral care and overall welfare to continuously improving every facet of the demanding commando-training regimen. Possibly due to his own combat experiences, Haydon understood that military forces cannot function at their peak unless the human elements are adequately cared for and developed.

By being attentive to the welfare of his troops and the professional development of his subordinate officers, Haydon attempted to cultivate a command climate of mutual respect, trust and commitment to excellence. Although operating under challenging circumstances, Haydon's leadership exemplified a balance of firm discipline and compassionate concern crucial for building cohesive highly motivated units like the commandos.

On 31 January 1941, Bob Laycock and 7, 8, and 11 commandos left the Special Service Brigade in Scotland and set sail for the Middle East as 'Force Z'. Nevertheless, when this hastily assembled formation arrived at its destination, it faced the same difficulties that plagued the other commando units.

4

The Guards Ethos

According to Field Marshal the Lord Guthrie of Craigiebank, GCB, LVO, OBE, DL, all regiments of the Household Division, the British monarch's personal troops, share some common qualities. They possess a remarkable esprit de corps, a strong sense of tradition and a forward-looking, versatile, can-do attitude.[1] Whether Foot Guards or Horse Guards, the regiments of the Household Division share one other quality: a commitment to being the best. In this chapter, we examine the Guards ethos, or 'special sauce', to use today's vernacular, which continues to transform ordinary civilians into guardsmen.[2]

The date generally recognised as the birth of the Household Division is 1660, the year of the restoration of King Charles II. The Household Division includes the Life Guards, the Blues and Royals of the Horse Guards, and five regiments of Foot Guards: the Grenadier Guards, Coldstream Guards, Scots Guards, Irish Guards, and Welsh Guards. Over the centuries, various composite formations of Foot Guards and Household Cavalry have also been temporarily established for specific conflicts, campaigns and operations.

The Life Guards is the senior regiment of the British Army. However, the Royal Horse Guards (now the Blue and Royals) and the Coldstream Guards were formed earlier than the Life Guards, as part of Oliver Cromwell's republican New Model Army. The Coldstream Regiment of Foot Guards is the oldest corps by continuous existence in the British Army.

In June 1650, Cromwell desired to confer a command on one of his staff officers, Colonel George Monck. In the autumn of 1658, Oliver Cromwell died. Monck, who held the post of general commanding the army in Scotland, moved his headquarters to the town of Coldstream, where his troops endured a bitter December of great hardship but apparently retained a cheerful spirit. Thereafter, Monck's troops were given the nickname 'Coldstreamers', in recognition of the regiment's steadfastness and endurance in the face of hardship.

On 1 January 1660, General Monck marched his troops south from Coldstream to London, whereupon the Coldstreamers helped to restore order following months of civil unrest in the capital. At the end of May 1660, King Charles II was restored to the throne of England. Monck was appointed captain general of land forces and made duke of Albemarle. Although Cromwell's New Model Army was disbanded, General Monck's Regiments of Horse and Foot were to be retained by the Crown.

On 14 February 1661, Monck's troops assembled at Tower Hill, where they were ordered to lay down their arms. Afterwards, the Regiment of Foot was immediately ordered to take up their arms again, but this time as the personal guards of the sovereign. In April 1670, George Monck died. In recognition of the Lord General's service to the Crown, his regiment was given the official title of Coldstream Guards.[3]

First and foremost, the soldiers of the Household Division are frontline combat troops. As the Sovereign's personal bodyguards, they hold an important ceremonial role during state occasions, safeguarding the royal palaces, with the Foot Guards performing the Ceremony of the Keys each night at the Tower of London. The ceremonial dress of the Household Regiments makes them instantly recognisable to the general public and conveys something of their histories. The Life Guards and Blues and Royal of the Household Cavalry wear a cuirass or armoured breast plate and backplate once worn by the cavalrymen of the English Civil War. They also wear a distinctive plumed helmet of the 1842 dragoon pattern while the white breeches and black leather riding boots hark back to the French Revolution and Napoleonic Wars of the early nineteenth century.

The ceremonial uniform of the Foot Guards, a scarlet tunic with a bearskin cap, makes them some of the most familiar troops the world over. Following the Battle of Waterloo (1815), the 1st Foot Guards had performed so well against the French Imperial Guards, who wore a bearskin cap, that the prince regent (later King George IV) decreed that they be known as the 1st Grenadier Regiment of Foot Guards and adopt the French style of headdress. In 1831, this distinction was extended to the Coldstream and Scots Guards. Bearskins were later adopted by the Irish Guards and the Welsh Guards when raised in 1900 and 1915, respectively.[4]

In 1959, a new military badge was introduced for the Household Brigade. It featured an eight-pointed star with the imperial crown at its centre and the motto 'Septem Juncta in Uno' [Seven Joined in One]. Initially, the term 'Household Brigade' referred explicitly to the Household Cavalry, while the Foot Guards had their own badge with the motto 'Tria Juncta in Uno' [Three Joined in One]. Over time, the Brigade of Guards expanded to include the Irish and Welsh Guards, leading to the revised motto 'Quinque Juncta in Uno' [Five Joined in One].[5]

The five regiments of Foot Guards can be distinguished from one another by the colour of the plume or hackle worn in their bearskins and by the spacing of buttons on their ceremonial scarlet tunics. See Figure 1.

Figure 1. Identification of Foot Guards by Ceremonial Dress Uniform.

Regiment	Tunic Buttons	Collar Badge	Shoulder Badge	Bearskin Hackle—colour and position
Grenadier Guards	Single	Grenade	Royal Cipher	White, worn on left-hand side
Coldstream Guards	Pairs	Garter Star	Rose	Red, worn on right-hand side
Scots Guards	Threes	Star, Order of Thistle	Thistle	None
Irish Guards	Fours	Shamrock	Star, Order of St Patrick	Blue, worn on right-hand side
Welsh Guards	Fives	Leek	Leek	White and green, worn on left-hand side

In June, troops of the Household Division perform the annual Trooping of the Colour ceremony on Horse Guards Parade, St James's Park, London to mark the sovereign's official birthday. The order in which all five regiments of Foot Guards form up when on parade together is (from right flank to left flank) Grenadiers, Welsh Guards, Scots Guards (in the centre and the reason they have no hackle), Irish Guards and Coldstream Guards.

Little Sparta

In his book *Fighting with the Guards*, author Keith Briant asks what makes guardsmen different from the infantrymen of other line regiments of the British Army. According to Briant:

> There is no reason to believe that the young men who enlist in the Guards are in any way braver, better, stronger or possessed of more stamina than any other young men. What, then, makes them into fighting men who, over a long period of military history, have been regarded as having extra quality—and having extra quality really only means the confidence that they will die where they are put rather than admit defeat?[6]

For over eighty years, the journey from civilian to guardsman started at Caterham or 'Little Sparta' as it was sometimes known. In 1877, the Guards Depot at Caterham-on-the-Hill, Surrey opened its gates. The depot cost £46,000 to build and incorporated every advance in military thinking to date, especially regarding health and hygiene. Up until then, army barracks had been filthy and overcrowded and a breeding ground for disease. Even in peacetime, the life expectancy of a British soldier based in the UK was shorter than that of the average civilian. The living conditions of soldiers stationed overseas were considerably worse. By comparison, Caterham was a beacon of modernity, constructed in the wake of the Crimean War, a conflict in which many British soldiers had died of disease due to inadequate clothing, food and shelter.

The depot was built adjacent to the Metropolitan Asylum for Imbeciles. In the nineteenth and early twentieth centuries, the word 'imbecile' was an official medical classification for someone with a low IQ (intelligence quotient). In 1920, the asylum was renamed Caterham Mental Hospital. For many bewildered recruits, it was said that the early days of training at the Guards Depot convinced them that they must have entered the asylum by mistake.[7]

In 1895, Major (later Major General) the Honourable H. H. Henniker prepared lecture notes for new recruits to the Brigade of Guards. After briefly explaining the chain of command from the sovereign downward to the individual guardsman, Henniker instructed the recruits on a variety of subjects including the importance of obedience, cleanliness, health, smartness, schooling (recruits were required to attend classes and attain a second-class certificate of education) and, lastly, discipline:

> The object of discipline is to develop a soldierly spirit; to help the soldier to bear fatigue, privation, and danger cheerfully; to imbue him with a sense of honour; to give him confidence in his superiors and comrades; to increase his powers of initiative, of self-confidence, and self-restraint; to train him to obey orders, or to act in the absence of orders, for the advantage of his corps in all conditions; to produce such a high degree of courage, disregard of self, and confidence in his armament, that in the stress of battle he will use his brain and his weapons coolly and to the best advantage; to impress upon him that, so long as he is physically capable of fighting, surrender to the enemy is a disgraceful act; and, finally, to teach him how to act in combination with his comrades in order to defeat the enemy. As soon as the recruit joins, he should be brought under influences which will tend to produce and increase such a spirit, and it is the duty of all officers and non-commissioned officers to assist in the attainment of this object by their conversation and example.[8]

The Process

Essentially, Caterham was a factory that turned civilians into guardsmen. The Brigade of Guards employed a brutally simple training process, refined over centuries to produce a very particular type of soldier. The Guards system of training sought to instil six basic qualities into its recruits, one layered upon the next, like bricks in a wall, until a steadfast guardsman was constructed.

The first quality the new recruits had to learn upon arrival at Caterham was cleanliness. The trainees were endlessly lectured and hectored about their seemingly shameful standards of personal hygiene, dress and deportment. Each recruit was also responsible for the cleanliness of his own personal bed space, the barrack room he occupied and all the equipment issued to him.

In the first weeks of training, the Guards' obsession with cleanliness transformed the recruits' lives into a misery of impromptu inspections and parades where they were forever failing to meet the required standards. Punishments swiftly followed the novices in every failure, mishap and minor infraction of the rules. However, gradually, painfully, the recruits found themselves standing straighter and looking smarter, with every item of equipment cleaned to perfection. At the same time, the natural resentment the trainees felt towards their instructors and tormentors slowly disappeared and was replaced by a feeling of pride.

To assist the recruits during basic training, a trained soldier, typically a seasoned guardsman, was assigned to each barrack room with the responsibility of instructing and helping the trainees meet the exacting standards. From an outsider's perspective, the challenges imposed on the recruits might seem nonsensical and even cruel, such as making them scrape the barrack room floor using razor blades to eliminate the tiniest speck of dirt. However, these seemingly pointless challenges aimed to create a fighting soldier who never overlooked the smallest detail or undertaking, no matter how fatigued they might be.

Following years of economic hardship during the 1930s, many novice guardsmen arrived at Caterham underweight and in poor physical condition. The Guards' training regimen aimed to improve the recruits' fitness levels with countless hours of parade-ground drill and intense periods of physical exercise. The constant pounding on the drill square also instilled in the recruits a habit of obeying orders quickly and without question. As the trainees' stamina and confidence increased, they realised that many of their once burdensome tasks became easier .

Psychology plays a significant role in military training, such as encouraging controlled aggression and helping to suppress the natural instinct for self-preservation. One of the objectives of the Guards training system was to cultivate a strong instinct for blind obedience in recruits to bolster their mental resilience in battle and decrease the chances of battle fatigue.

Once the novice guardsman had met the required standards of cleanliness, smartness and fitness, he started to feel more confident in his own abilities. Having overcome the many challenges of training and arrived at a point of competence in mastering a difficult job, recruits attained the fourth necessary quality for their transformation from civilians to guardsmen: pride. It was important for recruits to feel a sense of pride in themselves and their regiments. To help foster a deep emotional and psychological bond with their regiments, young guardsmen in training would visit the Guards Museum at Caterham. This museum was a vital educational tool, filled with relics, battle honours and reminders of the regiment's celebrated history and fighting prowess. Recruits were also rigorously tested on their regimental history, ensuring they internalised the traditions and legacy of their unit.

With a newfound pride in themselves and their regiment, the young trainees had to achieve the fifth essential quality of every guardsman: efficiency. They must strive to excel and be more efficient in all tasks than their peers. Schooled in the regiment's history and proud of its traditions, the young guardsman no longer needed to be bullied and cajoled by the training staff to reach high standards of effectiveness. Constantly reminded that the Guards were an elite fighting force, he became his own strict taskmaster, always pushing himself to be the best.[9]

During the 1930s and 1940s, the British Army held specific expectations for its soldiers. A good soldier exemplified loyalty to his regiment, adhered to strict discipline and promptly followed orders. Physical fitness was important, as soldiers needed strength, endurance and the ability to withstand challenging conditions. Proficiency in marksmanship, field craft and basic first aid was essential. Above all, teamwork formed the backbone of effective military operations, as soldiers relied on each other during combat. Although the training young guardsmen underwent at Caterham appeared unremarkable, the Brigade of Guards, fuelled by centuries of battlefield success, forged new soldiers with an unshakable belief in their own abilities.

Sir Terry Waite, a human rights activist and author, joined the Grenadier Guards in the 1950s. When Waite informed his father of his plan to join the Guards, his father tried to talk him out of it. Waite's father said, 'You do realise that Caterham is probably the toughest place in the British Army.' Undeterred, the teenage Terry Waite travelled to an army recruiting office in Liverpool, collected a travel warrant, and headed south to Caterham. Many years later, Waite travelled to war-torn Lebanon as special envoy for the Church of England. His mission was to try to secure the release of four Western hostages held captive by Islamic fundamentalist groups. On 20 January 1987, Waite was taken hostage. He remained in captivity for nearly five years until his release in November 1991. When he was finally released, after spending four years in total solitary confinement, Waite was transported to the Syrian Intelligence Headquarters, where an official asked if there was anything he required. Waite replied that he would like a haircut. According to Waite:

> I was determined to show the world I had not been defeated and would go out on public parade as well turned out as possible.
>
> Caterham? I can't say I loved the place, but it taught me valuable lessons. In fact, it certainly made a major contribution to my own survival. I've never gone back following my discharge, and now the Depot has moved. However, it lives on in my memory. My father was right. It was tough. But unknown to me, life was to deal me a tough hand and I shall always be grateful for what I learned there.[10]

In the foreword to the book *The Guards and Caterham*, His Royal Highness, Prince Philip, Duke of Edinburgh and Colonel of the Grenadier Guards, succinctly captured the transformative process that occurred at Caterham, turning civilians into guardsmen who believed they could 'beat the world'.

> We all remember the formative experiences in our lives. Some look back on them with affection and nostalgia, others would be happy to wipe them from their memories completely. The Guards Depot at Caterham-on-the-Hill provided a formidable experience for many hundreds of thousands of young men on their way to join their Regiments of the Brigade of Guards.

Caterham had to prepare young men for a wide variety of challenges. Anything from conventional infantry duties to armoured units, parachutists, the Long Range Desert Group and the Special Air Service Regiment, and it did it with great success. A training depot needs to do much more than develop discipline, fitness and basic military skills. It must also instill a sense of confidence and pride, which are essential for the morale and fighting spirit of every military unit. Whatever their personal views about the Guards Depot may have been, the proof of its methods is reflected in the outstanding military reputation, which the Guards Regiments achieved in small conflicts and world wars and in the precise discipline of their ceremonial duties.[11]

Caterham remained the official Guards Depot until 1960, when it relocated to Pirbright. However, guardsmen continued to be stationed at Caterham for another thirty-five years. On Thursday, 23 March 1995, the flag of Nijmegen Company, Grenadier Guards, was lowered for the last time, 118 years after the first guardsmen arrived.

Guards Officers

Until 1871, a gentleman could purchase a commission to become an officer in the British Army. A commission provided the purchaser opportunities for personal and professional advancement by ensuring access to the sovereign and London society. Before the establishment of the Royal Military Academy at Marlow in 1802, aspiring officers could attend privately run military colleges, but it was not compulsory. Traditionally, officers delegated the daily operations of their regiments to the non-commissioned officers and rarely interacted with the enlisted men.

Typically, the sons of the aristocracy and wealthy upper classes joined the Household Cavalry or Foot Guards to idle away their time on leisure pursuits such as hunting, gambling, drinking and womanising. It was unusual for junior officers to be married. When they decided to marry, they would usually quit the army because it was considered a vulgar, socially unacceptable occupation for a gentleman. To members of the aristocracy and Britain's social elites, the army was akin to working as a tradesman. The army was the destination for those second sons unlikely to inherit the family estate and not intelligent enough for a career in the law or the clergy.

Army reforms followed slowly in the wake of changes to British society rather than military necessity. However, as bastions of tradition, the Brigade of Guards and Household Cavalry did their best to resist change wherever possible. These regiments continued to draw their officer candidates almost exclusively from wealthy aristocratic families who sent their sons to public schools like Eton and Harrow. Guards' officers had to adhere to peculiar rules to emphasise their distinctiveness from regular line regiment officers, like never carrying parcels, never using public transportation, and never going anywhere without a hat. In his 1977 book *All the Queen's Men*, Russell Braddon's interviews reveal that the Household Division remained a socially elitist organisation throughout the 20th century.

> 'One doesn't like to be called a career officer,' a Welsh Guards officer explains, 'although, of course, one is. In the past, one was supposed to sustain the myth that we all had so much money and such vast estates that careers were beneath us, but not any longer. Actually, I personally have no money at all and no estates, and I will try jolly hard to do well in my Staff College exams so that a career is precisely what I have.'
>
> 'They're the Mafia of the British Army,' an Irish Guards officer slandered the Life Guards. 'One great big family with connections everywhere. If they want anything, their Lieutenant-Colonel rings their colonel, who rings his niece, who makes an offer no one can refuse.'
>
> The layman may not instantly take the Irishman's point—which is that the Colonel of the Life Guards is Admiral of the Fleet the Earl Mountbatten whose niece is Her Majesty Queen Elizabeth II.
>
> What the Irish Guards officer failed to mention is the Colonel of any of the Guards regiments who wants something simply has to call his mother, cousin or wife and they too would eventually be calling the Sovereign, who is Colonel in Chief of them all.[12]

Many aristocrats believed that a career in the army was vulgar and distasteful. Between the wars, Basil Liddell Hart, soldier, military historian and theorist, believed that the public took it largely for granted that an army commission was a symptom of idiocy. Public school boys being prepared for the Sandhurst Military Academy entrance exams were assumed to be the dimwits of the class. Junior Guards officers regarded the 'army' as 'a vague, remote, enormously incompetent authority' outside the Brigade of Guards and Household Cavalry. One's regiment mattered; the army did not.[13] Among the British Army regiments, the Foot Guards stood out with their arrogant, anti-intellectual, gentleman's-club mentality and loyalty, often leading to unhealthy isolationism and antagonism between units instead of harmony and cooperation.[14]

According to Richard Hart Sinnreich, retired US Army officer, independent consultant, columnist and military historian, the British Army regiment was a communal as well as an administrative and tactical organisation, and in the case of elite formations such as the Guards and Household Cavalry, were maintained as much for social and ceremonial functions as for potential combat operations. For officers, especially Guards officers, the regiment was a private, exclusive club, and a fitting home for gentlemen. It exerted a powerful cultural discipline above and beyond the military one. The more socially exclusive the regiment is, the more stringent its entry conditions are, requiring adherence to strict standards of dress, deportment and behaviour. In some respects, regiments, at least for their officers, were a convenient halfway house between English public school and marriage. By and large, the regiment was not the place to encourage the serious study of warfare.

In 1934, Tim Bishop joined the Life Guards at Windsor. He remembered that his commanding officer was noticeably absent, choosing to manage the regiment through his adjutant and NCOs. The commanding officer actively encouraged his officers to occupy themselves with leisure pursuits like hunting, race-riding and polo rather than spending time at Knightsbridge Barracks. Men like Robert Laycock, who took a keen interest in his profession, were very much in the minority in the Household Division.

Officer Recruitment

During the early years of the Second World War, officer recruitment was conducted by three-man command interview boards. Typically, candidates were quizzed about their family, social status and wealth rather than leadership qualities. Predictably, the aristocracy was keen to perpetuate the myth that only 'blue-blooded' men from the upper classes of society were born leaders. According to the social elite, leadership was an inherited trait and not a skill that could be taught to someone from a middle- or working-class background. Commonly used to describe British military leadership and perceived ineptitude during the First World War, the phrase 'lions led by donkeys' implied that brave working-class soldiers (lions) were led by incompetent upper-class commanders (donkeys). At the start of the Second World War, as the defeats mounted up, there was a widespread feeling of déjà vu, and that once again the ordinary soldier was being betrayed by an inept, indifferent leadership.

In 1942, the War Office introduced the General Service Corps (GSC) to act as a clearing house for all new recruits. During their time with the GSC, recruits received six weeks of basic military training. They were subjected to various intelligence and aptitude tests before being assigned to a specific branch of the army. The outdated and socially biased command interview board was replaced with the War Office selection board (WOSB) to select prospective officers for the army. Recruits identified as having leadership potential during their GSC evaluation were sent to a WOSB. The WOSB spent two or three days subjecting officer candidates to a barrage of tests and interviews designed to assess their intelligence, initiative, character and authority. Those candidates who passed the selection were sent to officer cadet training units (OCTUs) for several months' instruction.

Nearly half of all officer cadets selected by the command-interview-board system were washed out of training and returned to their units. By the end of 1942, the new system saw the number of officer candidates rated as above average increase from 22 per cent to 35 per cent. Only 15 per cent of OCTU graduates had attended a public school, while one in four new officers had no secondary education whatsoever. Having widened the social pool of officer candidates, the OCTU's failure rate fell to just 8 per cent.[15]

In his memoirs, Captain Christopher Bulteel, Coldstream Guards, recalled his early days as a cadet at the Royal Military College, Sandhurst. All the training staff at the college appeared to be guardsmen who gave the impression that anyone who was not a guardsman was hardly a soldier at all. Bulteel quickly learned that membership of the Brigade of Guards was an exclusive club, segregated from the ordinary world and quite convinced of its own superiority, that was reluctant to even speak to lesser breeds.[16]

Like Christopher Bulteel, the eminent military historian, Professor Michael Howard joined the Coldstream Guards as a young man. After officer training at Sandhurst, Howard was sent to the Guards Training Battalion at Pirbright, where he was introduced to the 'taboos of the tribe' as he described them, such as always referring to his formation as 'the Brigade', never 'the Guards'. At Pirbright, he learned from his fellow officers that fighting was their function. When not fighting, they should occupy their time with hunting, shooting, gambling and drinking and generally engage in traditional warrior pastimes as their forebears had done for generations. Few of his fellow officers expected to remain in the army once hostilities had ceased. Howard learned that most of his peers had attended Eton, and many were interrelated over many generations. Cowardice or any serious misbehaviour, known as 'putting up a black', would taint an officer for life and so simply did not happen. But anyone who took the army seriously as a profession, unless he possessed sterling compensatory qualities, was written off as a 'military shit'.[17]

In January 1939, Lord Carrington, a hereditary peer and later a Conservative politician, joined the 2nd Battalion, Grenadier Guards at Wellington Barracks, London. Having completed an officer training course at Sandhurst, Carrington joined his battalion as an Ensign (second lieutenant).[18] The Brigade of Guards had a strong ethos, with a focus on discipline, order, tradition and an exactly observed routine. The battalion was proud of its history and traditions, and many officers had fathers and grandfathers who were Grenadiers, including Carrington. The rigorous social conventions of the time were accepted as part of an unchanging order.

Officers were expected to dress correctly on every occasion, and there were strict rules about what to wear and how to behave. The atmosphere was formal and traditional, with a focus on propriety and correctness. According to Carrington, there was a certain infectious self-indulgence in the atmosphere, which led to softness of fibre where the reverse was needed. He believed that the shadow of the previous war hindered the battalion's ability to adapt to the changing circumstances of the new war. Carrington felt that the battalion's military training was inadequate, with too much focus on ceremonial duties and not enough on field training and military education.

In his memoirs, Lord Carrington reflects:

The theory in the Brigade of Guards—probably seldom articulated because they were not great theorists—was that officers and men who had been trained and disciplined to get every small personal detail right, whether in drill, dress, cleanliness or whatever, would similarly expect and observe the highest possible standards in every duty they were called on to perform. 'If it's worth doing, it's worth doing properly' was often heard, and so far as it goes it is a valid maxim. The trouble was that a lot of things were also worth doing which we didn't do at all. I must not exaggerate the inadequacy of our instruction: some principles were inculcated which were absolutely sound. In particular, we were left in no doubt that the interests and care of our men (when we had the chance to see them) came first, always: and our own concerns and comfort came last, always. We were very proud—indeed I suspect we often appeared arrogant in our pride—of how our battalion looked, drilled, responded to orders, did its duty. It was a fine battalion and there was not only first-class discipline but a splendid spirit within all ranks. We laughed at our deficiencies of equipment, mocked 'The Army', which we thought of as a vague, remote, enormously incompetent authority quite outside ourselves. We reckoned we were very good.[19]

Guards Officers and the Birth of Special Forces

Winston Churchill and the British government were keen to develop irregular forces at the start of the Second World War for several reasons. Firstly, after the fall of France in June 1940, Britain found itself alone, facing the threat of a German invasion. Churchill was determined to avoid a purely defensive mindset, which he believed had contributed to France's defeat. In a minute dated 3 June 1940, he wrote, 'The completely defensive habit of mind, which has ruined the French, must not be allowed to ruin all our initiative.'[20] He wanted to take the fight to the enemy and maintain an offensive spirit. Irregular forces like the independent companies and commandos offered a way to strike at German-occupied territories when Britain lacked the resources for large-scale operations.

Churchill saw raiding forces as a way to harass the enemy, tie down German troops along the occupied coastlines and gather intelligence. In his 5 June minute, he called for 'specially trained troops of the hunter class, who can develop a reign of terror down his coasts, first of all on the 'butcher and bolt' policy'. He believed these operations would boost British morale by demonstrating that the UK was still capable of offensive action. Irregular units could also be formed and deployed relatively quickly and cheaply compared to conventional forces. The prime minister hoped these raids would keep the Germans off-balance and force them to divert resources to coastal defence.[21]

At the outbreak of war, many officers and men from across the British Army, including elite units like the Guards, eagerly volunteered for the newly formed independent companies and commandos. These special forces promised immediate action, specialised training, and high-risk, high-reward operations that greatly appealed to ambitious and adventurous young servicemen. The volunteers were often driven by a simple desire to 'do their bit' and contribute to the war effort.

However, reality often fell short of the volunteers' expectations. Despite the enthusiasm and military zeal demonstrated by the volunteers, their hopes for getting into action and contributing meaningfully to the war effort were frequently frustrated. They encountered numerous obstacles, including entrenched military bureaucracy, severe lack of resources and poor strategic planning. Many operations were plagued by frequent postponements or outright cancellations, leaving eager troops idle and demoralised.

This situation is reflected in the Cabinet papers of the time. For instance, the prime minister's minute from 8 September 1940 expresses frustration at the lack of progress in deploying these special units: 'Unhappily, nothing has happened so far of which the troops are aware. They do not know they are not under sentence of disbandment. All recruiting has been stopped, although there is a waiting list.' This illustrates the disconnect between the volunteers' eagerness and the military establishment's ability to effectively utilise these new forces, highlighting the challenges faced by early special forces units in translating their potential into actual operational effectiveness.[22]

A curious and interesting paradox lies in the involvement of Guards officers in establishing these special forces units. Why were these officers, who belonged to regiments steeped in tradition and ceremony, and possessed of a certain disdain for professional soldiering, so prominent in the development of unconventional warfare?

One key factor was the social status and connections of Guards officers. In the early years of the war, the British government and military leadership were still dominated by the aristocracy and the landed gentry to a certain extent, notes historian David Cannadine. Prime Minister Winston Churchill was 'the descendant of Marlborough and a historian of past glories, the oldest strain of ruling tradition'.

Churchill was a strong advocate for the creation of irregular forces such as the commandos, and his support was crucial in overcoming resistance from more conservative elements in the military establishment. His support for these units was influenced by his own experiences of irregular warfare in South Africa and his admiration for the exploits of T. E. Lawrence during the Arab Revolt of the First World War. Churchill also hoped to avoid the excessive casualties of the previous war by fighting a more technological conflict.

However, overall, the Second World War marked a significant shift in Britain's social and political landscape, with the rise of trade unions, technocrats and businessmen as a new ruling class. The conflict was seen as a people's war, rather than a patrician struggle, and the aristocracy's role in it was ultimately transient and superficial.[23]

Guards officers, with their close ties to the aristocracy and the highest echelons of society, were well-positioned to leverage these connections to gain support and resources for their initiatives. As previously noted, the Guards regiments' unique access to the highest levels of power through their social and familial connections proved invaluable. This ability to bypass normal channels and appeal directly to those in power was a significant advantage for Guards officers seeking to establish special-forces units.[24]

Winston Churchill's favouritism towards specific units, particularly the Guards, was evident in his wartime actions as prime minister. This bias extended to special-forces units like the commandos, often drawing personnel from prestigious regiments. Churchill's personal interventions to protect these units demonstrate how his military background and class loyalties influenced strategic decision-making at the highest level.

In July 1941, when the commandos of Layforce were disbanded after suffering various setbacks in North Africa, Churchill personally intervened to reconstitute the force. In a personal minute dated 23 July 1941, he wrote, 'I wish the Commandos in the Middle East to be reconstituted as soon as possible,' and criticised Middle East command for having 'maltreated and thrown away this invaluable force'. He insisted on appointing Brigadier Robert Laycock as Director of Combined Operations and placed the force under General Auchinleck's direct command.[25]

This pattern of intervention by Churchill continued throughout the war. On two separate occasions, in June 1943 and again in 1944, Churchill directly intervened to protect the 6th Guards (Tank) Brigade from being disbanded, overriding the recommendations of his army commanders who needed infantry replacements.[26]

These interventions highlight how Churchill's personal affiliations and beliefs about elite units influenced his decision-making. By preserving the integrity of both Special Forces and Guards units against the recommendations of his field commanders, Churchill showed a willingness to prioritise what he perceived as high-quality specialised units over broader tactical requirements. This approach potentially impacted the flexibility of British forces during critical periods of the war, but also ensured the continuation of units that Churchill believed could make unique and valuable contributions to the war effort.

The Guards' elite status and unique ethos may have instilled in its officers a sense of superiority and a belief in their abilities to innovate and lead special units. Despite their focus on tradition and ceremony, the Guards prided themselves on being the best soldiers in the British Army. The Guards' distinctive combination of tradition and innovation, what Lord Guthrie described as their 'esprit de corps', combined with a 'can-do attitude', drove many to volunteer for special forces. This confidence in their abilities and a desire to prove themselves in battle may have driven Guards officers to seek new challenges and opportunities in unconventional warfare.

Early defeats suffered by the British Army during the war also played a role in the rise of special forces. As the army struggled with inadequate equipment, training and leadership, there was a growing recognition that new approaches were needed. Guards officers, with their social status and prestige, may have felt a particular responsibility to help turn the tide of the war. As Michael Howard, himself a Coldstream Guards officer, recalled, 'their function was to fight, and when not fighting they should occupy their time with hunting, shooting, gambling, drinking, and generally engage in traditional warrior pastimes as their forebears had done for generations'. This warrior ethos, combined with a sense of duty to king and country, likely motivated many Guards officers to seek opportunities to make a difference and actively contribute to the war effort.[27]

The creation of special forces allowed these officers to apply their skills and leadership abilities in a new and challenging context. As officer recruitment and training methods evolved to include more candidates from middle and lower-class backgrounds, Guards officers may have viewed special forces as a way to retain their elite status and influence within the military. By leading these highly selective, unconventional units, they could set themselves apart from the regular army, which they often despised, and prove their worth as warriors and 'natural' leaders.

Undoubtedly, there was an element of elitism and class-based conceit underpinning the enthusiasm of Guards officers for special forces. These men, predominantly drawn from the aristocracy and upper classes, often harboured a deep-seated belief in their own innate superiority and leadership abilities. This conviction stemmed from a long-standing tradition in British society that equated social status with natural talent and fitness to lead.

The literary portrayal of aristocratic and upper-class men from the Edwardian period through the interwar years often focused on three key archetypes: the gentleman adventurer, the officer and gentleman, and the sportsman. These depictions and real-life examples celebrated in the press reinforced a particular self-image for young men of privilege.

The gentleman adventurer archetype, exemplified in Sir H. Rider Haggard's Allan Quatermain series of popular novels, such as *King Solomon's Mines* (1885), presents aristocratic men as intrepid explorers facing exotic dangers with resourcefulness and bravery. This literary trope found real-world parallels in figures like Robert Falcon Scott, whose Antarctic expeditions captured the public imagination. *Scott's Last Expedition*, published in 1913, cemented the image of the stoic, determined British explorer.[28]

The officer and gentleman ideal, portrayed in works like John Buchan's Major General Sir Richard Hannay novels, such as *The Thirty-Nine Steps* (1915), depicted aristocratic men as natural military leaders combining martial skill with gentlemanly behaviour. T. E. Lawrence, or 'Lawrence of Arabia', embodied this archetype. His exploits during the Arab Revolt and his book, *Seven Pillars of Wisdom* (1926), fascinated the public and reinforced the image of the aristocratic officer.

Literature also frequently portrayed upper-class men as excellent sportsmen, emphasising their physical prowess and leadership qualities. P. G. Wodehouse's witty golf stories like *The Clicking of Cuthbert* (1922) often featured aristocratic characters excelling in sports. This literary theme was mirrored by real-life figures like Lord Burghley, who won the gold medal in the 400m hurdles at the 1928 Olympics, further reinforcing the image of the aristocrat as a natural athlete.

These ideals were bolstered by news coverage of real-life adventurers and soldiers. Sir Ernest Shackleton's Antarctic expeditions, the exploits of First World War flying aces and the 1924 British Mount Everest expedition captured the public imagination. Such stories, widely disseminated through books and news media, collectively shaped expectations for how young aristocratic and upper-class men should behave and what they should aspire to achieve. When Bill Stirling and Brian Mayfield recruited their team of experts to staff the commando training school at Inverailort House, the eclectic group of instructors included Olympic gold medallist Cyril Mackworth-Praed and explorers Freddie Spencer Chapman and Jimmy Scott. Frederick Browning, often referred to as the 'father of Airborne Forces', embodied the ideals of both officer and gentleman, as well as sportsman. In addition to his military career, Browning was an accomplished sailor and competed in the 1928 Winter Olympics.

The Guards officers, products of elite public schools and a regimental culture steeped in centuries of tradition, conceitedly viewed themselves as possessing unique, inborn leadership qualities that could not be easily replicated or taught to those from the lower classes. This mindset was not merely personal vanity but a reflection of broader societal attitudes of the time, where class distinctions were deeply ingrained and rarely questioned. Possibly, the eagerness of young Guards officers to join special units like the commandos can be seen, in part, as an extension of this belief. These elite groups provided a platform to test their perceived exceptional qualities. The exclusivity and prestige of such units aligned well with their self-image and social standing.

However, not everyone in the military establishment was convinced of the need for special forces. Some saw them as an unnecessary diversion of manpower and resources from the main war effort. As one critic argued, 'there should be no specialised commando units, on the grounds—with which I agree—that the existence of such units lowers the standards of training in the rest of the Army'. There was a belief among some that improving the overall quality and leadership of the army would negate the need for elite units to conduct unconventional operations.

In August 1940, Anthony Eden, secretary of state for war, wrote to Churchill, 'While I agree as to the need for having some troops specially trained for landings from boats, I also think it vital to raise to an ever higher level the fighting spirit and initiative of the average brigade and battalion. If I seem to you to be violently opposed to the Storm Trooper [a reference to German elite shock troops of the First World War] principle, it is only because I do not want the greater part of the British Army to become a dull, dead mass.'[29]

On 25 September 1941, the commander of UK Home Forces, General Alan Brooke, later 1st Viscount Alanbrooke, wrote that he felt the commandos should not have been separated from the army and each division should have its own battle patrol capable of commando work. Brooke confided to his diary that he remained convinced until the end of the war that 'the Commandos should never have been divorced from the army in the way they were.'[30] Instead, Brooke believed that most military operations could and should have been undertaken by specially trained troops from within regular army formations.

Despite these objections, the British Army ultimately developed a wide range of special forces in the early years of the war. In addition to the political support from figures like Churchill, this was largely due to the efforts and influence of Guards officers who championed these initiatives. Men like Robert Laycock, Shimi Lovat, Jock Lewes, Bill and David Stirling, all Household Division officers, who were instrumental in the creation and leadership of units like the commandos and the Special Air Service. Their social status, connections, ambitions, and genuine desire to help turn the tide of the war allowed them to overcome institutional resistance, enabling them to build these units into effective fighting forces.

In the end, the contribution of Guards officers to the establishment of British special forces in the Second World War was a product of their unique position within the military and wider British establishment. As members of elite regiments with a strong warrior ethos and close ties to the ruling class, they were well-suited to the task of creating and leading unconventional units. Despite resistance from some quarters, their efforts helped reshape the British Army and pave the way for a new era of military innovation and adaptation.

Layforce Goes East

After the defeat and evacuation of the BEF from the beaches of Dunkirk, the only place where British and Commonwealth forces could engage the Axis powers of Nazi Germany and fascist Italy was in the Mediterranean and North Africa. In December 1940, General Sir Archibald Wavell's Western Desert Force of 36,000 men attacked the Italians at Sidi Barrani in Egypt. On 7 February 1941, Wavell's offensive ended at El Agheila with the destruction of nine Italian divisions and the capture of 130,000 men. German Führer, Adolf Hitler, realised that he would have to support the Italians, and on 11 February 1941, Major General Erwin Rommel's well-trained and well-equipped *Afrika Korps* landed at Tripoli. Soon, the British Eighth Army found itself on the defensive.

The Desert War was primarily fought along a narrow corridor of the Libyan and Egyptian coasts with the Mediterranean Sea on one flank and the deep inhospitable desert on the other. The opposing forces fought up and down the coast road in a series of advances and retreats. Logistics dominated the Desert War. Throughout the campaign, both sides found that the further they advanced, the harder it was to supply their forces adequately. Both sides suffered shortages of fuel at crucial moments. The enemy's overstretched supply lines made an attractive target of opportunity for raiding forces. Therefore, 7, 8 and 11 commandos, collectively known as Force 'Z', were dispatched to the Middle East. On arrival, the force was joined by two locally raised units: 50 and 52 commandos.

Toward the end of January 1941, 8 Commando embarked on HMS *Glenroy*. Admiral Sir Roger Keyes and Brigadier Haydon boarded the ship to address the troops before departure. At 23.00hrs on 31 January 1941, HMS *Glenroy* slipped her moorings and set sail for North Africa, escorted by HMS *Kenya* and five destroyers. On the day of departure, the Brigade Major remarked gloomily to Lieutenant Colonel Laycock, 'You appear to be going to command a force of over 100 officers and 1,500 other ranks with one staff officer, a notebook, and eight wireless sets which nobody can work.'[1]

The first few days of the voyage were marred by stormy weather and rough sea conditions, resulting in widespread seasickness amongst the troops. Later, a debilitating outbreak of fever and diarrhoea swept through the ship, leaving many of the commandos in a weakened state. On 6 February, as HMS *Glenroy* made a brief stop at Freetown, the commandos were issued tropical uniforms and received a course of inoculations. On 13 February, the ship crossed the Equator before making port at Cape Town, South Africa, where shore leave was granted. Finally, at 17.00hrs on 7 March, the commandos arrived at Suez, Egypt.

On 10 March, Major General Evetts arrived on HMS *Glenroy* and announced that the commandos, now called Layforce, would form a Brigade within his 6th Division. Evetts told his audience that he foresaw an early opportunity for important and hazardous operations against the enemy, for which a month's hard training would be required. No. 8 Commando, now designated 'B' Battalion, was stationed at Camp 50, Geneifa, on the Great Bitter Lake, east of Cairo. Throughout March, Laycock spent his time between Geneifa and Cairo, conferring with the 6th Division about how Layforce might be usefully employed. At the same time, all ranks carried out daily training to restore the commandos' physical fitness after their draining sea voyage.

On 1 April 1941, the commandos started to prepare for Operation Cordite, the invasion of the Italian-held island of Rhodes. However, on 6 April 1941, the German Army attacked Greece and Yugoslavia to secure its Balkan flank prior to the invasion of the Soviet Union. Already overstretched and under-resourced in North Africa, the British dispatched 58,000 Commonwealth troops to Greece, severely weakening Wavell's forces. On 7 April, Operation Cordite was postponed. As part of an elaborate deception plan before Operation Cordite took place, Lieutenant Colonel Dudley Clarke had created the fictitious 1 Special Air Service Brigade. He sought to convince the Italians of a fictitious airborne threat and entice them to move their forces from the northern side of Rhodes, where landings were planned, to the southern side.

On 19 April 1941, 7 Commando boarded HMS *Glengyle* at Alexandria, Egypt and sailed for Bardia, Libya. The Bardia raid intended to harass the enemy's lines of communication and inflict as much damage as possible on supplies and material. Unfortunately, the operation achieved very little, although several technical and operational lessons were learned for future raids, such as the need for better navigational aids. The raid's main result was to cause the enemy to redeploy a significant number of troops and armour from Sollum to Bardia, thus easing pressure on the British Army's Western Desert Force.

By early May, it is clear from entries in the Layforce war diary that the formation had serious disciplinary and morale problems:

Repeated cancellations and postponements of Layforce is engendering an attitude of cynicism in all ranks which is exemplified by the following incidents brought to the notice of Col. Laycock.

The following inscription was found on one of the troop decks of HMS *Glengyle* after it had been vacated by A Battalion. "Never in the whole history of human endeavour have so few been so buggered about by so many." (N.B. Since formation this unit has been successively under command W.O., Home Forces, DCO, 1 SS Bde, GHQ ME, 6 Div, BTE, and Desforce).

The war diary suggests that Layforce was becoming something of a joke. One Royal Marine officer suggested that the formation change its name to 'Belayforce', as its planned operations were routinely postponed or cancelled.

On 20 May 1941, the Germans launched a combined airborne and amphibious assault on the island of Crete, codenamed Operation Mercury. At the same time, Layforce started to disintegrate. No. 11 Commando (C Battalion) was redeployed to Cyprus.

On 22 May, Laycock attended a meeting in Alexandria where the possibility of converting two battalions of the Special Service Brigade into new detachments of the Long Range Desert Group was discussed. Although Laycock agreed that his troops were suitable for conversion, he pointed out that the commandos had suffered considerable wastage and were no longer up to their war establishment or paper strength. He also pointed out that due to the peculiar terms of voluntary commando service, each individual soldier would have to agree to join the LRDG. The meeting concluded with the whole matter being deferred to a higher military authority. However, the events on Crete were to make any hypothetical discussions about the future of Layforce irrelevant.

On 25 May, Laycock attempted to land a force on Crete to reinforce the garrison, but bad weather caused the operation to be aborted. The following night, the commandos successfully landed at Suda Bay (Souda Bay) on the northwest coast of the island. However, rather than reinforce the garrison, the commandos had to cover a rather disorderly retreat and evacuation of British and Commonwealth forces. Between 27 and 31 May, the commandos fought a rearguard action, which enabled the main evacuation effort at Sphakia to take place. According to the Layforce war diary:

14:00hrs: Final orders from Creforce for evacuation (a) Layforce positions not to be held to the last man and last round but only as long as necessary to cover the withdrawal of other fighting forces. (b) No withdrawal before orders from H.Q. (c) Layforce to embark after other fighting forces but before stragglers.

The war diary entry for 22.00hrs reports that Colonel Laycock, under his own authority, ordered Layforce to evacuate the island. But by the time it was the commandos' turn to be evacuated, most of the ships and landing craft had already departed. Most of Laycock's forces were left to fend for themselves, although, controversially, he had already departed the island. Around six hundred commandos were killed, wounded, or taken prisoner on Crete.[2]

A certain amount of controversy has swirled around Bob Laycock's decision-making and leadership during the evacuation of Crete. In his book *Crete: The Battle and the Resistance*, Military Historian Anthony Beevor accuses Laycock of leaving the island prematurely, abandoning some of his men. He also suggests that Evelyn Waugh falsified the Layforce war diary to conceal the facts.[3] In contrast, Philip Eade's biography *Evelyn Waugh: A Life Revisited*, presents a more sympathetic view of Laycock and his decision-making during the chaotic evacuation. Eade contends that Beevor's accusations against Laycock and Waugh are based on supposition rather than historical facts.[4]

These conflicting interpretations highlight the complexities of wartime decision-making and the challenges historians and academics face when evaluating primary and secondary source materials. Whatever the truth of the matter, Laycock's superiors did not believe that he had done anything wrong during the evacuation of Crete, and this episode did not impede the progress of his military career.

In May 1941, a pro-Axis revolt in Iraq raised alarms that the Vichy French regime might allow German forces to establish bases in Syria, as promised by the Vichy Foreign Minister. Despite crushing the Iraqi revolt, General Wavell was sufficiently concerned that Germany would exploit Syrian facilities and communications to jeopardise wider British campaigns. Churchill pushed for a pre-emptive strike against Vichy French Syria before the Germans could make their move.

The invasion of Vichy French Syria called for three main thrusts, with the 7th Australian Division advancing towards Damascus and Beirut from Palestine. At the same time, two other forces invaded from Iraq: one towards Palmyra, the other along the Euphrates. A major obstacle for the brigade taking the coastal route to Beirut was the Litani River running east-west in a narrow gorge just north of Tyre. The plan was for Layforce's 11 Commando (C Battalion) to conduct an amphibious landing on beaches north of the river to seize and hold crossings until relieved by the 25th Brigade (Australia).

On 8 June 1941, around 04.00hrs, 11 Commando landed in several parties from the ship HMS *Glengyle*. Despite coming under fire, they were able to cross the beaches, capture enemy vehicles and seize the key Kafr Badr bridge and valley running east from it after fighting French troops. But the original plan went awry when the bridge itself was blown up by the French just before Australian forces arrived. No. 11 Commando fought fiercely throughout the night, beating back armoured counterattacks before finally being relieved by the Australians, who built a pontoon bridge. The battle to secure the Litani River crossings cost 11 Commando 123 casualties, about 25 per cent of its strength, but was regarded as a major success for Layforce.

While 11 Commando took part in the attack on Vichy French Syria, 8 Commando remained at Mersa Matruh in Egypt. Small detachments from 8 Commando were sent to the besieged port of Tobruk. The original plan was for these detachments to conduct raids on German lines from Tobruk and ultimately link up with a relieving force, but no such relief operation materialised. After spending about three weeks in Tobruk without being able to carry out their intended raiding role, the commandos returned to Mersa Matruh by sea in mid-May.

In June 1941, with British forces overstretched and fighting on multiple fronts, General Wavell decided to disband Layforce as an 'expensive commodity' that he could no longer afford. His replacement, General Sir Claude Auchinleck (later Field Marshal) agreed, and on 1 August 1941, Layforce was officially disbanded apart from 11 Commando, which returned to Cyprus. In July 1941, a party of volunteers from 8 Commando agreed to return to Tobruk, where they raided an Italian-held strongpoint situated on two small hills known as the Twin Pimples. The site overlooked the forward positions of the 18th Cavalry (India), which had been mechanised. Under the leadership of Captain Philip Dunne, a forty-man team stealthily moved through the Italian lines at night, aided by a diversion created by the Indian troops. In a fierce close-quarters battle, the commandos bombed and bayoneted the Italians, destroying ammunition dumps and mortars before withdrawing successfully with few casualties.

In October 1941, at a meeting at GHQ Cairo, the commandos were reconstituted using remnants of Layforce, the Special Boat Section, L Detachment, Special Air Service and other personnel. Reorganised into troops under Bob Laycock, it included the original 11 Commando as 3 Troop. In November, as General Auchinleck's Operation Crusader was getting underway, 11 Commando carried out a daring operation codenamed Flipper with the intention of killing or capturing General Erwin Rommel.

The raiding force set sail in two British submarines. The raiders came ashore in rubber dinghies, but only after some difficulty due to bad weather and the force was reduced in size. The commandos attacked what was thought to be Rommel's house and HQ near Sidi Rafa. However, despite their killing some German officers, it turned out Rommel was in Rome celebrating his wife's birthday. The raid ended in tragedy when the commander, Lieutenant Colonel Geoffrey Keyes, was killed storming the building, earning him a posthumous Victoria Cross. Most of the raiding force was either killed or captured.

After the raid, Bob Laycock and the beach party were unable to evacuate from the coast for two nights due to heavy seas that prevented a submarine from picking them up. On 20 November, as the enemy closed in, Laycock ordered his dwindling force to disperse into small groups and attempt to return to British lines. Laycock himself escaped with one other man, Sergeant Terry, finally reaching British forces on Christmas Day, after forty-one days in the enemy-occupied desert. Within a week of his return, Laycock was ordered back to England to take over command of the Special Service Brigade.[5]

Interviewed by the Imperial War Museum in 1993, George Jellicoe recalled his own experiences of Layforce. On reaching the Middle East, Jellicoe and a large contingent of 8 Commando went on board HMS *Aphis*. The commandos' mission was to attack a German airfield, but the ship was detected and nearly sunk before the troops could be put ashore; the raid was subsequently abandoned.

Jellicoe described the 'Aphis Mission' as a terribly clumsy way to attack an airfield. Overall, he believed that operational planning was very amateurish and the morale of the commandos assigned to Layforce quickly collapsed. After a month stationed at Tobruk, Jellicoe recalled, 8 Commando was disbanded, and he returned to the 3rd Battalion, Coldstream Guards. By July 1941, Jellicoe found himself gradually adjusting to regimental life and served with a Motor Battalion, although he did not see much action.[6]

In his book, *With Stirling's SAS in the Desert* (originally published under the title *When the Grass Stops Growing*), Carol Mather describes how Layforce chaotically disintegrated in the summer of 1941. He recalled that the remaining Guards officers gathered at the Cecil Hotel, Alexandria, to discuss what they might do. Some officers had already rejoined their parent regiments. Mather blamed GHQ Middle East for the officers' situation but conceded that the commandos had acquired a reputation for acting 'independently'. Mather writes that during this period, as Layforce disbanded, David Stirling started to recruit for his own raiding force that would be dropped by parachute close to enemy targets and then picked up by the Long Range Desert Group. When Stirling approached Mather about joining this new force, he declined. Mather believed Stirling's 'hare-brained scheme' was doomed to failure. Instead, Mather decided to join another Special Service unit, the GHQ Liaison Squadron, known as Phantom. The unit was tasked with providing up-to-date intelligence to the commander of the British Eighth Army so that he had a 'real-world' picture of the battlefield. Dermot Daly, Scots Guards, Mather's former troop leader, was in command. Mather commented on how the chaos of Layforce's last days contrasted with the confidence and clear sense of purpose he found with his new unit.[7]

The Origins of Failure

Layforce arrived in the Middle East when the British military situation was desperate. To make matters worse, General Wavell had to strip the Desert Army of men and material that he could ill afford to lose to support the defence of Greece. Unfortunately, GHQ Middle East had no understanding of special forces or how to use them, and did not have the luxury of time to learn. German air superiority over the skies of North Africa made seaborne commando raids extremely risky propositions, something the navy was loath to support. All but the fastest ships were vulnerable to Luftwaffe air attacks during daylight. When the commandos' assault ships and landing craft were redeployed, Layforce lost its only source of operational mobility. The Commando Brigade lacked its own logistical and heavy weapons support, so it could not be deployed as a traditional army formation. Instead, it became a general reserve for the Desert Army while being denied replacement troops to make good its losses.

Although limited in number, every operation that Layforce undertook drained its operational capacity. At the same time, the frequent postponement and cancellation of operations undermined the commandos' morale and discipline. There was a general feeling within the Desert Army that commandos were a waste of good troops who could be better employed with line regiments, especially when manpower was stretched to breaking point.

Understandably, GHQ Middle East found ways to syphon off men from Layforce for redeployment elsewhere, such as the defence of Tobruk. The final nail in the coffin for the commando experiment was when most of its men were sent to reinforce Crete, where they were used to cover the evacuation. Many of the men were taken prisoner, and Layforce was rendered useless. However, from the embers of 8 (Guards) Commando, a new force was about to spark into life.

Bob Laycock, the Strategic Commander

Today, the name Robert Laycock is largely forgotten except by military historians and academics. During the war, Laycock and his wife frequently appeared in newspapers and high-society magazines such as *Tatler*. Often referred to in the press as 'Lucky Laycock' and 'Britain's No. 1 Commando', his appointment as Chief of Combined Operations in October 1943 made front-page news.[1] The following year, a photographic portrait of Laycock appeared in *The Illustrated London News* as part of a series called 'Men Who Shape Our Destinies'.[2]

Laycock was deliberately portrayed in the British media as a heroic commando leader, the embodiment of special-forces prowess and aristocratic warrior traditions. Laycock's public persona served two main propaganda purposes. It boosted civilian morale during the challenging times of war, when victories were few and far between. It also emphasised the importance of commando operations to both the nation and military leadership.

His regular appearances with his socially connected wife (he was married to Angela Dudley Ward, younger daughter of William Dudley Ward, a Liberal politician and member of the Privy Council) in publications ranging from newspapers to society magazines reinforced his status as a recognisable military figure, helping cement and reinforce public support for special operations when their strategic value was still debated within conventional military circles. Later, this media strategy probably helped to ensure continued political and resource support for special operations whilst reinforcing British confidence in its military leadership during the critical invasion phase of 1944.

In March 1942, Laycock's appointment as commander of the special service brigade marked a significant advancement for British special forces operations. His prior experience commanding 8 Commando and leadership of Layforce had provided him with invaluable insight into the potential and limitations of unconventional warfare. Having demonstrated exceptional personal courage during Operation Flipper (the Rommel Raid) and his subsequent six-week evasion behind enemy lines, Laycock brought operational credibility to his new leadership role. The next three years would see him transform the commandos from an experimental small raiding force into a sophisticated military organisation, ultimately assuming responsibility for all Combined Operations at the highest strategic level.

Special Service Brigade, 1942–43

On 1 March 1942, Laycock was appointed commander of the special service brigade and promoted to acting brigadier. He took control of eight commandos (1, 2, 3, 4, 5, 6, 9 and 12) and established headquarters initially at Castle Douglas before relocating to Ardrossan in April. Laycock's leadership style emphasised organisational efficiency and front-line presence. He regularly visited his commanding officers, inspecting their units and attending exercises.

When presented with proposals to split the Brigade, Laycock firmly rejected the division of the force. His 27 March letter instead secured authorisation for an expanded headquarters staff, including a Brigade Second-in-Command (Colonel), Brigade Major, Staff Captain, and specialist officers. This demonstrated his preference for maintaining unified command whilst building sufficient staff capacity.

Laycock maintained high professional standards. Evelyn Waugh noted in his diary that following an exercise, Laycock delivered criticism 'without a sting' to troop leaders about weaknesses in training and discipline, threatening disbandment whilst 'commanding admiration' through his approach. This reflected his ability to deliver difficult messages without creating resentment.

In the spring of 1942, Laycock oversaw Operations Myrmidon and Abercrombie. In August 1942, the disastrous Operation Jubilee (Dieppe Raid) took place. The operation was an early dress rehearsal for the eventual full-scale invasion of France. The objective was to test the Germans' strength by briefly landing and holding a port. While the raid had been a resounding failure, many valuable lessons were learned that later informed the planning of Operation Overlord. No. 4 Commando achieved the only outright success of the raid when Lord Lovat's unit attacked a battery of six 150mm guns by Varengeville-sur-Mer.

Initially, the commandos had been founded to conduct small-scale raiding operations. By 1942, it was clear that the commandos' strategic purpose had now shifted to large-scale landing operations. The role of small-scale raiding was devolved to several specialised formations such as 10 (Inter-Allied) Commando, the Small Scale Raiding Force (62 Commando), 14 Commando for Norwegian operations and 30 Commando for intelligence-gathering operations.

Laycock's collaborative approach significantly benefited the development of American special forces. He established close professional relations with Lieutenant Colonel William Darby, treating the Americans as equals rather than inexperienced newcomers. This resulted in full cooperation; fifty rangers gained operational experience with 3 and 4 commandos at Dieppe.

In April 1943, Laycock initiated a comprehensive reorganisation of the Special Service Brigade. His paper 'Role of the Special Service Brigade and the Desirability of Reorganisation' recommended establishing a holding commando to rehabilitate units and dividing nine commandos into three operational groups.[3]

Reorganisation Initiatives

On 1 April 1943, Laycock submitted his paper on reorganising the Special Service Brigade to Mountbatten for consideration. This document proved pivotal in reshaping commando operations. Laycock identified the transition from small-scale raids to large-scale, strategically important operations.

Laycock proposed establishing a holding commando to address reinforcement issues highlighted by operations in Tunisia. He recommended creating three commando Groups, each containing three commandos, while specialist units remained under direct SS Brigade control. Mountbatten and the War Office accepted Laycock's reorganisation proposals in principle. Implementation began with establishing the Special Service Group in September 1943, with Major General R. G. Sturges RM assuming command as Laycock's responsibilities shifted to the Mediterranean theatre.

The reorganisation of the Special Service Brigades went beyond Laycock's original plan of three groups to four brigades. By December 1943, each brigade included army and Royal Marine commandos. This integration showed Laycock's focus on teamwork over inter-service differences and rivalries.[4]

Mediterranean Theatre, 1943

In May 1943, Laycock secured authorisation to lead commando forces in the Mediterranean, appointing Lord Lovat as acting commander in the UK. This reflected his preference for personal leadership in operational theatres rather than headquarters administration.

For Operation Husky (Sicily), Laycock commanded 3 Commando and 40 and 41 Royal Marine commandos. His force conducted successful landings near Punta Castellazzo on 10 July 1943, swiftly moving inland against modest opposition and securing all D-Day objectives by 06.00hrs. Following initial success at Sicily, Laycock directed Special Service Brigade elements in Operation Avalanche (Salerno). Commanding 2 Commando and 41 RM Commando, his force secured Vietri sul Mare and La Molina Pass despite determined German resistance. The Salerno operation demonstrated Laycock's capacity to maintain operational effectiveness under extreme pressure. Despite suffering 346 casualties (40 per cent of strength), his command delivered critical results, earning Lieutenant General McCreery's commendation for their contribution to morale and operational success.[5]

In biographical notes by Stuart Scheftel, he stated this about Laycock's leadership style:

> The American First Ranger Battalion under Col. Derby also played one of the leading roles in the initial stages of a tremendously important operation. Derby and Laycock have been the firmest friends ever since the First Ranger Battalion received their final training at the Commando basic training camp in northern Scotland.
>
> In Sicily, where he received the D.S.O., and at Salerno, Laycock was constantly in the thick of the worst fighting. An officer who was with him at Salerno paid him the following tribute: "Throughout, he remained absolutely calm and imperturbable in a situation which was always difficult and often critical. He had a knack of turning up just at the proper moment, at the proper place, right among the most hard-pressed of his forward troops, who were thus continually heartened by the presence of their Commanding Officer."[6]

Chief of Combined Operations, 1943–45

On 22 October 1943, Laycock was appointed Chief of Combined Operations, succeeding Lord Louis Mountbatten. At the age of thirty-six, he was promoted to major general, making him the youngest British general officer appointed during the war. This strategic appointment acknowledged his operational capability and organisational competence.

Laycock quickly demonstrated pragmatic leadership by implementing the Bottomley Report recommendations in January 1944. He reorganised COHQ into three functional directorates under the directors of combined operations (Naval, Military, and Air) while maintaining operational effectiveness during a critical planning period.

At the strategic level, Laycock's responsibilities expanded to formulating a combined operations doctrine across all theatres. His revised directive of September 1944 established that Directors of Combined Operations overseas would apply the doctrine he approved, ensuring a consistent approach to amphibious operations.

During Operation Overlord, Laycock observed American landings aboard USS *Augusta* with Rear Admiral Kirk and General Bradley, witnessing the challenges at Omaha Beach firsthand. His participation in high-level strategic conferences continued throughout 1944–45, including Quebec in September 1944, which he described as 'an unqualified success' regarding strategic agreements on operations in Italy and the Pacific.

In February 1945, Laycock attended the Yalta Conference before travelling to Moscow with Brigadier Head to obtain information on Soviet river-crossing techniques ahead of the Rhine operations. This technical intelligence-gathering mission demonstrated his detailed attention to tactical innovation.

Following Germany's surrender in May 1945, Laycock managed COHQ's transition to peacetime operations. He secured agreement from the chiefs of staff for measured staff reduction whilst maintaining essential capabilities. After Japan's surrender, he pragmatically oversaw the disbandment of army commandos and the transition to Royal Marine Commando Forces, accepting this reorganisation as necessary to preserve special forces çapabilities.

In June 1947, Laycock resigned his commission, ending his military career. His contributions were recognised through the Distinguished Service Order (September 1943), Companion of the Order of the Bath (1945), American Commander of the Legion of Merit, French Commander of the Legion d'honneur, Norwegian Commander with Star of the Order of St Olav, and Dutch Grand Officer of the Order of Orange Nassau with Swords.[7]

Robert Laycock embodied a pragmatic approach to special operations during the Second World War. He recognised the strategic and psychological value of special forces while skilfully navigating the complexities and obfuscations of Whitehall and the military brass hats that so frustrated Sir Roger Keyes. As a commando leader, Laycock believed in the effectiveness of elite forces executing targeted raids that could achieve significant impact with minimal resources. He understood the critical importance of offensive action during a period when Britain was mainly on the defensive, personally demonstrating the courage and initiative required for such operations.

One thing that distinguished Laycock was his ability to balance operational boldness with institutional diplomacy. While firmly committed to the commando concept, he worked effectively within established channels, cultivating valuable relationships with senior leadership that allowed special operations to gain acceptance and support. Laycock focused primarily on operational effectiveness and the practical integration of commandos into a broader military strategy rather than adopting a purely revolutionary stance against military orthodoxy. This balanced approach proved successful, enabling him to achieve significant influence and eventually rise to command Combined Operations, where he could implement his vision on a larger scale while maintaining the respect of conventional and special forces.

In many ways, Laycock advocated a distinctly British approach to warfare that leveraged what he saw as national character traits like individualism, self-discipline, daring and resourcefulness, rather than trying to match the German model of collective fanaticism. The portrayal of 'Lucky Laycock' as 'Britain's No. 1 Commando' alongside his glamorous wife proved highly effective in achieving specific wartime communication objectives. This carefully managed public image helped maintain public morale, generated support for special operations and elevated the status of Combined Operations during the last phase of the war.

The LRDG and SAS

A Legend is Born

On Friday, 14 February 1941, the front cover of *The Egyptian Gazette* was emblazoned with the headline:

MODERN "COMMANDOS" PENETRATE HUNDREDS OF MILES INSIDE LIBYA: *Amazing Story of The Long Range Desert Group.*

An amazing story has just been revealed of the work in the vast Libyan desert during the last six months of a small body of Commandos known as "The Long Range Desert Group" who, going out in small patrols usually of three cars, have consistently and successfully harassed Italian outposts, reduced isolated forts, interrupted communications and generally kept the Italian command guessing, playing a small but most important part in the eventual British sweep to Benghazi.

That well-armed parties of troops have made journeys of several thousand miles through enemy territory carrying with them their own supplies of petrol, food and even water to last them for many weeks at a time, constitutes something quite new in military history.[1]

At the outbreak of the war, Ralph Bagnold, a reservist, found himself recalled to the British Army. He was posted to East Africa, but en route, Bagnold's ship collided with another vessel travelling to Kenya, and he was rerouted to Egypt. Bagnold had served with the Royal Engineers during the First World War. In the 1930s, he pioneered desert exploration and carried out scientific work on the physics of sand and the movements of sand dunes. In 1932, he made the first recorded east-to-west crossing of the Libyan Desert. Bagnold completed his book *The Physics of Blown Sand and Desert Dunes* in 1939, and it was first published in June 1941. Incredibly, Bagnold's work has since helped to inform NASA's exploration of the planet Mars. In 2016, NASA paid tribute to Bagnold's pioneering work by naming a collection of sand dunes studied by the Mars rover *Curiosity* as The Bagnold Dunes.[2]

The primary role of the British Army in Egypt was to provide internal security and safeguard the Suez Canal, a key trade route between Britain and Asia. In Bagnold's opinion, the army was totally unprepared to defend Egypt's borders from the threat posed by fascist Italy. Bagnold had the idea to form a small reconnaissance unit capable of patrolling the 700-mile frontier with Libya and gathering information about the Italians' military dispositions and possible intentions. After seemingly indifferent officers rejected his idea several times within GHQ Middle East, Bagnold decided to write a note directly to General Sir Archibald Wavell, commander-in-chief (C-in-C) Middle East. In the note, he condemned the army's lack of preparedness to meet the Italian threat.

It seems Bagnold's note did the trick. General Wavell immediately summoned Bagnold and asked him to explain his idea of a small scouting force that could penetrate the desert to the west of Egypt and assess what the Italians were doing. According to Bagnold, a stern-faced Wavell asked, 'What if your force finds the Italians are not preparing for an offensive?' In reply, Bagnold told Wavell that his force would conduct some 'piracy on the high desert', attacking targets of opportunity. Wavell liked what he heard. Years later, Bagnold remembered the change in Wavell's demeanour as his face lit up with a broad grin and he asked if the scouting force could be ready for action in six weeks. Both Bagnold and Wavell foresaw that bureaucratic red tape might strangle at birth the new reconnaissance force. In response, Wavell had his Chief of Staff prepare a letter for Bagnold, which said:

> I wish that any request made by Major Bagnold in person should be met immediately and without question.[3]

Bagnold recalled that armed with Wavell's talisman, he had complete carte blanche to do anything he wanted to ensure the assembly of his new desert scouting force by the six-week deadline. He formed a small HQ and three patrols, each consisting of two officers and around thirty men carried in eleven vehicles. He also created a small supply section of three large trucks for building forward dumps to stockpile water, petrol and other essential items required for desert operations. Crucially, he secured the transfer of 120 officers and men, all volunteers, from the Divisional Cavalry Regiment (New Zealand). According to Bagnold, the New Zealanders proved ideal for the task. Many of the volunteers were farmers in civilian life, accustomed to outdoor living, and as responsible owner-drivers, they recognised the value of keeping vehicles and equipment in good condition. Above all, Bagnold wanted reliable, self-disciplined and independently minded volunteers who could think on their feet when confronted by the unexpected.

Bagnold gathered a team of specialists, including Pat Clayton, originally from the Egyptian desert survey, Bill Kennedy Shaw for navigation, Tim Heywood for signals and Captain Edmundson for medical support. The immense task of equipping the unit began with vehicles sourced mainly from civilian stocks and specialised gear often obtained by Bagnold from his friends within the Egyptian government.

Training commenced immediately, covering essential skills like navigation, signalling, and medical care. Bagnold's attention to detail became evident in his innovations, such as developing a unique desert camouflage pattern and modifying the Vickers machine guns to reduce stoppages when firing at enemy aircraft. In addition, Bagnold is credited with developing a sun-compass for desert navigation, a condenser that saved precious water when a vehicle's radiator boiled over, and various techniques for driving with reduced tyre pressures over loose sand and at speed over sand dunes.

Remarkably, Bagnold's Long Range Patrol (LRP) was operational just six weeks after receiving Wavell's approval. The patrols left Cairo on their first mission on 3 September 1940, a testament to Bagnold's organisational skills and vision. In November 1940, the LRP was expanded and renamed the Long Range Desert Group (LRDG). This expansion saw the addition of three new patrols: Guards, Yeomanry, and Rhodesian. The formation of the LRDG stands as a tribute to Bagnold's ingenuity and leadership. He not only conceived the idea but also inspired those under his command to bring it to fruition, creating a unit renowned for its extraordinary spirit and effectiveness in desert warfare.[4]

G (Guards) Patrol

In his history of the Scots Guards, David Erskine describes the 'G' (Foot Guards) Patrol of the Long Range Desert Group as the most remarkable group of guardsmen in the entire war. This patrol, formed in December 1940, consisted of volunteers from the 2nd Battalion, Scots Guards, and the 3rd Battalion, Coldstream Guards.[5] As the LRDG sought to expand, it is understandable that Ralph Bagnold went looking for volunteers from amongst Rhodesian and Yeomanry regiments. During the Second World War, Southern Rhodesia (modern-day Zimbabwe) was a self-governing colony of the United Kingdom, and many of its troops were tough, self-reliant settler-farmers in civilian life.

Traditionally, a yeoman was a tenant farmer who followed his overlord into battle at times of national crisis. In 1940, although no longer vassals to the landed gentry, Yeomanry regiments mainly recruited from Britain's rural counties and agricultural communities. Like their New Zealand and Rhodesian counterparts,

Yeomen were perceived as more independent, practical and resourceful than troops from urban areas. So, why did Ralph Bagnold search for potential LRDG volunteers from amongst the bearskins and scarlet tunics of the Brigade of Guards?

According to Jimmy Patch, an LRDG veteran, guardsmen were regarded as self-reliant, highly trained and self-disciplined, making them attractive candidates for special forces. However, the Scots and Coldstream Guards were also a convenient source of LRDG recruits, having been stationed in Egypt for almost a year before the outbreak of hostilities.[6]

Spencer Seadon joined the Coldstream Guards to escape the poverty and lack of opportunities in his native Suffolk. Spencer had wanted to join the local police service for better pay and prospects, but there were few vacancies and strong competition. One way to be assured entrance into the Suffolk constabulary was to have served in one of the regiments of Foot Guards, so Spencer joined up.

In 1938, he was sent to Egypt for what should have been a two-year posting, joining the 3rd Battalion, Coldstream Guards, the 1st Guards Brigade. Unfortunately, war broke out just months before his battalion was scheduled to return to the UK, leaving Spencer stuck in Egypt indefinitely. Sometime later, Spencer found himself in a LOB (left out of battle) camp while he recovered from a leg injury. Bored, with little to occupy his time other than a daily drill parade, Spencer applied and was accepted by the LRDG as a replacement machine gunner.

Spencer was assigned to G2 patrol under Captain J. A. L. Timpson, Scots Guards. Operating from Kufra and the Siwa Oasis, G2 patrols were principally tasked with conducting road watches, covertly observing enemy transport movements and reporting them to GHQ Middle East via radio. While some of the guardsmen in the 3rd Battalion saw joining the LRDG as a 'suicide squad', Spencer had a different opinion. Spencer noted that the guards were always sent to the worst trouble spots, where they were expected to recover the situation, which usually meant heavy casualties. Therefore, he believed he was safer operating behind enemy lines with the LRDG than if he remained with his battalion.[7]

According to the regimental history *The Coldstream Guards 1920–1946*, the 3rd Battalion suffered 744 casualties, either killed, wounded or taken prisoner, between 1940 and 1943.[8] Captain Michael Crichton-Stuart, Scots Guards, recalled that G Patrol was drawn mostly from townsmen compared with the rest of the LRDG, who were nearly all countrymen, maturer in years and responsible in outlook. In extreme contrast, guardsmen were the product of the most rigid system of instilled discipline. In his book *G Patrol*, Crichton-Stuart writes:

> The aim of the system was to produce the best soldier in battle; and where it was best put into effect, in a good battalion, it was a poor guardsman who was not determined to go into battle with his battalion.

Therefore, most guardsmen within G Patrol thought of themselves as only being on temporary detachment from their parent battalions. Crichton-Stuart viewed joining the LRDG as a welcome escape from the monotony of garrison duty. Many guardsmen who volunteered viewed it as a way to occupy their time until their battalions were sent into action. After accepting the job of commanding G Patrol, Crichton-Stuart did start to wonder if guardsmen were not a bit out of place in the middle of the Libyan desert. He considered guardsmen capable of taking on any job asked of them but questioned whether it was possible to make the best irregular soldiers out of the best regulars. David Lloyd Owen, commander of Yeomanry Patrol, wrote that 'even the worst of Guardsmen are good, and let it suffice to say that we were fortunate in that we had the best'.

According to Crichton-Stuart, the selection process for G Patrol recruits was far from infallible, and mistakes were made. However, the unremitting challenges of operating in the deep desert quickly revealed any shortcomings in a new member of a patrol, and such individuals were quickly returned to their parent units. Many of the New Zealanders in the LRDG had learned the importance of resourcefulness, resilience, and independence from growing up on remote sheep stations and farms. At Caterham, guardsmen were forged through a time-honoured process, virtually unchanged since Waterloo, creating soldiers renowned for their steadfastness, discipline, and meticulous attention to detail— men who took pride in executing their duties to perfection. In Crichton-Stuart's words, it was no accident that the man whose gun was always ready for action despite the desert dust, the driver whose truck tyres were always at the right pressure, the reliable guard on solitary night watch was, in barracks, among 'the smartest on the square'.[9]

In the spring of 1943, as the Desert War approached its conclusion, G Patrol completed its final operations. Although some guardsmen decided to stay with the LRDG after G Patrol was disbanded and went on to serve in the Dodecanese, Italian and Adriatic campaigns, many more returned to their parent battalions, which had suffered heavy casualties in recent fighting. Michael Crichton-Stuart noted that guardsmen saw joining the LRDG as a chance to escape the tedium of military routine and an opportunity to actively contribute to the war effort. Yet, their primary loyalty remained with their regiments.

Former desert explorer and LRDG Intelligence Officer, Bill Kennedy Shaw, speculated why men volunteered for the unit. In his book *Long Range Desert Group: Behind Enemy Lines in North Africa*, Kennedy Shaw sets down what he believed were the pros and cons of joining the LRDG in a simple decision balance sheet:

Assets	Liabilities
The best food in the Middle East.	The strain of operating almost continuously behind enemy lines.
A job which was always interesting and often exciting.	Never returning to base for a long refit and rest, and suffering as a result from weariness, desert sores and occasional cafard (a feeling of depression or apathy).[10]
Almost complete freedom from drills, guards and fatigues.	
A minimum of being 'mucked about'.	

Layforce, the LRDG and Disbandment

The commandos were formed to conduct small-scale amphibious raids on the coasts of occupied Europe from bases within the UK. Volunteers joined the commandos for a six-month term of service, after which they could choose to return to their parent units in Britain. Foreign service was never part of the initial agreement.

As the war progressed, however, circumstances changed. Nos. 7, 8 and 11 commandos were combined to become 'Z Force' (later Layforce) and were sent to the Mediterranean to conduct raiding operations on the island of Rhodes. Despite efforts, organising and executing amphibious raiding operations in the Mediterranean proved impractical due to their complexity and vulnerability to air attacks. After losing its assault ships, Layforce became little more than a general reserve of reinforcements for the Desert Army. By the summer of 1941, the adjutant general's office found itself in a quandary over what to do with the commandos stationed in the Mediterranean and North Africa. The decision to disband Layforce sparked a heated debate within the high command about the commandos' conditions of service.

In May 1941, one potential option considered was to divert Layforce personnel into the Long Range Desert Group. However, the LRDG preferred to continue recruiting from New Zealand and South African units. Despite the commandos being generally suitable for LRDG service, they would require extensive training, and the expansion would necessitate additional vehicles and equipment that

GHQ Middle East could not afford. Having conducted a feasibility study, the idea was deemed impractical and abandoned.

As the summer wore on, the adjutant general's office decided not to honour the commandos' original conditions of service. No troops would be returned to the UK, contrary to the initial War Office agreement. Instead, officers and other ranks were asked where they would like to be reassigned upon Layforce's disbandment.[11]

On 24 June 1941, the officer commanding G Troop, A Battalion (7 Commando), Layforce wrote to Bob Laycock about the impending disbandment of his unit. Although the letter is unsigned, it is probable that Captain Frank Nicholls, Royal Artillery wrote it. He would be killed the following year while serving in Burma with Special Service Detachment 1.

Captain Nicholls begins by expressing his belief that Lieutenant Colonel Laycock was unlikely to form a new commando unit or Long Range Desert Group from the remnants of A, B and D Battalions. Despite this, Captain Nicholls makes it clear to Laycock that he and his men would be willing to serve under Laycock's command if the opportunity presented itself. He then outlines his two main reasons for submitting this statement: firstly, his sense of responsibility towards his men, whom he recruited from their parent regiments with certain promises that had not been fulfilled, and secondly, his belief that disbanding the troop would be a waste of their specialised training.

Clearly disappointed and a little resentful at the prospect of seeing his troop disbanded, Captain Nicholls writes:

> When I first formed my troop in England a year ago I took them away from their own regiments by leading them to believe, as I had been led to believe, that they would see action in the immediate future that they would have under certain conditions (Allowances, etc.), and that at the end of six months or the conclusion of any one operation they would be at liberty to return to their units in the UK. There was no question of foreign service.
>
> Owing to various circumstances these conditions have one, after the other, gone by the board. The feeling of the majority of the men now is that they wish to stick together as a troop, rather than be scattered among various units in the Middle East; many of them having the prospect of going to a different regiment altogether.
>
> For the reasons given above I feel to a very great degree responsible for them and I wish to do all I can to see that they get a square deal.

Captain Nicholls then discusses the troop's morale in detail:

> In spite of many setbacks and disappointments, their morale is exceptionally high. From the very beginning, they felt that they were the pick of the British Army and 'second to none'; this feeling has been the foundation of their discipline.

He provides two specific examples of their high morale in action:

> At Bardia, when we landed it seemed almost impossible that we could be taken off again; we left the boat aground on a rock in a heavy surf and the Naval Officer i/c told me that he had very little hope of getting it off. This had no effect whatever on the spirits of the men; one private soldier was heard to remark that anyway he hadn't enjoyed the trip in much and he didn't suppose he would like the trip back to the ship any better.

And in Crete:

> On the last night of the evacuation, we were ordered to hold a position covering the beach and told that our chances of being taken off were almost nil. From our position, we could see men being taken off the beach all through the night, and throughout this period, the men remained at their posts and in excellent spirits.

Captain Nicholls then details G Troop's training and specialised skills:

> The main object I have tried to achieve is a first-class 'all-round' soldier. The foundation of all our training has been Infantry section Leading so that all ranks, whether Gunner, R.A.S.C. or Infantrymen, have a sound knowledge of elementary tactics, fieldcraft, etc., and, of course, thoroughly know all the Infantry weapons they have to handle and also a good deal about weapons they were not equipped with.

He lists their specialised skills, including demolition, map reading, driving, combined operations with naval personnel and various types of landing craft, rock climbing and languages.

The letter concludes with three suggestions for the troop's future:

(1) That if there is a possibility of fighting in the Far East I might be allowed to take my troop out there as a guerrilla unit.
(2) That I might command my troop as a unit or sub-unit of the Long Range Desert Group.
(3) That my troop might be attached to the Navy for co-operation with submarines.[12]

In July, Geoffrey Keyes, C Battalion (11 Scottish Commando), wrote to Bob Laycock explaining the situation within his command as he contemplated disbandment. He notes that half of his men are undecided about where to be reassigned. Some were requesting transfers to units or services for which they had no qualifications or experience. Keyes illustrates his point with an amusing anecdote:

> A man, whose military service consists of 2 months in an I.T.C., 12 months with us, and who was previously a farm labourer, puts into go 1st choice R.A.F., 2nd choice Navy. His chances of getting either are presumably too remote to be entertained.

Keyes also mentioned that a small group of 'malcontents' had requested transfers to the merchant navy, while others volunteered for service in Burma. He estimates that about 240 officers and other ranks wanted to remain commandos, if possible, while a quarter of all ranks wished to return to their parent corps or units stationed in the Middle East.

Initially, Layforce troops were asked where they would prefer to be reassigned, with the understanding that none would be sent home. Many opted to return to their parent units in the Middle East rather than stay with the commandos. However, due to a sudden change of plan, some commandos were earmarked to return to the UK. This created a dilemma for the High Command. They feared that once word got out that some troops who had chosen to stay with the commandos were being sent home, those who had elected to transfer to other units would feel the army had deliberately misled them. To avoid potential unrest and morale issues, the commander-in-chief ultimately decided to keep all Layforce troops in the Middle East, with exceptions made only for those returning to the UK on compassionate grounds or those who had volunteered for service in Burma or China.

However, there was one additional choice: all ranks could volunteer for duty with a 'special S.S. unit'. The Commando Depot's commanding officer was informed that Captain A. D. Stirling would visit the camp to explain the purpose of his mysterious new unit and interview applicants.[13]

A New Special Service Unit

On 6 May 1941, Bob Laycock wrote to Lieutenant General Sir Arthur Smith, Chief of Staff, Middle East Command suggesting that if Layforce was not to be used to conduct raiding operations, it should be disbanded. A week later, Laycock cabled Lieutenant Colonel Dermot Daly, commanding officer of B Battalion (8 Commando), instructing him to organise a small group of men to be dropped by parachute to coincide with RAF raids on Gazala and Derna. The parachute operation never took place.

In his book *David Stirling, The Phoney Major*, historian Gavin Mortimer explains that Jock Lewes, upon hearing about the cancelled parachute mission, approached Laycock for permission to establish his own group of parachutists. One of the men to join Jock's group was David Stirling. Although the idea of expanding the LRDG by transferring men from Layforce had been abandoned, David Stirling believed there was still a need for a small raiding force that could operate independently behind enemy lines.

David Stirling and Jock Lewes were two very different personalities. David Stirling was a louche young man who was superficially charming, manipulative and socially well-connected. Lewes was handsome, intelligent, thoughtful but self-righteous. Nevertheless, despite their differences, the aspiring parachutists performed several practice jumps from an ageing Valencia aircraft. Both Stirling and Lewes suffered injuries on the practice jumps, and the idea of forming a parachute unit was abandoned. Upon his recovery, Jock was posted to the besieged port of Tobruk. While convalescing in the hospital, David Stirling started to refine his ideas for a small parachute force.[14]

David Stirling's memorandum on the 'Training of Parachute Troops' called for the formation of a small unit capable of prosecuting raids on enemy lines of communication, aerodromes, oil dumps and other enemy dispositions on which damage could be inflicted. Stirling believed that small teams of saboteurs, dropped by parachute at night, could succeed where large-scale commando raids requiring extensive naval and air support had proven impractical in the Mediterranean (See Appendix A). In his memorandum, Stirling is keen to extol the double virtues of the men from 8 Commando as the perfect candidates for his new parachute force. All the men of 8 (Guards) Commando were fully trained Special Service troops capable of operating at night and were familiar with the use of explosives for sabotage. The men of 8 Commando also had the benefit of a guardsman's training, with the resulting high standard of routine efficiency and discipline.[15]

David's elder brother, Bill Stirling, probably co-wrote the 'Parachute Troops' memorandum and then presented the idea to Lieutenant General Sir Arthur Smith for review. The Stirling brothers certainly knew how to use the socially elite 'old boy's network' of the British establishment to bypass bureaucracy and get what they wanted. Smith had been commissioned into the Coldstream Guards in 1910, served in France during the First World War and had been General Staff Officer for the London District and then adjutant at the Royal Military College, Sandhurst during the inter-war years. In 1942, he would be appointed major general commanding the Brigade of Guards and general officer commanding London district. As the Stirling brothers were Guards officers, they had confidence that Smith would be receptive to their proposal of creating a small airborne unit mainly composed of guardsmen. Smith liked the Stirling brothers' memorandum enough to pass it along to his boss, Sir Claude Auchinleck, C-in-C Middle East Command.

After a discussion between General Auchinleck, General Smith and General Neil Ritchie, it was decided that David Stirling would be authorised to raise a small airborne unit of six officers and sixty other ranks. It is likely that the decision to allow Stirling to proceed with his project was influenced by a demonstration witnessed by Auchinleck and Ritchie in December 1940. During this display, a small force of parachutists from 11 Special Air Service Battalion (formerly 2 Commando) successfully overcame a group of defenders in prepared positions through speed and surprise.

On 10 February 1941, X Troop of the 11th Special Air Service Battalion undertook the British Army's first airborne raid of the war, codenamed Operation Colossus. The intention of the raid was to destroy the Tragino Aqueduct, a vital piece of infrastructure located near Calitri in southern Italy. The aqueduct supplied fresh water to both industry and a large portion of the Italian population. The raiders successfully damaged the aqueduct, but it was quickly repaired. To exfiltrate, the parachutists had to march for 60 miles to rendezvous with a Royal Navy submarine. However, the submarine was recalled, the rendezvous never took place, and X Troop went into captivity.[16]

Operation Colossus, while not achieving its strategic objectives, compelled the Italian military to reallocate forces to protect vital infrastructure, thereby thinning their front-line defences. More importantly, it showcased the innovative military tactic of deploying airborne forces to disrupt enemy operations, a concept that was still in its infancy. The media coverage generated by the raid made front-page news in the London-based *Sunday Pictorial*, with the bold headline 'THEY WERE OURS! British Parachute Troops' Daring Drop into Italy', boosted morale and demonstrated to the public and allies alike the daring capabilities of the British forces. This positive propaganda effect likely influenced General Sir Claude Auchinleck's decision to establish David Stirling's small parachute unit in the Middle East.[17]

Toward the end of May, Colonel Laycock informed the members of 8 (Guards) Commando that they were to be disbanded. Many guardsmen, disillusioned with 'special service', elected to return to their parent units in the Mediterranean. In July 1941, George Jellicoe, for example, returned to the 3rd Battalion, Coldstream Guards, where he served with the Motor Battalion. After a spell in hospital, Jellicoe was recruited into the fledgling Special Air Service by David Stirling to help improve the unit's administration. Jellicoe thought that David Stirling was a man of great imagination, foresight and strong leadership skills. While Stirling possessed the vision to drive the SAS forward, Jellicoe believed Jock Lewes was largely responsible for the organisation and training of the unit in its early days. According to Jellicoe, David Stirling had a high opinion of Lewes.[18]

Having received the official sanction to raise a small parachute unit, David Stirling was able to start recruiting officers and men:

Volunteers for special S.S. Unit (GHQ MEF, CRME/1668/AG1), 8 August 1941, OC, 'C' Bn LAYFORCE.

Copy to: Capt. A.D. Stirling

Will you please allow Capt. A.D. Stirling to visit 'C' Bn LAYFORCE with a view to finding out if there are any volunteers for a special S.S. unit, which he is forming.

Capt. Stirling will explain the purpose of this new unit.

Any officers or other ranks who volunteer and who can be spared by you, will be replaced, provided 'C' Bn is not disbanded.

Capt. Stirling will submit a nominal roll to this HQ of the volunteers he wishes for this new unit.

Signed G.M. Kinmount, Major. For Maj-Gen, DAG.[19]

On 28 August 1941, Stirling's unit was officially formed as 'L' Detachment, Special Air Service Brigade. Its primary function was to conduct sabotage and the destruction of military equipment behind enemy lines in the Mediterranean theatre of operations.

The unit's name was the brainchild of Brigadier Dudley Clarke. One of Clarke's tasks was to deceive the enemy about the Desert Army's true capabilities and intentions. To this end, Clarke was keen to mislead the enemy into believing the British Army had sent a full airborne brigade to Egypt. Stirling's new L Detachment helped sell the deception by giving the impression it was part of a larger formation.

Two of Stirling's first recruits were Jock Lewes, formerly of 8 Commando, and Robert Blair 'Paddy' Mayne, 11 Commando. The unit formed at Kabrit, Egypt. Jock Lewes, as Stirling's second-in-command, assumed the role of principal training officer. Lewes established a gruelling programme at Kabrit, which included physical exercise, parachute training and instruction in various skills such as desert survival, navigation, first aid, observation and demolitions.

To simulate a parachute landing, for example, Lewes came up with the unorthodox and dangerous idea of having volunteers leap from a moving truck. This training method led to several broken bones and numerous other injuries. Physical conditioning included forced marches progressing from ten to 100 miles with full packs and minimal water. Those men who successfully endured the rigorous training would advance from parachuting theory to making their first jump from an RAF Bristol Bombay aircraft.

In November 1941, L Detachment got its first mission. The intention of the raid was to launch an attack on the enemy airfields located in Gazala and Tmimi, Libya, in support of Auchinleck's Operation Crusader. However, L Detachment's first and only parachute operation in the Western Desert proved unsuccessful due to severe weather conditions, including heavy rain and high winds. The operation resulted in significant casualties, with only twenty-two of the sixty-two parachutists dropped returning to Kabrit. The only part of the raid deemed successful was the rendezvous and exfiltration of the survivors by the LRDG. Further parachute operations in the Western Desert were judged too hazardous and inadvisable. The unit subsequently shifted its focus to long-range ground operations, relying on the LRDG for transportation to and from its targets, which proved more successful.[20]

In December, L Detachment attacked enemy airfields at Tamet and Sirte. They successfully destroyed numerous aircraft on the ground along with fuel and ammunition dumps. On 30 December 1941, the unit suffered a major blow with the death of Jock Lewes, who was killed when an enemy aircraft attacked his vehicle. On 20 November 1942, David Stirling wrote a letter of condolence to Mr Lewes, explaining Jock's role in the formation of L Detachment and the circumstances of his death.

> There is no doubt that any success this Unit has achieved up to the time of Jock's death, and after it, was, and is, almost wholly due to Jock's work. Our training programmes [sic] and methods are and always will be entirely based on the syllabuses he produced for us. This must show the extent of his influence.[21]

As Stirling's second-in-command, Jock Lewes was largely responsible for the day-to-day running of L Detachment, as well as being the architect of its innovative training methods. In the months following the unit's formation, it was Jock who helped establish the Special Air Service's unique culture. At the same time, David Stirling was waging his own war with the bureaucrats of GHQ Middle East who sought to throttle the fledgling unit before it could take flight. Stirling described the administration of the Desert Army as 'ludicrously swollen, unnecessarily big, and wholly obstructive to anything that would look like a new idea'.[22]

The relationship between David Stirling and Jock Lewes, and their respective contributions to the formation and success of L Detachment, presents an interesting study in complementary skills and leadership styles.

Stirling, with his aristocratic background and social connections, was the visionary and political operator of the pair. He possessed a remarkable ability to navigate the complex hierarchies of the British military establishment. His membership in the Brigade of Guards gave him a certain cachet and access to senior officers that proved invaluable. Stirling's genius lay in his ability to sell the concept of the SAS, bypassing traditional chains of command when necessary, and securing the resources and permissions needed for the unit to operate. He was, in essence, the public face and advocate for the SAS in 1941.

Lewes, on the other hand, was the pragmatic organiser and tactical innovator. While Stirling was networking with generals and securing political backing, Lewes was on the ground developing the innovative training regimes and operational procedures that would define the SAS. His background as a Guards officer and

Oxford rowing Blue and his time spent in pre-war Germany gave him a unique perspective on physical fitness and military tactics. Lewes was responsible for creating the gruelling training program that would produce the kind of soldiers capable of carrying out SAS raids. He also developed innovative equipment, most notably the Lewes Bomb, which proved crucial in early SAS operations against Axis airfields.

Their partnership was one of vision, meeting practical application. Stirling's ability to open doors and secure support was matched by Lewes's capacity to turn that support into tangible results on the ground. Without Stirling's political acumen, charm and cunning, the SAS might never have gotten off the ground. Without Lewes's organisational skills and tactical innovations, it might not have survived its early missions.

It is worth noting that their relationship, while productive, was not without tension. Stirling's often cavalier attitude and penchant for bending rules clashed with Lewes's more disciplined approach. In fact, Jock despised the type of 'playboy' Guards officers that he had encountered in 8 Commando, who were more interested in drinking and gambling than prosecuting the war. However, these differences ultimately contributed to the unit's success, providing a balance between daring and discipline that became a hallmark of SAS operations.

Interviewed by the Imperial War Museum, Carol Mather's account of his time in the SAS paints a vivid picture of the unit's early days and operations. Joining in May 1942 at the Kabrit camp, Mather found himself part of a small but elite force. 'We were mainly tasked with spoiling operations,' he recalled, 'such as attacking enemy airfields, shooting up road traffic and blowing up telegraph poles.'

These daring raids often took them deep into enemy territory, with patrols operating around a hundred miles behind enemy lines for weeks at a time. But gradually, sleep deprivation robbed a patrol of its effectiveness. 'After a couple of weeks without any proper sleep,' Mather noted, 'my reflexes and situational awareness deteriorated.' Some soldiers resorted to taking Benzedrine tablets to stay alert, but this had its own drawbacks, leaving men 'like zombies after two or three weeks'.

David Stirling's leadership style left a lasting impression on Mather. Rather than barking orders, Stirling would ask, 'Would you like to do this or that operation?' It is an approach we recognise today as permission-based leadership, fostering motivation through relationships rather than rank. As we have already seen, there were numerous officers within GHQ Middle East who opposed the use of special-service troops. Mather recalled that 'Montgomery thought Stirling was mad', though the general grudgingly admitted that 'there was room for mad people in wartime.' The RAF, on the other hand, was more appreciative. After all, as Mather pointed out, 'for every enemy aircraft destroyed on the ground by the SAS was one less for the pilots of the Desert Air Force to worry about.'

Despite the dangers, encounters with German patrols were surprisingly rare. Mather explained that 'the German army did not like to venture into the desert', making most encounters accidental rather than planned. In 1942, the unit started using its own heavily armed, specially modified jeeps, giving it greater operational flexibility. Throughout the North African campaign, the unit was credited with destroying hundreds of enemy aircraft and critical supplies while providing valuable intelligence to Allied forces.[23]

The Guardsman Effect

As Guards officers, Bob Laycock, David Stirling and Jock Lewes quite naturally favoured recruiting guardsmen for their special service units due to the unique qualities these soldiers brought to the table. Guardsmen were renowned for their exceptional discipline, high standards of professionalism, and excellent physical fitness—all crucial attributes for the demanding nature of special operations, especially in harsh environments like the North African desert. Their meticulous attention to detail, hammered home from the first day at Caterham and honed through ceremonial duties, translated well to the precision required in special operations planning and execution. Moreover, the strong esprit de corps cultivated in the Guards was invaluable for maintaining morale in small teams operating behind enemy lines.

The preference for guardsmen also stemmed from practical considerations. Guards regiments attracted some of the best recruits in the British Army, providing a high-quality pool of potential candidates. Their adaptability, despite a reputation for parade-ground soldiering, made them well-suited for the ever-changing scenarios of special operations. It is worth noting that Stirling's personal experience in the Scots Guards likely influenced this preference.

However, while the commandos, LRDG and SAS favoured guardsmen, they also recruited capable soldiers from other regiments, focusing on individuals who could operate effectively in small, independent units under challenging conditions. This predilection for guardsmen in early special-forces units helped establish a tradition that continues in British special forces recruitment until today.

The Parachute Regiment

Storming Eagles

In May 1941, German airborne and amphibious forces successfully invaded the Greek island of Crete. Codenamed Operation Mercury, the German assault was a military victory and a propaganda coup. At a victory parade in Germany, General Kurt Student, the father of German airborne forces, praised his Fallschirmjäger [paratroops]:

> Our victory banners wave over Crete. You, my paratroopers and airborne troops, have, under your proven leaders, achieved unprecedented feats. Paratroopers! Filled with an unstoppable offensive spirit you, entirely on your own, defeated the numerically superior enemy in an heroic, bitter struggle. Wherever you landed on Crete you both stormed heroically and held stubbornly.

However, after the war, General Student confessed that the operation to capture Crete was a Pyrrhic victory:

> I find it very hard to write about Crete. For me, the commander of the German airborne forces, the name of Crete conjures up bitter memories. I miscalculated when I proposed the operation, and my mistakes caused not only the loss of very many paratroopers—whom I looked upon as my sons—but in the long run led to the demise of the German airborne arm which I created.

During his post-war interrogation, Student confessed: 'Crete was the grave of the German parachutists.' For weeks after the battle, newspapers all over Germany published black-bordered statements announcing the names of the dead.

The Battle of Crete was a disaster for the German airborne forces, with estimated casualties ranging from 4,000 to 6,500 troops. The Luftwaffe's transport fleet suffered heavy losses, with over two hundred and seventy Ju-52 transport aircraft lost or damaged.

When Hitler learned the true cost of Operation Mercury, he told General Student, 'The day of the paratrooper is over! The parachute arm is a surprise weapon, and without the element of surprise, there can be no future for the airborne forces.' Student said, 'After the Crete operation, no German parachute division was committed in airborne operations as a whole unit.'

In his biography *Hitler's Paratrooper: The Life and Battles of Rudolf Witzig*, author Gilberto N. Villahermosa contests that Hitler was correct in his assessment that the ongoing cost of maintaining elite airborne forces outweighed their value and utility. Instead, until the war's end, German airborne forces were used as fire brigades of elite infantry to attack or defend, wherever the fighting was fiercest. Nevertheless, the British and Americans felt that they could provide the manpower and technology required to ensure the success of future large-scale airborne operations.[1]

A year before Operation Mercury, German paratroopers had captured key strategic locations in Scandinavia, Belgium and the Netherlands, achieving complete surprise. However, the margin between success and failure of these early airborne operations had been wafer-thin. Nevertheless, the British seem to have been beguiled by the potential of airborne operations.

In July 1941, a month after Operation Mercury, the Royal Air Force prepared a paper to help familiarise commanders and staff with paratroops. The document's introduction states: 'It is hoped that it will assist them not only to train and fight with our own paratroops but also to protect themselves and their formations from those of the enemy.'

While the first few paragraphs focus on the success of German airborne operations in Holland, the paper maintains that the paratroops' effectiveness lay in their ability to prevent bridge demolitions and hold positions until ground forces arrived:

> The success of paratroops in Holland showed how decisive they can be, put down where most inconvenient for the enemy, so that he has to fight not only on his front but also on his flanks and in his rear, along his lines of communication and supply, at his railheads, vehicle parks, dumps and workshops and inside the headquarters of his field formations.

The paper concludes that the success of German airborne operations in Holland demonstrated their game-changing potential as a strategic military force. The paper's dual focus, championing the offensive potential of airborne forces while also discussing defensive countermeasures, might appear contradictory. However, the authors were engaged in the kind of comprehensive analysis essential for military doctrine development. This balanced approach proved prescient. While German airborne operations had proved decisive in Holland in 1940, they could also be disastrous, as would be shown by Operation Market Garden in 1944. The paper's authors were attempting to describe both sides of an emerging military capability, allowing readers to understand the pros and cons of airborne operations.

Beginnings

On 5 June 1940, Winston Churchill called for a British parachute force to be raised following the success of German airborne operations during the invasion of the Low Countries. On 22 June 1940, Churchill wrote a note to General Ismay, his chief military assistant, requesting that the British Army take a leaf from the Luftwaffe's book and establish a corps of 5,000 parachute troops:

> We ought to have a corps of at least 5,000 parachute troops, including a proportion of Australians, New Zealanders and Canadians, together with some trustworthy people from Norway and France. I see more difficulty in selecting and employing Danes, Dutch and Belgians. I hear something is being done already to form such a corps but only I believe on a very small scale. Advantage must be taken of the summer to train three forces, who can, none the less, play their part meanwhile as shock troops in home defences. Prey let me have a note from the War Office on the subject.[2]

Raised in the summer of 1940, 2 (Parachute) Commando was the British Army's first airborne formation.[3]

On 21 June 1940, following Churchill's directive to create a corps of parachutists, a Central Landing School was established at RAF Ringway near Manchester. Commanded by Squadron Leader Louis A. Strange, Ringway was primarily designed as a parachute training centre and research and development facility. On 19 September, the school was expanded into the Central Landing Establishment (CLE) RAF, which comprised a parachute training school, a technical unit, and a glider training squadron. The main objectives of this establishment included training parachute troops, glider pilots and aircrews for airborne operations, developing effective tactics for managing airborne troops, conducting technical research and recommending necessary equipment and procedures. In September 1941, the Central Landing Establishment was renamed the Airborne Forces Establishment.[4]

No. 2 Commando was stationed at Knutsford, Cheshire, near Ringway. On 3 July 1940, on his appointment as commanding officer of 2 Commando, Major Charles 'Ivor' Jackson was promoted to Lieutenant Colonel. Jackson joined the Royal Tank Corps (later the Royal Tank Regiment) in 1925. He was seconded to the Royal Air Force twice between 1927 and 1936, serving with 4 (Army Co-operation) Squadron. As 2 Commando took shape, Jackson's men arrived wearing their parent-unit uniforms and cap badges. The men's only common bond was that they had all volunteered for special service and were keen to get at the enemy. The Tatton Park estate, north of Knutsford and southwest of Ringway, was selected as a suitable drop zone for parachute training descents.[5]

Ground-based training for the fledgling paratroops began in early July. The first parachute descents occurred on 13 July. The RAF had no purpose-built aircraft for parachutists. After some trial and error, most parachute jumps were executed from slightly modified Armstrong Whitworth Whitley bombers. The intrepid parachutists exited the aircraft by dropping through a three-foot hole in the fuselage floor. With some practice, a 'stick' of eight fully equipped paratroopers could exit an aircraft in around ten seconds. A 'static line' attached to a cable inside the aircraft fuselage automatically deployed the parachute canopy. When paratroopers jumped, a 12-foot line paid out behind them until snapping tight, pulling the parachute canopy out of its bag.

Major Miles Whitelock described his first parachute descent from a Whitley in Max Arthur's book *Men of the Red Beret*:

> The plane slowly circled the dropping zone. I threw my legs over the hole and watched—green light, down the hand 'Go' and through the hole I jumped into space and possible oblivion. Almost before I could draw breath, I felt a jerk on my back, and, as if by magic, I saw above me the reassuring canopy of silk opened out and I began to float gently to earth.[6]

On 25 July 1940, the unit suffered its first fatality when Driver Ralph Evans, originally of the Royal Army Service Corps (RASC), was killed during a practice jump. He became entangled in the rigging lines of his parachute, which prevented the canopy from deploying properly. As a result of the training accident, modifications were made to the parachute deployment system, reducing the chances of similar accidents taking place. Nevertheless, a second fatal training accident occurred at the end of August, when Trooper Watts, Household Cavalry was killed due to another parachute malfunction.[7]

Within two months, twenty-one officers and 132 other ranks of 2 Commando had completed the parachute course at Ringway. Around thirty volunteers washed out for various reasons, such as refusing to jump, and were returned to their parent units. By the end of 1940, about five hundred soldiers had completed their qualifying parachute jumps. To qualify as a parachutist, a volunteer was required to complete five jumps, the first from 800 feet, the next two from 500 feet and the final two in 'sticks' at the same height. Upon qualification, the parachutists received their 'wings' badges to be sewn onto their uniforms. They received additional parachute pay of four shillings per day for officers and two for other ranks. The extra jump pay was often referred to as 'danger money'.

An anti-aircraft barrage balloon was pressed into service to supplement the severe lack of aircraft available for parachute training. The balloon was winched to a height of between 600 and 700 feet. The trainee parachutists were suspended in a basket under the balloon. Although the balloon increased the number of practice jumps possible, many trainees found the 'balloon jump' experience unpleasant. By June 1941, Ringway had clocked up around seven thousand practice parachute descents.[8]

11th Special Air Service Battalion

On 21 November 1940, 2 Commando was re-designated as the 11th Special Air Service (SAS) Battalion, containing a headquarters, a parachute wing and a glider wing. Lieutenant Colonel Jackson remained in command of the unit. The battalion remained based at Knutsford, close to Ringway. A peculiarity of the commandos' terms of service was that all ranks were billeted in civilian homes rather than barracks. Therefore, the Royal George Inn served as the officers' mess. The headquarters was next to a fish-and-chip shop, and parades were held at the aptly named Jail Square.

Originally, the unit was organised into four troops. This was later expanded to approximately four hundred and fifty personnel and reorganised into ten troops. The new troops were sourced from various commands across the UK. However, the rejection rate of volunteers was high due to jump refusals, injuries and disciplinary issues. The battalion's section size increased from eight to ten paratroopers to match the Whitley's load capacity.

As with other commando units, a lack of operational activity undermined morale and affected discipline. Conducting a series of exercises with regular units and performing parachute demonstrations for senior military officers and civilian dignitaries only undermined morale further. Some men requested they be returned to their units, some of whom were fighting in Egypt. In January 1941, Lieutenant Colonel Jackson paraded the whole unit on Shaw Heath in Knutsford and asked for volunteers for a dangerous mission; everybody volunteered. The officers and men selected for the mission were formed into X Troop.

After six weeks of rehearsals and training, the first British parachute operation of the war was undertaken by seven officers and twenty-eight men with a raid on the Tragino aqueduct in Italy on the night of 10/11 February 1941. The intention was to destroy the aqueduct, which supplied water to three major ports.

The RAF provided eight Whitley bombers, six carrying paratroopers and two conducting a diversionary raid. Despite setbacks, the team blew up a section of the aqueduct, but the damage was quickly repaired. The men of X Troop were supposed to rendezvous with a submarine for extraction, but it was recalled, leaving them stranded and taken prisoner. Although a strategic failure, the mission demonstrated Britain's resolve and provided valuable lessons for future airborne operations. In the next section, we will examine the Tragino aqueduct raid in more depth.[9]

The loss of X Troop led to a draft of guardsmen from the commando training centre at Achnacarry joining Captain Peter Bromley-Martin's L Troop. In January 1941, sixty Grenadier Guardsmen had arrived at Achnacarry for commando training alongside contingents from the South Wales Borderers and Lancashire Fusiliers. Lieutenant Arthur Kellas, who commanded these guardsmen, described them as 'big sturdy men'—the kind of physically imposing soldiers needed for the demanding role of airborne operations. His colourful descriptions paint a picture of impressive physical specimens: Sergeant White with his 'fat red countenance and richly curling whiskers' and Lance Corporal Rayment 'tall as a lamp post'. Then there was Guardsman Saunders, a professional wrestler standing at six feet three inches.

The selection of guardsmen was more than just about their physical attributes. The Guards regiments were known for their exceptional discipline and high standards, which would prove crucial in developing Britain's airborne forces. This was demonstrated throughout their training, particularly during the infamous 'Pemmican March'—a gruelling three-day trial of endurance across the Scottish Highlands that tested their physical and mental toughness.

What is particularly interesting is to see how the Guards' influence shaped the character of the early airborne forces. We see this clearly in an account from Captain Peter Bromley-Martin's L Troop. After one particularly demanding march, while other troops collapsed on a grass verge to rest, L Troop, mainly composed of guardsmen, finished with rifles at the slope and executed a perfect drill movement. This blend of elite fighting capability with ceremonial precision and a touch of bravado became a hallmark of British airborne forces.[10]

The Guards' connection to airborne forces grew even stronger over time. By November 1941, the newly promoted Major General Frederick 'Boy' Browning, himself a Grenadier Guard, took command of the parachute troops and airborne division, bringing with him two more Grenadiers as staff officers. This unique combination—the discipline and standards of the Guards and the innovative spirit of the new airborne concept—helped create something special in British military history. The formation of L Troop was more than just about filling a gap left by the loss of X Troop during Operation Colossus: it was about setting a standard for what airborne forces could become.

In June 1941, Lieutenant Colonel (later Lieutenant General) Ernest Edward 'Eric' Down took command of 11th Special Air Service Battalion from Lieutenant Colonel Jackson. In September, the unit was redesignated the 1st Parachute Battalion. By all accounts, Down was a man of enormous energy, drive and tenacity. Initially, he was almost universally disliked by officers and other ranks. However, over time, he earned the respect and affection of everyone he led.

Originally, 2 Commando had been conceived as a small raiding force. Colonel Down began to transform the battalion into a more conventionally trained light infantry unit. Down was appalled at the unit's incompetence and indiscipline.

He pictured a highly trained attacking infantry unit requiring a different type of recruit and training. Some of the original founding members of 2 Commando were returned to their units and replaced by a new intake of more regular, infantry-minded people. Next, Down moved the battalion to Bury for two months of intensive training. With help from the Lancashire Fusiliers, he focused on improving the battalion's weapons skills and platoon tactics. A routine of seemingly endless marches gradually improved the unit's fitness and stamina. Upon completing the training, Down marched his men the 25 miles back to Knutsford.[11]

Guardsman Reg Curtis recalled that Down was an unpopular officer who was immediately nicknamed 'Dracula'. Curtis thought Down was overzealous but confessed that he rather admired the man's enthusiasm. In addition to continuing to hone their infantry fighting skills, the battalion served as a testing ground for various equipment innovations, including air-dropping heavy weapons containers. Reg recalled another invention was the 'jump bag', allowing parachutists to jump with a kit bag of personal supplies attached to their leg. Once their parachute opened, they would release the bag on a length of rope, allowing it to hang below them and hit the ground first. This method allowed soldiers to carry an extra 100lb of vital supplies, essential for isolated parachute troops.[12]

In September 1941, the 1st Parachute Battalion (previously known as the 11th Special Air Service Battalion) was ordered to Hardwick Hall, where the 1st Parachute Brigade was being assembled under the command of Brigadier Richard Nelson 'Windy' Gale. The new brigade was to form part of the 1st Airborne Division, comprised of parachute and glider troops commanded by Major General Frederick 'Boy' Browning. A tall, always immaculately dressed Grenadier Guards officer, Browning intended to infuse the new parachute regiment with the spirit of the Brigade of Guards.

According to Hilary St George Saunders, author of *The Red Beret*:

By the time the aspiring parachute soldier had passed through Hardwick and Ringway, he was a toughened athlete, physically and mentally alert. Hardwick became for the parachute soldier "what Caterham is for the Brigade of Guards, a place of trial but not error".[13]

Guardsmen Volunteers

Having been one of the 300,000 souls rescued from the Dunkirk beaches during Operation Dynamo, Grenadier Guardsman Reg Curtis was rewarded with two weeks' leave. When he returned to duty, Reg was sent to Lough near Grimsby. In October 1940, Reg's battalion was paraded in front of the regimental sergeant major (RSM), who announced that the army was looking for volunteers to be trained as commandos and parachutists.

Reg recalled that the RSM read out the War Office notice with sneering derision, stating: 'Now I know that you would not wish to desert the Regiment, but anyone wishing to volunteer, one pace forward, march!' Glaring at the assembled guardsmen, his voice full of mocking contempt, the RSM continued, 'Well? You all chicken, then?' Reg recalled that no one in the parade made a sound or moved a muscle in response to the call for special service volunteers until he summoned the courage to take a pace forward. Reg was ordered to report to the 11th Special Air Service Battalion a few days after Christmas.

Reg was not the only guardsman to volunteer for special service during the summer and autumn months of 1940. On 19 July 1940, a report from the officer commanding the left flank of the 1st Battalion Scots Guards records that twenty-eight guardsmen expressed their willingness to volunteer for special service, with thirteen of them ready to undergo parachute training.[14] The war diary of the 1st Battalion, Scots Guards confirms that one officer and twenty-two other ranks were transferred to 8 (Guards) Commando for special service between the end of July and the start of August 1940.[15]

Reg joined his new unit at Congleton, southeast of Knutsford, where he found more volunteers from the Guards and other assorted regiments. Reg was assigned to L Troop, which was composed mainly of guardsmen and was commanded by Captain Peter Bromley-Martin of the Grenadier Guards. Reg recalled, 'The other volunteers included quite a few guardsmen from the Welsh, Coldstream and Irish Regiments, and all had seen active service.' After a few weeks at Ringway, Reg and his comrades were sent to Fort William, Scotland, for commando training. After passing various endurance tests in the bleak Scottish Highlands, the volunteers returned to Ringway to start their parachute training.

At the start of 1941, British parachute training was still in its infancy, dependent on a certain amount of trial and error. To practice landing correctly, Reg was required to throw himself from the back of a moving truck, a training method that was quickly abolished owing to broken bones among the novices. Next, the guardsmen completed a series of practice jumps from a Whitley bomber and a barrage balloon. Finally, Reg jumped as part of a stick of eight parachutists, half of them guardsmen. Within weeks, the guardsmen had completed seven parachute jumps and qualified as paratroopers. In his memoir, Reg wrote, 'We could not wait to sew those blue wings on the right arm of the battledress blouse.'[16]

In May of 1940, Guardsman John Morgan-Griffiths, 2nd Battalion Irish Guards saw action in France, taking part in the defence of Boulogne before being evacuated back to Britain. As part of the 22nd Guards Brigade, the 2nd Battalion settled into a period of home defence in anticipation of a German invasion of the British Isles. When the Germans did not materialise, John and several fellow guardsmen volunteered for special service. After attending a selection interview at Bulford Camp near Stonehenge, Salisbury, he was posted to Hardwick Hall for a toughening course and pre-jump training as a member of the 11th Special Air Service Battalion. Hardwick Camp was adjacent to the main house. The camp's training facilities included various assault courses, a parachute jump tower and a trapeze. When pre-jump training was completed, the recruits had to speed-march approximately 50 miles to join the parachute course at RAF Ringway.

In 1995, John was interviewed by the Imperial War Museum for its oral history project. During the interview, he recalled that the commandos liked to recruit guardsmen because they were 'hefty fellows'. John was a member of his battalion's boxing team, played rugby and always enjoyed keeping physically fit. However, the training staff were not keen on 'Guards discipline', which they thought tended to stifle rather than encourage a recruit's initiative. John remembered a large sign posted at the entrance of Harwick Camp that read, 'Bullshit Baffles Brains.'

The camp was a hive of activity. The recruits were required to run everywhere. After six hectic weeks of ground training focused mainly on jumping and landing from various platforms and towers, John moved to Ringway for his parachute training. According to John's account, he had to complete seven parachute jumps—five from an aircraft and two from a balloon—to qualify for his blue wings and earn an extra four shillings per day in jump pay. He recalled that the Whitley bomber was a poor choice of aircraft for parachute training. If a trainee failed to exit the aircraft cleanly through the small opening in the fuselage floor, there was a good chance of breaking one's nose or knocking oneself unconscious—an event commonly referred to as 'ringing the bell'. However, it was the balloon jumps that most trainees really hated.[17]

Operation Colossus

Towards the end of 1940, at a meeting in London, a decision was taken based on information from the civil engineering firm George Kent and Sons that an attack on the Tragino aqueduct in southern Italy might severely damage the Italian war effort. The aqueduct supplied water to three major ports: Taranto, Brindisi and Bari. Various methods of attacking the aqueduct were considered. Eventually, it was decided that a small raiding force inserted by parachute would likely have the best chance of achieving the objective. The mission was assigned to Britain's only parachute unit, the 11th Special Air Service Battalion, formed from 2 Commando.[18]

The men of 2 Commando were assembled, and volunteers were called for a dangerous mission. The volunteers were assembled into X Troop, commanded by Major Trevor Allan Gordon 'Tag' Pritchard of the Royal Welch Fusiliers. Sergeant Ernie Chinnery, 2 Commando, explained the selection process:

> Then, X Troop, a composite troop, was formed from among our ranks. It wasn't a question of us all volunteering and then being selected; each man was picked individually and the troop was segregated from us, doing their training in Tatton Park. We all wanted to be involved, but a lot of the men were chosen for their experience in demolition.[19]

After months of training in the UK, the X Troop volunteers were deployed to an advanced operating base in Malta. They flew across occupied France in a group of Whitley bombers to reach Malta. The mission, codenamed Operation Colossus, aimed to drop X Troop by parachute. The objective was to sabotage the Tragino aqueduct. Following this, the troops would march to the coast, where they would be picked up by a Royal Navy submarine.

Lieutenant Anthony (later Major General) Deane-Drummond, Royal Signals recalled his own part in preparations for Operation Colossus:

> The first operation I did was the first British Airborne parachute operation of the war in February 1941. We prepared for about two months before (the Operation), I suppose. And I was sent off ahead of the main party to Malta, which is to be the base from which the aeroplanes then fly to southern Italy. I arrived in Malta; I suppose it must have been at the beginning of February '41. My job was, in fact, to find suitable accommodation for one or two nights for the main party of No. 2 Commando, who were flying out from Lincolnshire to Malta, which in those days was something of a dodgy set-up because the twin-engine Whitley was an aircraft that was operating almost at extreme range, so I believe. Anyway, they all landed in Malta. From there, we used the same aircraft to drop into southern Italy.

On 7 February 1941, Admiral Sir Roger Keyes, Director of Combined Operations came to give the men an official send-off. The mood was sombre. One soldier standing near the Admiral heard him say to himself, 'A pity, a damned pity'. Apparently, Admiral Keyes regarded the mission as ill-conceived and detrimental to the health of the troops involved.[20]

The operation began on the evening of 10 February, when eight Whitley bombers took off from Malta. Six carried the parachutists, while two were assigned to create a diversion by bombing the railway yards at Foggia. The first aircraft arrived over the target in bright moonlight at 21.42hrs. Lieutenant Deane-Drummond's stick landed within 250 yards of the aqueduct. However, one aircraft, carrying Captain Gerrard Daly, Royal Engineers and his demolition team, became lost and dropped its men in the wrong valley. In Raymond Foxall's book *The Guinea-Pigs: Britain's First Paratroop Raid*, he recounts what happened to Daly and his men in the moments leading up to the jump and after:

> Daly was acting as despatcher. He sent all four of his men out and pressed the button to release the containers. Nothing happened. He tried again. No joy. He jumped. Daly and his men were indeed floating down into the wrong valley. Many miles and a great mountain separated them from the aqueduct and their comrades. It meant that the senior engineer officer, the man who was to mastermind the blowing of the aqueduct, would not be there to go into action.[21]

According to Anthony Deane-Drummond, after a mix-up in the jump order on board his aircraft, he found himself the first paratrooper on the ground from his 'stick' and landed very close to the Tragino aqueduct. He recalled that it took the other aircraft about an hour to drop their loads, and eventually, they all regrouped. In an interview recorded after the war, Deane-Drummond explained what happened to him immediately after landing:

> Well, there was one Sapper (combat engineer) who was there. I can't remember his name, but it doesn't matter. On inspection of the actual bridge, instead of being in bricks and mortar, it was, in fact, reinforced concrete, which was a much more difficult thing to blow up. So, he put all the explosives that we had onto the one pier and blow me down; he did blow it up, but a couple of hours later. In the meantime, and I've been there after the war and seen the old aqueduct, which had been repaired, of course, within about a month, I think, of when we blew it up. But it did excite the Italians, and I think they deployed an additional division of protection for all, not only that sort of aqueduct but lots of other places all up and down the length of Italy.[22]

Deane-Drummond was correct when he said the aqueduct was constructed of reinforced concrete rather than the masonry the saboteurs had anticipated. Despite having less explosives than initially planned due to equipment container losses and misdropped personnel, around six to seven hundred pounds of gun cotton were placed against the westernmost pier of the aqueduct by 2nd Lieutenant George Robert Paterson, Royal Engineers. According to Raymond Foxall, a grave-faced Paterson reported to Major Pritchard that the aqueduct was 'one hell of a sight stronger than expected, but he would do his best.'[23]

At around 00.30hrs on 11 February, after moving some Italian civilians to safety, the charges were detonated. The explosion of the aqueduct was a spectacular demonstration of the power of airborne forces. The men of X Troop had undergone pioneering training in Britain and had come a long way to participate in this spectacular sabotage. In his book *The Guinea-Pigs*, Raymond Foxall describes the scene immediately after the aqueduct was blown:

> The major and lieutenant halted some ten paces from where the explosives had been stacked—and what they saw made them momentarily inarticulate with excitement. Half the aqueduct was down. One pier had gone altogether. Another leaned at a crazy angle. Huge breaches cut gaping wounds into the concrete water runway. From these, water cascaded into the Tragino valley.[24]

After successfully completing its mission, X Troop split into three groups to escape to a designated meeting point with the British submarine HMS *Triumph* at the mouth of the Sele river. However, back in the UK, the news that Operation Colossus had apparently failed provoked a decision that would have far-reaching consequences for the men of X Troop. On 13 February, the Chiefs of Staff Committee met in Whitehall. According to the minutes of the meeting, it was agreed by those present that the enemy was probably aware of X Troop's planned rendezvous with HMS *Triumph* due to one of the Whitley bombers having sent a distress message in simple code that the Italians were likely to have deciphered. Therefore, it was agreed to cancel the rescue mission, recall the submarine, and effectively abandon X Troop to its fate.[25]

Years later, Deane-Drummond described the events on the ground following the attack on the aqueduct:

> And then we had to get away. The plan was, in fact, to walk about 60 miles to the western coast to be picked up by a submarine from the mouth of the river Sele. I had become friendly with the captains of the submarines because that's where the submarines were based in Malta, and it was, in fact, HMS *Triumph*. And, but, unfortunately, after we had landed, after we had blown it up, which wasn't in fact seen by even air photographs back in the UK, but it did, in fact, blow up. They had all this later. But anyway, they thought that the effort had been carried out successfully; we'd carried the explosives; we'd apparently blown it up. The task of getting 60 miles to the coast was almost impossible. And I don't think any of us managed that at all.
>
> "Tag" Pritchard and myself, we divided ourselves into three parties. The job was finished. We were on our way. We ended up on a hillside, not all that far, about ten to twenty miles, from where we had blown up this thing. There were a lot of people around us. They were all black-coated women and dozens of children. So there were about two to three hundred of them all around us. This applied to the other parties, which were doing it slightly differently but were going the same way. And then, behind the women and the children, who appeared to be all black and dressed in black things because that was the normal clothing for peasants in southern Italy at the

time, there was a group of policemen: Carabinieri. And then behind that, the army was there [laugh quietly]. And so "Tag" Pritchard asked me if we should shoot our way out of it. And I said, well, judging by the experience we'd had getting this far, it was rather a useless performance. So, in the end, we surrendered, which was a very uncomfortable thing to do anyway. However, we were all taken off to various places. We were in Naples for a bit on the airfield, and we were taken to Sulmona, which was the first camp, the first prisoner of war camp.[26]

All the men of X Troop had been captured within days of the operation. The unit's Italian civilian interpreter, Fortunato Picchi, was executed by the Fascist militia after being tortured. The raiders were imprisoned, first in Italy and later, after Italy's surrender, in Germany. While the damage to the aqueduct was slight and quickly repaired and had no discernible effect on the war effort, the psychological impact on Italian morale was more significant. The raid led to increased security measures throughout Italy and demonstrated that Britain could strike deep behind enemy lines.

It was 8 January 1941 when General Ismay had written to the prime minister outlining a proposal by the director of Combined Operations to cut off the water supply to the towns in southern Italy by 'dropping parachutists to destroy the Apulian Aqueduct'. General Ismay informed the prime minister that the chiefs of staff had reviewed the project and believed it had a reasonable chance of success. Therefore, he recommended that the operation, originally known as Project 'T', be approved. The following day, the prime minister approved Operation Colossus. However, when initial reports from Malta immediately after the operation suggested that Colossus had failed, the prime minister, to distance himself from any political repercussions from the operation, mendaciously claimed no knowledge of it. On 15 February, the prime minister wrote to General Ismay from 10 Downing Street:

> I do not remember having been consulted in any way upon the proposal to land parachute troops in Italy. I remember hearing about the project to land men from a submarine to attack bridges from the coast. The use of parachute troops was a serious step to take, in view of the invasion aspect here, and I would rather not have opened this chapter, raising as it does all sorts of questions about the status and uniform of these troops.
>
> Let me have a report as soon as possible upon the preparation and execution of this plan, showing exactly what authorities were consulted. Make sure that for the future my initial is obtained to all projects of this character.

On the same day, 15 February, a functionary from the office of the minister of defence coldly rebutted the prime minister's assertion that he knew nothing about preparations for Colossus:

I attach a Minute (Flag "B") which was submitted to you outlining the Operation. In paragraph 1 of the Minute reference was made to the proposal to land parachutists. You will see that you approved the Operation on 9th February.

On 13 February, Wing Commander Sir Nigel Norman prepared an initial report on the lessons learned from Operation Colossus, which he regarded as a failure at the time of writing. Norman speculated that having the latest intelligence, including aerial reconnaissance, was crucial to planning operations effectively. The parachutists and aircrew needed more time to study and memorise the terrain before launching an operation. Dropping parachute troops at night on an unfamiliar target took longer than initially anticipated, and their presence caused significant disturbances in the target area, which seemed unavoidable. Norman also suggested several improvements for future operations, such as contact between the commanders of both air and ground forces for better decision-making, sufficient time for army personnel to familiarise themselves with the aircraft they would use during operations and the redesign of air-dropped equipment containers.

At Combined Operations, Sir Roger Keyes, who had apparently always regarded Colossus as something of a suicide mission for those involved, was angry and bitter about the decision to recall the submarine, leaving X Troop stranded. On 13 February 1941, Keyes wrote to the prime minister in protest at what he saw as the abandonment of his men: 'I consider our failure to make any effort to carry out the salvage arrangements promised to the parachutists a clear breach of faith.' The text of the prime minister's personal notes regarding Operation Colossus and its immediate aftermath can be found in Appendix B.[27]

After the rather gloomy assessments of the first few days, Operation Colossus was deemed at least a partial success for Britain's inexperienced airborne forces. Thought the Tragino aqueduct had been damaged and not destroyed, the operation proved a much-needed propaganda victory. However, Sir Roger Keyes clearly antagonised the wrong people with his accusations. Like many of the men who had joined the commandos, Keyes found himself constantly frustrated as planned operations were frequently postponed or cancelled. Perhaps lacking the skill to navigate the shark-infested waters of Whitehall, Keyes resigned as director of Combined Operations on 27 October 1941. He was replaced by a member of the Royal Family and pillar of the establishment, Captain Lord Louis Mountbatten, who was immediately promoted to the rank of commodore.

On 14 February, Rome issued a communiqué regarding the landing of British paratroopers, which was reported in every major newspaper. In response, London's Ministry of Information released a brief but cautious statement concerning the operation. The Italian communiqué received significant coverage in the United

States, with radio commentators interpreting the raid as a sign of Britain's aggressiveness and increasing offensive spirit and capabilities. Aside from the evident propaganda value of the news reports, they stood as the first clear indication to the War Office that Operation Colossus had achieved some level of success.

On 16 February, the front page of *Sunday Pictorial* was emblazoned with a banner headline: 'THEY WERE OURS!—official. British Parachute Troops' Daring Drop into Italy.' The headline was illustrated with a large photograph of parachutists descending from a cloud-filled sky. The body copy of the article continued:

THE VEIL IS LIFTED THIS MORNING ON AN AMAZING BRITISH WAR SECRET.

Without a word leaking out WE have trained parachute troops—and we have dropped them in Italy. They were sent to carry out a daring operation, and this official news confirms the Italian authorities' statement that British parachute troops had arrived. Our men did not go to their great adventure disguised in enemy uniforms.

THEY WENT OUT TO DO THE JOB AS SOLDIERS, IN MILITARY UNIFORM.

What their tasks were, and how many got back cannot be told. But the Government now officially released the news that the troops reported in Italy were British. Before this announcement, the Italians claimed that they had captured eighteen Britons—who dropped by parachute in the "toe" of Italy.

A report reaching America from Rome suggests that the captured men reached at least some of their objectives—"They must have got down to the job," it says. Although an official statement from Rome last night said that these invaders would be treated as prisoners of war, there had already been talk in Italy of "treating them as spies." If this is anything more than talk, there should be another thing coming to the Fascist Government.[28]

The *New York Herald Tribune* also reported the story that day, confirming that British authorities had admitted to dropping parachute troops in southern Italy.[29]

A summary from the War Office of reports regarding Operation Colossus included the following:

On 14 March 1941, a correspondent of the *Chicago Daily News*, who had recently returned from Rome, stated that the Apulian Aqueduct was blown up by our parachutists and repaired in two and a half days. The American Military Attache visited the captured parachutists, whose morale was "terrific". They said they had blown up a railway bridge, besides damaging the aqueduct.

Local inhabitants carried their dynamite, under the impression that they were Germans. They intended to escape at the first opportunity.[30]

Many of the men who participated in the ill-fated raid and were taken prisoner went on to enjoy distinguished military careers. Major 'Tag' Pritchard received the Distinguished Service Order (DSO), while several others received military decorations after the war, including the Military Cross and Military Medal.

In the final judgement, Operation Colossus tested the capability of Britain's new airborne forces, provided valuable operational experience and proved that British paratroopers could successfully reach and, at least partially, destroy a target deep inside enemy territory. The operation marked the start of British airborne operations during the Second World War. While its strategic impact was limited, it taught valuable lessons that would influence the development of airborne forces throughout the rest of the war.[31]

Early Airborne Policy

According to William F. Buckingham's book *Paras*, the War Office was actually ahead of Churchill in exploring the use of parachute forces. They began their preliminary investigations before Churchill's June 1940 directive to create a force of 5,000 parachute troops. It seems that the prime minister's decision to set the target at 5,000 parachutists was completely arbitrary. The directive did not indicate the force's strategic purpose or mention the use of gliders.

In April 1940, Sir John Dill was appointed CIGS. He remarked that Churchill was often full of ideas, many of them brilliant, but most of them impractical. Possibly, given the vagueness of Churchill's directive, it was not pursued with great vigour. Between December 1940 and January 1941, the Air Ministry and War Office significantly disagreed over the future direction of airborne forces development.[1]

Before the prime minister's note to General Ismay, the chiefs of staff agreed to assess the feasibility of raising an airborne force. On 8 June 1940, the director of plans at the Air Ministry issued a memorandum addressing the development of parachute forces. The Air Ministry identified several immediate obstacles to fulfilling Churchill's demands. These included a lack of suitable aircraft, insufficient personnel and no clear policy regarding the force's purpose. As a result, they deemed the original target of 5,000 parachutists impractical and recommended reducing the number to 500 troops.[2]

Unlike the German model, British parachute troops would be under army command rather than that of the air force. Together, the War Office and Air Ministry would oversee training. The air force's role was limited to providing instructors and aircraft. Since no purpose-built aircraft existed for parachute operations, and none were planned, slightly modified bomber aircraft were requisitioned for training. Unsurprisingly, the Air Ministry took a dim view of having to divert bomber aircraft away from their primary task of attacking the enemy.

Within days of the memorandum's circulation, an outline of operational doctrine emerged. Two main deployment methods were proposed: direct assault, or coup de main, and 'offset drop', whereby troops landed at a distance from the target. This second approach prioritised tactical surprise by avoiding immediate contact with the enemy, but required troops to move cross-country to reach their objective. Four main types of parachute operation were envisaged: sabotage attacks against infrastructure (described as 'suicide attacks' in the document), holding attacks to secure strategic objectives, reinforcement of ground forces, and disruptive attacks on enemy rear areas, lines of communication and flanks.[3]

Two days after Churchill issued his fateful directive, Major (later Lieutenant Colonel) J. F. Rock, Royal Engineers was summoned to the War Office and ordered to take charge of the military organisation of airborne force. However, Rock received no clear direction on policy or task. Rock was a regular soldier without prior knowledge of parachuting or gliders. Nevertheless, he and his RAF colleagues—Squadron Leader Louis Strange, Wing Commander (later Air Commodore) Sir Nigel Norman and Group Captain L. G. Harvey—quickly established the Central Landing School at Ringway, Manchester.[4]

On 12 August 1940, the Air Ministry issued an air staff memorandum titled 'Present Situation Regarding the Development of Parachute Training', clearly outlining its pessimistic views on using parachute troops:

> We are beginning to incline to the view that dropping troops from the air by parachute is a clumsy and obsolescent method and that there are far more important possibilities in gliders. The Germans made excellent use of their parachute troops in the Low Countries by exploiting surprise, and by the fact that they had practically no opposition. But it seems to us at least possible that this may be the last time that parachute troops are used on a serious scale in major operations.[5]

A year later, following the disastrous losses suffered by German *Fallschirmjäger* units during the invasion of Crete, Adolf Hitler came to the same conclusion as Britain's Air Ministry: that parachute troops should not be used for large-scale military operations.

In the early days, most fledgling parachutists came from the newly formed 2 Commando. Various types of 'synthetic' ground-training equipment were developed to simulate the different stages of a parachute descent. Mock-up aircraft fuselages were constructed, allowing students to practice entry and exit procedures. Various platforms and trapeze-like apparatuses enabled trainees to practice every phase of a parachute descent and landing in a controlled environment. As we have already seen, at the end of November 1940, the infamous barrage balloon was pressed into service as an alternative platform for practice parachute jumps due to the lack of training aircraft.[6]

On Wednesday, 11 December 1940, the Air Ministry outlined a policy regarding the establishment and training of airborne forces. Although the target of training 500 parachutists—reduced from Churchill's original requirement of 5,000 paratroopers—was expected to be met by the spring of 1941, other objectives for the newly formed airborne forces were likely to be missed. These included the development of gliders, the recruitment and training of glider pilots and the availability of suitable transport aircraft.[7]

On 26 April 1941, Churchill visited Ringway to review airborne forces and assess progress. What he witnessed was a rather disappointing spectacle of around sixty parachutists dropped from a handful of ageing Whiteley bombers and a flying display by a single Hotspur glider. Although airborne troops came under the army's command, Churchill had failed to nominate a single ministry, office or department to coordinate the many services required to create an effective airborne capability. Therefore, the project lacked the clear leadership needed to move forward quickly. As we have seen, a certain amount of inter-service rivalry between the army and the air force undoubtedly hampered the project's progress.[8]

On 26 May 1941, following the German airborne invasion of Crete, the prime minister wrote to General Ismay. He expressed concern about the Air Ministry's hesitance to proceed with the development of Britain's own airborne forces. While the Air Ministry believed that gliders were the most effective means of air landing troops rather than parachutes, the prime minister highlighted that very little had been done to develop the necessary glider force. Pessimistically, Churchill confided to Ismay, 'Thus we are always found behind-hand by the enemy.' Instead of the 5,000 parachute troops and an Airborne Division imagined by Churchill a year before, the army had only one trained battalion.[9]

As the threat of invasion of the British Isles faded and Germany's 'Blitz' bombing campaign tapered off, the War Office was eager to shift from a defensive posture to offensive operations. Between July and September 1941, the War Office refined its airborne requirement, aiming for a brigade-sized force, but paid little attention to practical matters such as purpose, composition, recruitment, and training.

On July 4, 1941, the War Office announced plans to expand the airborne forces by 1,800 men. However, Lieutenant General Haining, Assistant Chief of the Imperial General Staff (ACIGS), opposed this plan, citing concerns about manpower shortages. He suggested postponing the expansion. Despite his objections, his superior, Sir John Dill, ordered the immediate formation of two additional parachute battalions.

In February 1941, J. F. Rock was promoted to Lieutenant Colonel and proposed five recruitment options to address manpower availability while continuing to expand airborne forces. His first suggestion was to take volunteers from across the army, or specifically from infantry units, but he acknowledged that this approach would require time. Another idea was to start with a cadre of volunteer officers and non-commissioned officers (NCOs) before adding new recruits. The fourth option involved recruiting primarily from a single infantry regiment.

The final and boldest plan proposed converting entire infantry battalions into parachute units, although he recognised that there would be some wastage, as not every soldier would be physically or psychologically suited for parachuting. Ultimately, he recommended a combination of voluntary recruitment and the wholesale conversion of existing infantry battalions. Rock acknowledged that while forced conversion was controversial, it offered the fastest path to meeting urgent wartime expansion needs.

The commandos, which included the 11th Special Air Service Battalion, operated under unique terms of service that emphasised independence and self-reliance. Volunteers retained the right to withdraw from 'special-service' duties and return to their original units after any operation. Commandos were classified as 'irregular soldiers'. Although they were subject to military discipline, they were expected to be independent and self-sufficient. Unlike most regular army units, commando soldiers were responsible for arranging their own accommodation, food and travel.

On 23 July, at a War Office conference, it was decided the commandos' original terms of service would be replaced by parachute pay. Rock hoped that the new parachute allowance would offset the loss of commando privileges. The 11th Special Air Service Battalion had developed a reputation for being a maverick unit and was at risk of disbandment. However, in August 1941, the unit was reorganised into a conventional infantry battalion. In September of the same year, it was renamed the 1st Parachute Battalion and became part of the 1st Parachute Brigade.[10]

On 2 December 1941, Major General F. A. M. Browning, Commander of the 1st Airborne Division, wrote to GHQ Home Forces on the subject of the 1st Parachute Battalion and its continued unruly behaviour:

> 1 Battalion, formed from the old Parachute Commando, must be concentrated out of billets immediately if it is to have any chance of becoming a disciplined, well-administered and trained unit within measurable time. If it remains in its present location or is spread out in billets, it cannot improve to any real extent and may even deteriorate.[11]

On 28 August 1941, the assistant adjutant general sent an airborne-forces recruitment circular to all field forces, infantry, rifle and machine-gun battalions in the UK. The circular specified that volunteers had to be aged between twenty and thirty-two (with exemptions for qualified officers and NCOs), maintain A1 fitness, weigh under 196lb and meet specific eyesight and dental standards. Signals and mortar officers were prioritised, and captains were required to hold company command qualifications. The new terms of service replaced commando privileges with basic parachute pay (4 shillings weekly for officers, 2 shillings for other ranks after completing three qualifying jumps). To avoid weakening existing units by taking their best soldiers, battalions were limited to providing ten volunteers each, with nominations due by mid-September 1941.[12]

Initially, the basic physical screening for parachute recruits focused on practical considerations, including a soldier's weight (which should not exceed 250lb when lightly equipped), the ability to exit an aircraft through a 3-foot opening, and the thickness of a man's skull, along with the strength of his ankles, to endure hard landings. Later, despite the establishment of clear minimum medical standards for parachute volunteers, individuals who were neither physically nor psychologically prepared for the demands of training continued to arrive. It is possible, even likely, that some units viewed the request for parachute volunteers as an opportunity to offload subpar soldiers, as had happened during commando recruitment.[13]

In October 1941, Brigadier Richard 'Windy' Gale, who led the 1st Parachute Brigade, wrote to the War Office following a visit by Group Captain Craig, Principal Medical Officer (PMO), RAF Bracknell. Craig reported on medical procedures for parachute volunteers and highlighted several ongoing issues: some volunteers arrived without any medical examination, prompting calls for disciplinary action. He recommended the introduction of secondary medical checks at parachute units since their doctors had more relevant experience.

Craig found several cases of men who, when faced with the fact of having to hurl themselves from an aeroplane or balloon, were psychologically incapable of doing the act. He recommended that psychological testing be considered to screen out those unsuitable for jumping. Cases of airsickness also proved to be a significant problem that could incapacitate troops. Finally, training units needed proper equipment to test for colour blindness. Craig's report reflects some of the early challenges of establishing proper medical standards and procedures for Britain's newly formed parachute forces.[14]

The airborne training regime expanded significantly in the autumn of 1941, as the War Office aimed to produce 100 parachutists weekly (5,200 annually). The training syllabus encompassed physical fitness, unarmed combat, technical skills, aircraft familiarisation, parachute instruction and tactics. Training facilities grew to include elementary flying training schools, glider training schools, and specialised parachute exercise squadrons.[15]

A War Office letter dated 29 October 1941 stated that the Army Council had agreed on the policy for an airborne establishment of 2,500 parachutists, probably to be increased later, and an air-landed independent brigade group, including heavy weapons, engineers, medical and logistics. The provision of air-landed armoured fighting vehicles was still under investigation, but the lightly armoured Bren Gun Carrier was being considered because of its 'good fighting power' and its load-carrying capabilities.[16]

The War Office planned to move beyond small-scale raiding to create forces capable of supporting major conventional operations, much like the German *Fallschirmjäger*, who had successfully seized crucial objectives in Norway and the Low Countries in 1940. This meant developing larger formations capable of capturing and holding strategic points, such as bridges and road junctions, ahead of advancing ground forces.

The War Office's expanded vision of airborne forces required significant organisational changes: transitioning from battalion to brigade-sized units, developing new tactical doctrines and establishing robust training programs. This evolution demanded greater air transport resources and closer coordination with RAF Bomber Command, which controlled the aircraft needed for large-scale drops. These requirements often created tensions with the Air Ministry, which prioritised strategic bombing over airborne operations.

By late 1941, the War Office's ambitions began to take shape with the formation of the 1st Airborne Division, although achieving full operational capability would require considerable time. The transition highlighted the challenges of scaling up specialised raid-focused units into larger conventional forces while maintaining their elite status and effectiveness. The War Office's vision for expanding airborne forces reflected a broader strategic shift. While small raids like Operation Colossus demonstrated tactical utility, military planners increasingly saw the potential for airborne forces to support large-scale conventional operations, particularly in preparation for a future invasion of Europe.

The Father of Airborne Forces

Regarded by many as the 'father of Britain's airborne forces', Frederick Arthur Montague Browning was born on 20 December 1896. As a child, friends and family alike referred to Browning by the nickname Tommy. His mother and paternal grandparents were devout Christians, and from an early age, he became a regular churchgoer. He maintained his Christian faith and ethics throughout his life.

Aged nine, a boisterous young Browning was packed off to West Downs boarding school, Winchester. Sports played an important role in the life of the school, and Tommy participated in cricket and football and won several awards for diving. In the classroom, he proved to be an academically average student. In 1910, he moved to Eton College Public School. In 1913, he joined the Army Class, which was created to prepare young men for a regular commission in the British Army. Browning's biographer Richard Mead noted:

> The old Etonian network has always been extraordinarily influential, and the connections which Tommy established during his time at school, particularly through membership of Pop [the Eton Society reserved for elite, waistcoat-wearing prefects], were to be of benefit throughout his life.[1]

Browning's school contemporaries included a future prime minister, Anthony Eden, and several politicians who would go on to serve in Churchill's wartime government. This network of connections would prove invaluable throughout his career, with one American officer later wearily observing that 'as usual, the admiral, the Governor, the Governor-General and everyone else of consequence had been to school with, played polo with, sailed with or fought in World War I with Browning'.[2]

On 28 June 1914, Archduke Franz Ferdinand, the heir to the throne of Austria-Hungary, was assassinated by a Serbian radical. Due to the various interconnecting alliances between European nations, the dominoes started to fall, with Austria-Hungary declaring war on Serbia, Russia becoming involved and then Germany. On 4 August 1914, Britain declared war on Germany after it invaded neutral Belgium.

On 24 November, Browning sat the Sandhurst Military College entrance exam but failed to pass all of the required subjects. It appeared that Browning's ambitions for a military career had faltered at the outset until the headmaster of Eton stepped in, recommending him as a candidate for officer training to the Army Council. On 27 December, Browning entered Sandhurst as a gentleman cadet seeking a regular commission. He successfully graduated on 16 June 1915 and was gazetted (i.e., listed in the *London Gazette*) as a second lieutenant in the Grenadier Guards. Entry into the elite regiment was fiercely competitive; despite mounting casualties at the front, gaining an interview with the regimental colonel still required a personal recommendation from someone influential within the British establishment.

Browning was posted to the newly formed 4th Battalion. However, when the battalion was shipped to France, he was transferred to the training battalion due to his youth and inexperience. Although the Grenadier Guards were the epitome of strict discipline and military precision, it was customary for all officers up to the rank of major to address one another by their first names. The regiment's officers were also inordinately fond of nicknames. The exact origin of his nickname is unknown, but he would be known as 'Boy' Browning for the rest of his military career. Nevertheless, among close friends and family, he would remain Tommy.

On 13 October, Browning left Chelsea Barracks in London for France, reporting for duty three days later at the 2nd Battalion Grenadier Guards, 4 Guards Brigade, 2nd Division. A month later, Browning was joined in the trenches by Major Winston Churchill, MP, who temporarily joined the battalion on secondment. Churchill served as the first lord of the Admiralty at the outbreak of war. In 1915, he played a key role in planning the disastrous Dardanelles naval campaign and the military landings at Gallipoli, both of which resulted in heavy casualties. Following the failure of these campaigns, Churchill resigned from his government post. He then became an officer in the army and served on the Western Front. Churchill remained with the Grenadiers until January 1916, when he took command of the 6th Battalion, Royal Scots Fusiliers. During his time with the Grenadier Guards, Churchill developed great admiration and affection for the regiment.

On 6 January 1916, Browning was hospitalised and returned to Britain, showing symptoms of trench fever. Lice typically transmit the disease to their human hosts. Symptoms vary in presentation from headache, rash, malaise and joint pain to life-threatening inflammation of the heart's inner lining (endocarditis). The unsanitary conditions of trench life created a perfect breeding ground for head and body lice, leading to over a million cases of the disease by the end of the conflict. Browning was in the hospital for about a month and spent the following eight weeks on sick leave. He was sent on attachment to the Guards

Depot, Caterham, where he remained for seven months before being passed fit for active duty and returned to the front. The 2nd Battalion had repeatedly been in action and suffered heavy casualties while Browning was absent.[3]

Following bitter fighting to capture Gauche Wood on 1 December 1917, Browning was awarded the Distinguished Service Order (DSO) for conspicuous gallantry and devotion to duty. According to an article in the 2017 edition of *The Grenadiers Gazette*, 'Browning was profoundly affected by the confusion and carnage of Gauche Wood. For the rest of his life, he would have recurrent nightmares and wake up shouting.' After the battle, an officer of the 18th Bengal Lancers wrote:

> I have now seen His Majesty's Guards in action and fought alongside them. They can die like gentlemen without a groan. Four of our men were carrying a Guardsman who appeared to be suffering considerably. I asked him who he was, and he instinctively straightened himself as best he could and said, 'A Grenadier, ' his tone implying how proud he was to be one.[4]

A month after the action at Gauche Wood, Browning was promoted to captain and took command of 1 Company. In the autumn of 1918, he served as aide-de-camp (ADC) to the general officer commanding (GOC) Fourth Army, Sir Henry Rawlinson, before rejoining the Grenadiers for the war's final days.

Peace meant the army was rapidly downsized and returned to policing the British Empire. Opportunities for career advancement for a regular army officer were rare and difficult to come by. In November 1921, Browning returned to Caterham as the Grenadiers' captain in residence. He also took up the sporting pursuits of archery, athletics and bobsleigh. He narrowly missed qualifying for the 1924 Olympic team when he suffered a severe injury in a bobsleigh accident just before the inaugural Winter Olympics but ultimately competed in the 1928 Winter Olympics in St Moritz, Switzerland. His five-man bobsleigh team, Great Britain II, came tenth. Given his privileged upbringing, it is unsurprising that Browning was an accomplished horseman, keen sailor and skilled marksman. In 1927, he won the Officers' Jumping Competition at the Royal Tournament.[5]

In April 1923, Browning was in Cornwall to collect his boat, which he had moored on the River Fowey for the winter. He heard that the young novelist Daphne du Maurier was convalescing nearby after an appendectomy and invited her to go sailing with him. He had read du Maurier's novel, *The Loving Spirit* and had been impressed by her descriptions of the Cornish coastline. She was ten years his junior; nevertheless, a romance blossomed.

In Richard Mead's biography, *General 'BOY'*, he writes that 'on the face of it, Boy and Daphne were not obviously suited to one another'. Browning was every inch the army officer: forthright, practical, confident and outgoing, with a wide circle of friends and acquaintances. Daphne was quiet, withdrawn, highly imaginative and creative. They did share one common passion: a love of the sea and sailing. In what would today be termed a 'whirlwind romance', the couple married in July.[6]

In 1924, Boy was appointed adjutant at the Royal Military College, Sandhurst. During his tenure, officers like the future commando leader Bob Laycock passed through Sandhurst. Browning established the tradition of the adjutant riding his horse up the steps of Old College, a feat that became one of his claims to fame.[7] In April 1928, he returned to his regiment. However, the next few years of his career were somewhat marred by ill health, primarily bouts of nervous exhaustion. His health problems cost him a coveted place at Staff College, a prerequisite for officers seeking senior command appointments. His father's death and the Wall Street crash of 1929 left the family finances in a perilous state. Browning found himself almost entirely dependent on his army pay, and being a Guards officer could be ruinously expensive.

His marriage to a literary celebrity allowed Browning to add an artistic circle to his formidable political and military contacts. However, the relationship would face strains due to his military commitments. Indeed, unbeknownst to Browning, du Maurier began an affair with their landlord at Hitchin during a particularly demanding period of his career in 1942. Browning's frequent absences, travelling to various military installations and engagements, put significant pressure on their marriage. His all-consuming dedication to establishing the airborne forces left little time for family life.[8]

In 1939, Browning was appointed assistant commandant of the Small Arms School and was quickly promoted to brigadier and commandant. Although he held an important position, he would have preferred serving with one of the Grenadier battalions in France. In mid-May 1940, he took command of the 128th (Hampshire) Infantry Brigade. The formation was preparing to join the British Expeditionary Force when the Dunkirk evacuation happened. Despite challenges like equipment shortages, Browning impressed his superiors, leading to recommendations for a divisional command. In February 1941, he assumed command of the 24th Guards Brigade Group, which was tasked with defending London.

Towards the end of May 1941, the War Office and Air Ministry submitted a joint paper on the future development of airborne forces. The paper proposed the formation of two parachute and two airlanding brigades, one of each to be deployed in the UK and the others in the Middle East. This led to the formation of 1 Parachute Brigade, which included the 11th Special Air Service Battalion, renamed the 1st Parachute Battalion. In October, 31 Independent Brigade Group was converted into 1 Airlanding Brigade Group. Around this time, the War Office decided that a separate headquarters was necessary to organise and run the expanding airborne forces.

It appears that Commander-in-Chief, Home Forces, General Sir Alan Brooke (later Field Marshal, 1st Viscount Alanbrooke) was encouraged by his cousin, Sir Bertram Sergison-Brooke, Major General commanding the Brigade of Guards and GOC London District, to appoint Browning as commander of Britain's fledgling airborne forces. It is clear from General Alan Brooke's diaries that he and his cousin were close and socialised frequently. The two men had worked together to bring the Guards Armoured Division into creation, and Sergison-Brooke recommended Oliver Leese as the new formation's commander.[9]

General Brooke had been particularly impressed by Browning during a demonstration of 'attacks on tanks' that he observed in October 1941, describing it in his diary as 'a first-class show very well staged and full of useful lessons'. Brooke was so impressed that he arranged to have the demonstration made into a training film. At this event, Brooke informed Browning that he had been selected for command of the Airborne Division.[10]

Browning appointed two Grenadier Guards officers to his new staff, Lieutenant Colonel John Goschen as his assistant adjutant and quartermaster general (AA & QMG) and Major Richard des Voeux, General Staff Officer 2 (GSO2) (Operations).

According to Richard Mead, Brooke saw Browning as the ideal candidate to take control of Britain's new airborne forces:

> He was known to be determined and energetic but also personally ambitious, which meant he could be counted on to throw himself into the role and make a success of it. He was a natural leader, who would inspire those under his command. He was a good organiser, who would overcome any obstacle put in his way. Whilst no intellectual, he was entirely open to new ideas, unlike many of his contemporaries. Finally, he was very well connected, not only to Brooke himself, who was about to become the professional head of the British Army as CIGS, but to other senior officers and politicians, even to Churchill himself. He had been known for many years to the Royal Family.[11]

Although appointed by Brooke to command British airborne forces partly due to his social connections and personal ambition, it appears Browning could still overstep his boundaries. In David Fraser's biography of the 1st Viscount Alanbrooke, he recounts an episode when Browning was called to meet the Chief of the Imperial General Staff for a reprimand:

> He had been 'writing to politicians', said Brooke. Browning was himself a formidable superior, but he emerged from a few minutes' interview, scarlet in the face, gathered his Staff Officer waiting in the outer office and hastened away. 'Come on,' he said, 'I've had the biggest dressing down of my life—but My God he's a great man!'[12]

Promoted to acting major general on assuming the role of GOC of the 1st Airborne Division, Browning decided to concentrate his new command close to the army training grounds on Salisbury Plain. Syrencot House was selected as the divisional headquarters. There were suitable grass airfields nearby at Upavon and Netheravon, providing ample space to conduct exercises. In January 1942, two exercise squadrons, 296 for glider training and 297 for parachute training, were combined to form 38 Wing, which was commanded by Nigel Norman, who was promoted to Group Captain. Browning and Norman quickly established a good working relationship. In April 1942, 1 Parachute Brigade moved south from Hardwick Camp. However, a shortage of suitable aircraft for either towing gliders or dropping parachutists remained an obstacle to training.

While Browning is frequently credited with single-handedly expanding British airborne forces to divisional size and beyond (and often referred to as the 'father of British airborne forces'), official records show that the War Office, along with senior officers like Dill and Alan Brooke, were working toward expanding the airborne force well before Browning became involved.

There are arguably stronger candidates for the title of 'father of airborne forces'. One such candidate is Richard Gale, who played a key role in transforming the British parachute effort into a recognised airborne force. He also led the 6th Airborne Division during the Normandy invasion, which is considered the most significant and successful British airborne operation ever conducted. Another noteworthy figure is Lieutenant Colonel John Rock of the Royal Engineers, who oversaw British airborne training, research, and development from its inception until he was tragically killed in a glider accident in October 1942.

Certainly, Browning brought limited operational expertise to his new command. Before this appointment, his major claims to fame were establishing the tradition of the adjutant riding his horse up the steps to the Old College at Sandhurst and his marriage to Daphne du Maurier. It may also be significant that Browning did not receive an operational command at the outbreak of war in 1939. This suggests that he was selected to command the 1st Airborne Division HQ primarily because he was a well-connected Guards officer who could effectively fight for the airborne cause in Whitehall.[13]

As we have seen, the original parachute force was composed of special service volunteers from 2 Commando. Many of these 'originals' of the airborne forces were rebellious nonconformists who had joined the commandos to escape the tedium of army life and parade-ground discipline. As a small raiding force, the commandos sought independently minded, maverick characters who could think on their feet and operate alone if necessary. Browning now required quite the opposite. He wanted a highly disciplined, large-scale fighting force that could be utilised in a conventional order of battle. Anyone unwilling or unable to accept Browning's ambitions for airborne forces was returned to their parent units.

Commando Training, unarmed combat, No. 2 Dutch Troop, 10 Inter Allied Commando, August 1943. (*National Archives of the Netherlands*)

Commando Training, men attacking through a smokescreen, No. 2 Dutch Troop, 10 Inter Allied Commando, August 1943. (*National Archives of the Netherlands*)

Commando Training, exercise briefing, No. 2 Dutch Troop, 10 Inter Allied Commando, July 1943. (*National Archives of the Netherlands*)

Commando Training, the result of several pounds of high explosive being detonated, No. 2 Dutch Troop, 10 Inter Allied Commando, July 1943. (*National Archives of the Netherlands*)

Commando Training, on parade, 1st Lieutenant P. J. Mulders, No. 2 Dutch Troop, 10 Inter Allied Commando, July 1943. (*National Archives of the Netherlands*)

The Guards Depot ('Little Sparta'), Caterham, September 1939. (*East Surrey Museum*)

Joseph Charles Haydon, Irish Guards, during the First World War, later became the commander of the Special Service Brigade. (*IWM*)

Major General Sir Robert 'Lucky' Laycock, Chief of Combined Operations, May 1944. (*IWM*)

LRDG Jeep equipped with twin Vickers machine guns, Overlord Show, 2024. (*By the author*)

Lieutenant Colonel David Stirling
DSO, Special Air Service, 1943.
(*IWM*)

Lieutenant General Sir Oliver Leese (left) speaking to Lieutenant General Sir Bertram Sergison-Brooke (right), 1944. (*IWM*)

Lieutenant General Sir Frederick 'Boy' Browning. (*Airborne Assault Limited*)

'L' Troop 11 SAS Battalion, 1941. (*Airborne Assault Limited*)

1st Parachute
Battalion parading
in 'stick' order next
to a Whitley at RAF
Ringway, late 1941 /
early 1942. (*Airborne
Assault Limited*)

British Airborne Forces
re-enactors, Overlord Show,
2024. (*By the author*)

The grave of Lieutenant Colonel
Sir William Richard De B. Des
Voeux, Grenadier Guards, Arnhem
Oosterbeek War Cemetery, a
member of General Browning's
staff in the early days of the
airborne movement, July 2025.
(*By the author*)

Grenadier Guards, Queen's Birthday Parade, Trooping the Colour, London, 8 June 2019. (*U.S. Navy Petty Officer 1st Class Dominique A. Pineiro, Flickr*)

A Trooper of the Life Guards, Household Cavalry, Horse Guards, May 2024. (*David Rodrigues, Pexels*)

The new parachute and airlanding battalions were comprised of volunteers from every regiment of the British Army, including a mix of regular soldiers, conscripts and officers commissioned on emergency wartime assignments, effectively civilians in uniform. Browning's primary challenge was to unify these diverse groups into a single, efficient unit with a shared identity and objective. To achieve this, he needed to establish a clear vision and core values that everyone could rally around and create standardised training programs to ensure everyone was on the same page. With consistent effort and a clear plan, Browning believed he could transform this diverse group into a unified and effective organisation. For Browning, a dyed-in-the-wool Guards officer, discipline was the cornerstone of military success. To ensure that every member of airborne forces met a uniformly high standard of military discipline, he brought in several NCOs from the Brigade of Guards to help realise his vision and impose his will.[14]

This approach was not universally welcomed. Many volunteers who joined the parachute units expected to be treated as an elite force, 'men in a higher drawer than the ordinary soldier', as one paratrooper put it. Instead, they were subjected to what Lance Corporal Maybury of B Company called 'a psychological blow'— intensive parade-ground marching, spit and polish, and traditional drills. Sergeant Eddie Hancock, a 21-year-old Londoner, condemned Browning as a martinet who, 'as a result of his Guards background,' thought that 'hard-line, mindless, Regular Army techniques should be applied to men who were, at heart, civilians in uniform'. Hancock believed those volunteering for such dangerous duty were extremely individualistic and didn't take kindly to such treatment.

Browning's persona, when in command, was described by one subordinate as one of 'mannered arrogance,' and many serving under him felt his privileged background made him aloof and distant. This led to occasional tensions, with soldiers at times protesting what they called 'too much bullshit' when they had joined for action. In one incident, soldiers fed up with parade-ground drills and kit inspections marched on their company office with homemade protest placards.[15]

Browning understood the importance of esprit de corps and wanted everyone within the airborne forces to identify with the whole organisation, not just their part of it. He wanted everyone to wear the same uniform and insignia and take pride in the organisation's achievements. Browning was a man who took pride in his appearance and was always meticulously turned out, whatever the circumstances. He understood the importance of presentation. Therefore, he reasoned that one method of distinguishing airborne troops from others was how they were dressed. He decided to introduce a distinctive coloured beret to be worn by all members of the formation. He organised a committee to produce berets of various colours, which were paraded by Guards NCOs at Wellington Barracks in a headdress fashion parade. After some deliberation, the maroon beret was selected and promptly introduced. Browning also introduced a distinctive insignia to be worn on the battledress of every soldier within airborne forces. The selected badge design featured the Greek mythology hero Bellerophon riding the winged horse Pegasus. This image was set against a maroon fabric background with the word 'AIRBORNE' emblazoned in capital letters. Introduced in 1942, the camouflaged Denison smock and rimless paratrooper helmet further distinguished British airborne forces from other army formations.

Leading by example, Browning thought it only correct that he should learn to parachute. He made a couple of parachute jumps and injured himself on both occasions. Unlike many airborne commanders, including American Major General Matthew Ridgway, who volunteered to make a parachute jump despite not being required to do so, Browning never qualified as a parachutist. He did, however, learn to fly at 46 years of age, going solo after just eight and a half hours of instruction, and trained as a glider pilot. It should be noted that he qualified on the General Aircraft Hotspur, which was little more than a glorified sports glider and, therefore, nothing like the heavier and more demanding types flown into combat by the Glider Pilot Regiment.[16]

The first test for airborne forces under Browning was Operation Biting, a raid on a German coastal radar installation at Bruneval in northern France. On 27 February 1942, a landing party of paratroopers under the command of Major John Frost was dropped a few miles from the installation. The raiders successfully seized a top-secret Würzburg radar array before being evacuated by sea.

This operation revealed something of Browning's leadership style. He personally selected C Company, 2nd Parachute Battalion for the raid but left his liaison officer, a Grenadier named Peter Bromley-Martin, formerly of L Troop, to act in his stead. When Major Frost questioned the rigid plan that had been drawn up, Bromley-Martin bluntly informed him that he would be replaced if he refused to accept the plan without modification. Frost complied, though his reservations proved justified when two sticks of paratroopers were dropped astray during the operation. Fortunately, the mission succeeded through luck and the men's initiative on the ground, but this pattern of Browning overseeing the imposition of unsuitable plans with little regard for the opinions of those tasked to carry them out would be repeated later in the war, with far more serious consequences.[17]

Compared with Operation Colossus, the Bruneval Raid was a complete success. The airborne troops suffered few casualties: three killed, two missing and seven wounded. Together with a captured German radar technician, the radar equipment they retrieved enabled British scientists to study enemy advancements in radar technology and devise new countermeasures against them.

By the summer of 1942, the equipping of Britain's first airborne division was going well, except for a shortage of transport aircraft and gliders. Browning's efforts to instil some esprit de corps into his troops started paying dividends.

Discipline was improving, and morale was rising. However, the parachute battalions raised so far remained unaffiliated with a parent regiment. In August 1942, the War Office formed a new unit called the Parachute Regiment, to which the parachute battalions would be attached. On Wednesday, 9 December 1942, the front page of the *Daily Herald* newspaper featured a small notice tucked away at the bottom, informing its readers:

OUR PARACHUTE REGIMENT

First official mention of the Parachute Regiment as the title of Britain's paratroops was made last night in an announcement that Field-Marshal Sir John Dill has been appointed its Colonel-Commandant.

Another important arm of the Army Air Corps, the Glider Pilot Regiment, has General Sir Alan Brooke, Chief of Imperial General Staff, as Colonel-Commandant.

These appointments date from November 12. Both Sir John Dill and Sir Alan Brooke retain their present positions.[18]

Browning's ambition and political skill are clear from the speed with which he climbed the airborne ladder. By mid-1942, he was the official British adviser on airborne forces to the commanders in chief in all theatres of war. In May 1943, he was appointed major general airborne forces, and shortly thereafter, he acted as airborne forces adviser to all headquarters in North Africa, including Eisenhower's Allied Force Headquarters in Algiers.

As he lacked any operational airborne experience, his value as an adviser is questionable, especially considering that US airborne development and experience were at least equal to that of the British and, in some instances, more advanced. There was also the fact that the British were almost totally reliant on USAAF transport aircraft. However, this did not prevent Browning from acting extremely high-handedly and arrogantly toward his American allies.

Shortly after the US 82nd Airborne Division commander, Major General Matthew B. Ridgway, arrived in North Africa, Browning turned up unannounced at his HQ. Although they were nominally equal in rank, Browning demanded to see the Americans' plan for the upcoming Sicily operation, leaving him with no doubt that he (Browning) was in charge. Browning reinforced the impression that he viewed the US airborne force as part of his personal fiefdom a few days later when he cavalierly decided to inspect the US 509th Parachute Infantry Battalion without reference to Ridgway or anyone else in the US chain of command. He then added insult to injury by attempting to have the 509th made honorary members of the British airborne forces, complete with maroon berets.

The enmity between Browning and Ridgway came to a head in November 1943 when Browning, in the presence of US Colonel James M. Gavin, snidely criticised

Ridgway for not having parachuted into Sicily with his division. This was both ill-mannered and hypocritical, given Browning's own lack of operational parachute experience. The true reason for Browning's antipathy toward Ridgway appears to have been that the American was more qualified for the overall airborne command Browning coveted and, therefore, threatened his ambition.[19]

In General James Gavin's wartime diaries, published in 2022, he recalls some of the personal enmity between General Ridgway and Browning:

Wednesday, 17 November 1943

Before my departure Gen. R warned me of the machinations of Maj. Gen. Browning, stating that he was intelligent, charming, and very close to Mr. Churchill. Further that he was unprincipled and ruthless in his efforts to align every operation and every piece of equipment to the complete benefit of the British Empire at our expense. Worse still, he had completely taken in Gen. Lee, who thought his word was law. This is just about entirely true, and Browning must be handled cautiously but firmly.

Three days later, General Gavin ran into Browning at a meeting in London. Gavin recalled that they talked for quite a while, noting that Browning was "as smooth as ever" but generally distrusted by American high commanders. After the meeting, General Barker cautioned Gavin about Browning's ambitions as an empire builder.[20]

During Browning's tenure as airborne commander, he had significant clashes with British officers, most notably Lieutenant Colonel Bill Stirling of the 2nd Special Air Service (2SAS). In the lead-up to the D-Day landings in 1944, Stirling strongly objected to plans by the 21st Army Group to use SAS troops tactically just beyond the Normandy beachhead. He argued instead that they should be deployed strategically, deep behind enemy lines. General Montgomery's notion that the SAS should be 'sprinkled like confetti in front of the Normandy landings' was considered suicidal by those in 2SAS. Determined to prevent this misuse of his unit, Stirling demanded and secured an interview with Browning to argue his case.

The confrontation between Stirling and Browning was uncompromising. According to Major Pat Hart, 'Stirling simply told Browning in no uncertain terms that he, Bill, had no confidence in him and he didn't know what he was doing, everything he had in mind for us was wrong, and that Bill wouldn't stand for it.' Browning interpreted this as insubordination of the highest order and immediately dismissed Stirling. As Stirling departed Browning's office, he quipped, 'Is there a special sort of maroon coloured Airborne bowler hat?' (To be 'bowler-hatted' was military jargon for being summarily dismissed.)

Stirling's dismissal caused significant distress throughout 2SAS, with many officers and men threatening to resign in protest. Corporal Bill Robinson recalled,

'Everyone went mad when they heard about Bill Stirling's resignation.' Sergeant Fred Rhodes expressed similar indignation, believing that 'what Stirling did was right... Stirling was protecting the men in his regiment, that was his sole objective, not to have specialised troops used in a manner opposed to what they had been trained for.' Despite the immediate consequences, Stirling's stand ultimately proved effective—the initial operational order was cancelled, and the SAS were eventually deployed strategically, exactly as Stirling had advocated.[21]

Pat Hart, who served as deputy assistant adjutant and quartermaster general (DAA MG) of the SAS brigade, confirmed the significant tension between Browning and the SAS. He noted that SAS leaders were deeply concerned about how their unit would be used under Browning's command:

> Because of all this, there was a tremendous anti Airborne feeling building up. None of the desert SAS wanted to wear a red beret and to have AC flashes on their shoulders.

Hart further explained that the SAS resisted being categorised as airborne troops:

> They didn't want to be considered to be airborne troops, because everybody would find out after the first raid that the parachute was only a way of getting to the targets, and their actual function was not of airborne troops at all.

Hart characterised Browning's support of the SAS as fundamentally self-serving:

> He was a supporter of anything which supported Browning, and the SAS was a useful extra leg for his Army Air Corps to stand on. He wasn't a supporter of the SAS in the sense of being a devoted exponent or follower of the idea of small party/deep penetration operations.[22]

Whatever Browning's motivations, British airborne forces continued to grow in size and capability under his control. Nevertheless, frustrations and disasters lay ahead before victory in Europe was finally achieved in 1945. Between 6 June and 9 September 1944, fifteen airborne operations were planned to support Allied ground operations in France, Belgium and Holland. All of these were cancelled.

In September 1944, Operation Market Garden was planned to airdrop a carpet of 34,600 troops, allowing ground forces to advance and secure a crossing over the Rhine River. As deputy commander of the 1st Allied Airborne Army, Browning was one of the main drivers behind the operation, and critically, he approved the Arnhem air plan (which placed landing zones far from the objectives) despite the fact that it 'flew in the face of all airborne experience to date.' Browning's decision to accompany the Market force to Holland has been criticised as driven more by personal ambition than military necessity.

The operation ultimately ended in bitter failure and recrimination. The most salient reason for the 1st Airborne Division's failure at Arnhem was the distance between the landing zones and the bridge, which was the division's objective. Most accounts acknowledge that the RAF planners chose these zones and that their choice was allowed to stand despite the misgivings and, in some cases, outright objections from the airborne soldiers involved. However, this was not an isolated occurrence but rather an official policy dating back to the beginning of the British airborne force, when the Air Ministry secured untrammelled control over the air side of airborne operations as the price for its cooperation in the project.[23]

When the operation failed, Browning was instrumental in shifting the blame onto others, particularly Major General Stanislaw Sosabowski and the 1st Polish Independent Parachute Brigade. On 17 October, in a letter to CIGS Alan Brooke, Field Marshal Montgomery criticised the Polish brigade for an unwillingness to take risks and demanded Sosabowski be removed from command. On 20 November, Browning sent a report to the Deputy CIGS claiming that Sosabowski had been incapable of grasping the urgency of the situation at Driel, was needlessly argumentative and was unwilling to obey orders. The report recommended Sosabowski's removal due to his 'temperament and inability to co-operate'.

There was not a shred of truth in these allegations, which were a blatant and shameful attempt to conceal the British incompetence that sealed the fate of Market Garden. The fact that the Polish brigade lost a quarter of its strength, including ninety-two dead, gives the lie to Montgomery's allegations. Quite simply, Sosabowski was pilloried for no other reason than being an obstacle to Browning's ambitions, having repeatedly rebuffed Browning's attempts to gain control over his brigade and publicly pointing out the flaws in the Market Garden plan.

Market Garden cost the American airborne divisions around 4,000 casualties, while the British 1st Airborne Division was nearly wiped out. Over 10,000 Commonwealth and Polish troops were dropped at Arnhem, resulting in 1,500 killed and more than 6,500 captured during nine days of fighting.

In the aftermath of Market Garden, Browning lost his deputy command of the 1st Allied Airborne Army to the more competent Major General Gale, and never held an operational command again. Before 1944 was out, he had been dispatched to Burma to act as chief-of-staff to Supreme Commander, South-East Asia Command, Lord Louis Mountbatten, a far more appropriate employment for his political talents. In 1946, he was sidelined to the War Office, where he served as military secretary, and two years later, he was quietly removed from the active list and made controller and treasurer to Princess Elizabeth's Household, a position he held until his retirement in 1952.[24]

Perhaps more than anything, actor Dirk Bogarde's portrayal of General Browning in the 1977 war film *A Bridge Too Far*, which depicts Operation Market Garden, has fixed his place in history as the chillingly ambitious leader responsible for the destruction of the 1st Airborne Division. Certainly, General Browning's temperament, motives, and actions between 1941 and 1944 will undoubtedly continue to excite debate and divide the opinions of historians, academics and history enthusiasts.

The Pros and Cons of Special Forces during the Second World War

In the summer of 1940, with the collapse of France and the gallant evacuation from Dunkirk, Britain found itself standing alone against the military power of Nazi Germany. Unable to challenge Nazi supremacy directly, Britain turned to irregular methods of warfare to demonstrate its ability to resist, by launching small-scale raids on the occupied coastlines of Europe, which also served as a weapon of morale-boosting propaganda. This chapter examines the complex legacy of the British special forces during the Second World War.

Formations such as the LRDG and SAS evoke images of daring raids behind enemy lines, but their actual utility, cost-effectiveness and proper application were subjects of intense debate both during and after the war. We will examine the advantages and disadvantages of these elite units, including their improper use and underutilization, their contribution to the Allied victory and propaganda value, and the burden they placed on an increasingly strained British Army faced with manpower shortages.

Problems of Employment

The employment of special forces presented a persistent challenge throughout the war. As Colin Gray, a writer on geopolitics and professor of international relations and strategic studies at the University of Reading, noted, specialist formations were 'probably uniquely vulnerable to misunderstanding and misapplication'.

Almost every special force unit experienced either inappropriate tasking or periods of idleness that undermined their value. Initially created for raiding operations, the army commandos frequently found themselves misused as conventional infantry. In North Africa, 1 and 6 commandos were employed in sustained defensive positions for which they were neither equipped nor trained. One commando officer reported that this misuse stemmed from the 'ignorance of all staffs to understand the roles of commandos'.

As we have already seen, Layforce was initially tasked with conducting raids to disrupt Axis lines of communication in the Mediterranean. However, due to the deteriorating strategic situation, the commandos were diverted from their original role and used primarily to reinforce regular troops. This misuse of Layforce, coupled with heavy casualties and a lack of proper support, led to its disbandment. Colonel Laycock, who would later become Chief of Combined Operations, observed that force commanders were 'only too willing to use commandos to their best advantage during the initial landings, but that subsequently they regard them as unwanted and unnecessary units', leading to their employment in roles better suited to regular infantry.

The LRDG experienced a similar mishandling during the summer of 1941 when it was deployed in tactical reconnaissance and static defensive positions at Kufra, roles inappropriate for a mobile, long-range reconnaissance force. However, these deployments proved instructive, and the unit was seldom again used on tasks best carried out by reconnaissance aircraft or armoured cars.

Possibly the worst misuse of British special forces occurred in the Aegean in late 1943. The LRDG, a unit uniquely designed for desert reconnaissance, was ordered to conduct an assault to recapture the island of Levitha, an operation completely unsuited to their capabilities and training. Despite strong objections, the raid proceeded with devastating results: forty-one experienced operators were lost, more casualties than the unit had sustained in the previous three years combined. David Lloyd Owen of the LRDG described it as a 'wicked and misplaced' operation, motivated by political considerations rather than sound military judgment. This misuse continued when the LRDG was tasked with garrison duties on Leros, resulting in further heavy losses, including the unit's commander and approximately one hundred men being captured. The LRDG war diary acknowledged this as 'a gross misuse of LRDG Patrols who were trained and equipped for special tasks, and not for mere garrison duties, the job of the normal infantryman'.

The issue of disuse, the holding back of valuable formations for indeterminable periods, was equally problematic. The Middle East Commando (later known as 1st SS Regiment) suffered from an identity crisis and a lack of a clearly defined role. The unit remained largely underutilised despite attempts to find employment, including attachment to the LRDG. GHQ Middle East noted it was 'wasteful to keep first-class material in units whose opportunities for employment are exceedingly rare', with General Auchinleck likening this neglect to 'keeping a valuable cow and milking it once or twice a year'. A year before the formation's disbandment, Bob Laycock warned that there were 'too many commandos and not enough work' in the Middle East.[1]

British airborne forces also faced challenges regarding their proper employment. The 1st Airborne Division spent only seventeen days in combat throughout the entire war. It trained for nearly a year (September 1943–September 1944) before being deployed to Arnhem, where it suffered devastating losses.

The repeated cancellation of operations in support of 21st Army Group, combined with the threat of being deployed as regular infantry or disbanded, appears to have fostered a reckless eagerness among the British commanders of airborne forces, particularly General Browning, to engage in battle at any cost.[2]

Measuring the Success of Special Forces

Determining the actual impact of special forces on the broader war effort presents significant challenges. John Ferris, an author and professor of history at the University of Calgary, remarked on intelligence operations, 'one rarely has the equivalent of a laboratory experiment in which all other variables remain constant and one can gauge with precision the effect of changes in intelligence'. The same holds true for special operations more generally.

The LRDG made perhaps its most significant contribution through intelligence gathering rather than offensive action. Its 'road watch' operations, which physically charted east and west-bound traffic along coastal roads, built an exceptionally detailed and therefore valuable picture of the supply and reinforcement situation of the Axis forces. Brigadier T. S. Airey, director of Military Intelligence at GHQ Middle East, considered these operations of 'quite exceptional importance', providing 'an indispensable basis for certain facts on which calculation of enemy strength can be based'. When General Ritter von Thoma, Rommel's deputy, was captured, he was shocked to learn that General Montgomery knew more about the supply status of the *Afrika Korps* than he did.

The SAS achieved its greatest impact in the Desert War, where it claimed to have destroyed some 350 enemy aircraft. This achievement was undoubtedly significantly and greatly aided the beleaguered Desert Air Force by materially helping 'to tilt the balance of air power in the Mediterranean Theatre'. Even Erwin Rommel acknowledged in his diary that the SAS 'caused us more damage than any other British unit of equal strength'. However, it is important to remember that these actions were not decisive in the campaign's outcome but ancillary operations that contributed to the final victory in North Africa.[3]

Special forces also contributed by compelling the enemy to divert resources to defensive measures. The LRDG was raised partly to create 'the impression of British ubiquity throughout the interior of Libya'. Even small-scale operations could have disproportionate effects by forcing the enemy to strengthen defences and divert resources from the front. Wavell noted that the LRDG made 'an important contribution towards keeping Italian forces in back areas on the alert and adding to the anxieties and difficulties of our enemy'. General Hackett believed, 'The aim [...] in using these special forces is to hinder the most effective application of the enemy's resources in war and to secure advantages on the employment of our own.'

The commando raid on Vaagso in January 1942 played on German insecurities, contributing (alongside other factors) to Hitler's decision to reinforce Norway. By D-Day, some ten German divisions were left idle in Norway, although this outcome was perhaps more attributable to the Fortitude North deception schemes than to commando operations alone. The psychological impact of special forces extended to the enemy's morale. In the Aegean, raiding forces 'created a reign of terror' among German island garrisons, leading to the surrender of 1,200 well-fortified troops on Samos to 'a trifling Allied force because they were literally frightened for their lives of Raiding Forces'. Reg Seekings of the SAS believed that special forces status gave units a psychological edge. Reg suggested, 'If British troops knew they were up against German paratroopers, they were half beaten already'.[4]

For airborne forces specifically, their impact has been debated. While critics like military historian Dr John Peaty argue they had limited operational use, with only five major airborne operations during the liberation of Europe, defenders point to significant tactical successes. The 6th Airborne Division's D-Day operation successfully secured the eastern flank of the Normandy landings, and the 2nd Independent Parachute Brigade rendered 'sterling service' in the Mediterranean theatre. Military historian and author William F. Buckingham argues that airborne forces served as a 'force multiplier' by obliging the enemy to divert resources into guarding against airborne attack, what he calls 'a land warfare equivalent to the concept of a fleet in being'.[5]

Morale and Propaganda Value

Special forces played a significant role in boosting home front morale, particularly during the darkest periods of the war. As historian and academic John Newsinger observed regarding the SAS: 'The story of the SAS in the Second World War is an adventure story. Young ex-public-school boys, the cream of the British race, leading their men in daring, sometimes foolhardy exploits against a brutal enemy'.

Special operations offered welcome escapism from the realities of industrial warfare; they personalised the conflict and created heroes, serving as 'a tonic for both conventional defeat and inactivity'. They rekindled the spirit of Colonel T. E. Lawrence (Lawrence of Arabia) and allayed fears of another stalemated trench war like the First World War. Churchill himself recognised this value, writing that 'small scale raids by the Commandos [...] not only gave us confidence and experience, but showed the world that although beset on all sides we were not content with passive defence'. The early commando raids were undertaken, as much as for any other reason, simply 'to cheer-up everyone at home'.

These operations also had political value, helping to protect Britain against accusations of passivity regarding opening a second front. Well-publicised raids served as 'a showpiece for the Americans [...] to dispel the impression of passivity and defensiveness that was doing so much to erode the good opinion of British fighting resolve'.[6]

Propaganda played an explicit role in the development of airborne forces. Both direct and indirect propaganda were used to attract volunteers. Direct propaganda involved official War Office material aimed at serving soldiers, encouraging men to volunteer for parachute or glider training. Indirect propaganda ensured that 'suitably targeted articles on parachuting and airborne forces appeared regularly in national periodicals, publications, and featured on national newsreels and in films'.[7]

Cost-Effectiveness and Manpower Considerations

Critics argue that special forces were 'expensive, wasteful, and unnecessary', as Field Marshal Slim famously stated. The principle criticism centred on the drain these units represented to scarce manpower reserves, particularly for the infantry. John Terraine, military historian and television screenwriter, criticised all specialist formations as 'not legitimate, or even sensible', viewing the commandos as the 'most famous' of the 'offenders' and contending that the LRDG and SAS, though few in numbers, 'helped to compound the felony'.

John Peaty, studying the British Army manpower shortage of 1944, claimed that the proliferation of special forces 'distorted the British Army's manpower distribution and contributed to its manpower problems', concluding that 'on any rational assessment the inflated and under-employed Special Forces which the British Army possessed during WWII were not cost-effective. Quite simply, the benefits did not match the costs.' However, these criticisms often rely on an overly broad definition of special forces. When restricted to actual commando and special forces units (excluding airborne forces, mountain troops, and specialised regular battalions), the British had approximately 13,000 men in such formations by mid-1944.

The quality of personnel absorbed by special forces was perhaps more concerning than the quantity. These units attracted 'warriors': enterprising, physically fit individuals with initiative who would likely have made excellent NCOs or junior officers in regular formations. This 'leadership drain' was exacerbated by high casualty rates, creating what one analyst called a 'selection-destruction cycle that leads to depletion of assets that are not readily replaceable'. Lieutenant Colonel J. P. O'Brian Twohig, writing in *The Army Quarterly* journal, emphasised that the 'gallantry and skill the commandos displayed did not compensate for the dearth of good junior leaders to which their existence was a big contributing factor'.[8]

While British airborne forces achieved some remarkable tactical successes and captured the public imagination, their creation and expansion came at a considerable cost to the broader British Army at a time when infantry manpower was increasingly scarce. When existing infantry battalions were designated for transformation into airborne units, the wastage rates were staggering. When the 10th Battalion, The Green Howards, converted to become the 12th Parachute Battalion, only about 25 per cent of the original personnel successfully completed the transition. Similarly, when the 2/4 Battalion of The South Lancashire Regiment was converted into the 13th Parachute Battalion, less than 30 per cent of the original men made the grade. These statistics paint a stark picture: established infantry formations with existing unit cohesion were effectively dismantled, with most of their personnel deemed unsuitable for airborne operations.

This approach was particularly questionable because these converted battalions still required substantial reinforcement from volunteers drawn from other infantry units across the army to reach their establishment figures. Even accounting for the smaller size of parachute battalions (approximately four hundred and fifty men compared to standard infantry battalions), the converted units only achieved between 35 and 50 per cent of their required strength from the original battalion personnel. This created a double drain on infantry manpower through the disruption of established battalions and the continued need for volunteers from elsewhere in the army.

Possibly most concerning was the pattern of successful conversions. Over 50 per cent of officers successfully transitioned to airborne forces; among other ranks, a high proportion of those who passed were experienced NCOS. This meant that the original units' hierarchical structure and leadership backbone were being systematically stripped away, concentrating experienced leadership in airborne formations while leaving conventional infantry units bereft of their most capable officers and NCOs.

This selective extraction of leadership talent occurred precisely when the British Army began to face its most acute manpower challenges. By 1944, the army was experiencing a significant manpower crisis, particularly in infantry units. The continued prioritisation of airborne forces exacerbated this problem by directing scarce human resources away from the conventional formations that would bear the brunt of the fighting in Northwest Europe. The situation created a paradoxical imbalance.

While conventional infantry units struggled with shortages of experienced leaders and high-quality personnel, the airborne forces were frequently underutilised despite their elite status and rigorous selection processes. As we have already seen, the 1st Airborne Division, with a war establishment of over 12,000 men, spent only seventeen days in combat throughout the entire war, while the 6th Airborne Division spent almost two-thirds of the Northwest Europe campaign employed as conventional infantry rather than in their specialist airborne role.

One might reasonably question whether the creation of these elite formations, particularly at the scale undertaken by the British Army, represented an efficient use of limited manpower resources. While certain airborne operations were successful, such as the 6th Airborne Division's securing of the eastern flank of the Normandy landings, the overall strategic impact of airborne forces was arguably limited compared to the investment made in their creation and maintenance.

General Sir Brian Horrocks summed up the fundamental problem when he observed that out of a section of ten men, typically two would be leaders, seven would follow and one would prefer not to be there at all. By extracting the natural leaders for special formations, conventional units lost the personnel who made them effective fighting formations. As Horrocks noted, in special units, 'each leader represented only himself as they were all of the same type; but in his regiment, he was worth almost a whole section, for he was the man the others would follow.'

The policy appears even more questionable given that, after the war, examination revealed that many converted airborne battalions performed no better than those raised entirely from volunteers. This suggests that the disruption of existing infantry formations might have been unnecessary and that a more measured approach to building airborne capabilities could have better balanced the competing demands for quality personnel across the army.[9]

The LRDG stands as a prime example of cost-effectiveness. The unit remained small (never exceeding 250 men), made modest demands on equipment and resources and was almost continuously employed. General Thompson suggested it should be considered 'the yardstick by which one should gauge those that came after them'. Its achievements in intelligence gathering, reconnaissance, pathfinding and occasional offensive action represented excellent value for the investment.

The SAS also demonstrated remarkable cost-effectiveness, especially during its early operations in the Desert War. Its destruction of enemy aircraft far outweighed the personal score achieved by any aircrew, whose training was both long and costly, and who attacked in expensive aircraft maintained by a large number of ground crew. In the later stages of the Desert War, the SAS started to show diminishing returns and higher casualties. As Lloyd Owen described, 'the balance sheet showed too great an excess of expenditure over achievement'.

Even as the SAS expanded from sixty men at its inception to a multinational brigade of approximately 2,500 by mid-1944, it generally maintained its cost-effectiveness, though not at the same extraordinary level as in its earliest operations. Nevertheless, its tally in France was impressive, accounting for 7,753 enemy casualties, 4,764 prisoners taken, and somewhere between 400 and 1,000 vehicles destroyed or captured. The SAS also cut numerous road, rail and telephone links, destroyed bridges and generally disrupted enemy lines of communication. The butcher's bill for its 49 operations was 345 killed or missing and 115 wounded.[10]

Social Connections, Patronage, and the 'Old Boy Network'

Social connections, patronage, and the 'old boy network' featured prominently in the development of British special forces. As an American OSS officer observed in Yugoslavia:

> All [Fitzroy Maclean's] officers appeared to be old friends and several had been together in North Africa fighting against Rommel's forces. These British officers who were drawn to irregular operations seemed not only to have been together in early wartime operations but also to have had many close school and family ties.[11]

According to Dr Andrew Hargreaves, the British pattern of special forces formation typically involved an 'errant captain', a relatively junior officer with social connections who would conceive of a unit and prove instrumental in its creation and operations. This individual would require backing from a sympathetic 'champion', a well-placed senior officer willing to lift the red tape of orthodoxy. Without such support, these formations would never have developed.

Ralph Bagnold's creation of the LRDG exemplifies this pattern. Despite having his proposals rejected twice, Bagnold's 'driving power and importunity' for his concept, combined with General Wavell's patronage, enabled the LRDG to be established quickly. Similarly, David Stirling's ability to bypass normal channels and present his proposal for the SAS directly to General Auchinleck and General Ritchie demonstrated the importance of personal connections.[12]

Like the Stirling brothers and Simon Fraser, the 15th Lord Lovat, Fitzroy Maclean was a member of the Scottish minor nobility. Maclean's arrangement to deploy special forces to Yugoslavia provides another clear example of social connections at work. Maclean personally assessed the potential for special operations with former SAS comrades and arranged 2 Commando's deployment to the island of Vis simply by meeting Brigadier Tom Churchill at a New Year's Eve party. All arrangements were made before approaching General Alexander, Irish Guards, for authorisation, who subsequently lent Maclean his own aeroplane so he could fly to meet Churchill to discuss the scheme.

According to Williamson Murray, historian and author, the appointment of General 'Boy' Browning as the commander of the 1st Airborne Division had little to do with his military qualifications, leadership or organisational skills. Browning had the right political and social connections to advance the War Office's agenda for developing large-scale airborne forces. Murray contends that General Sir Alan Brooke assigned Browning to his airborne position because Guards regiments needed representation among the general officer corps.[13]

Post-War Legacy

The experiences of British special forces during the Second World War established precedents and lessons that would influence post-war military thinking. While the war confirmed Field Marshal Slim's assertion that 'armies do not win wars by means of a few bodies of super-soldiers but by the average quality of their standard units', it also demonstrated that specialist formations had unique value when properly employed.

The cost-effectiveness debate ultimately came down to ensuring that specialist forces were used as designed. Colonel Laycock, reflecting after the war, wrote that 'the answer to the question as to whether or not you require "specialist" troops for raiding is "Yes". But the lesson is: don't raise too many; don't form odd units for odd jobs, because if they are worth their salt, they ought to be quite capable of carrying out any particular type of raid'.

The essential principle was proportionality in the number of formations raised and the scale of each unit, combined with their utility in terms of frequency, duration and significance of employment. As David Lloyd Owen of the LRDG stated regarding the use of regular units for specialist tasks:

> I would willingly have undertaken many of the tasks we carried out with the men of a regular unit. But I could not have done it without rejecting those who were not physically fit, those who were not temperamentally suited... To have tried this type of raid and other tasks without specially trained and selected men would have been madness. For not only would you virtually destroy the structure of a normal unit in transforming it for a specialised task but also you would be diverting it from its main purpose.[14]

According to Alan Allport, social historian and author, 'Britain was in a class of its own when it came to the creation of private armies during the Second World War.' The British Empire allocated more soldiers to Special Forces than any other great power of the period. The British appear to have been particularly beguiled by Germany's use of airborne forces, despite half of these troops being killed, wounded or captured during Operation Mercury, the invasion of Crete.

Over 28,000 soldiers were committed to the British Army's two parachute divisions and one independent parachute brigade, but of the four large-scale operations undertaken by airborne forces, only the D-Day drop was successful. The operations in Sicily, Holland and the Rhineland were, respectively, a tragic fiasco, a noble failure and an expensive sideshow. Airborne forces represented the equivalent of twenty standard infantry battalions, and every talented soldier attracted to special forces was one denied to the infantry.[15]

Despite the controversies during the war, 'the world's major armies have retained a significant parachute element since 1945' because 'no one has yet come up with a better method of getting battle-ready troops on the ground at short notice and over long distances than the parachute'. Modern airborne units have 'a relatively small logistical tail and are thus trained, equipped, and configured for rapid deployment at short notice, which explains their high profile in military operations since 1945'.[16]

British special forces during the Second World War represented a valuable, if imperfect innovation. Though they consumed resources, absorbed talented personnel and were frequently misused, they nonetheless provided capabilities that conventional forces could not replicate within the same constraints. Their value lay not in war-winning decisive actions but in their ability to expand military options, create opportunities for conventional forces, gather crucial intelligence and maintain morale during the darkest periods of the conflict.

The debate over their utility touches on fundamental questions of military organisation and resource allocation during a time of national emergency. While critics raised valid concerns about their cost in manpower and resources, defenders could point to tangible achievements in intelligence gathering, operational flexibility and psychological impact on the enemy and home front morale. Perhaps most importantly, the lessons learned through their establishment, employment and occasional misuse formed the foundation for modern special operations doctrine and continue to influence military thinking today.

The Guards Parachute Company and G Squadron SAS

The Guards Parachute Company represents a unique chapter in British military history, combining the high standards of the Household Division with the daring of airborne forces. This unique unit bridged two proud military traditions, creating a formation that would serve with distinction in numerous operations while maintaining the highest standards of both parent organisations.

Origins: From Battalion to Company

After the Second World War, the 1st Airborne Division was disbanded, and the 6th Airborne Division was deployed to the Middle East as the British Army reorganised and downsized following the conflict. As part of this process, the 1st (Guards) Parachute Battalion was formed under the command of Lieutenant Colonel John Nelson, a Grenadier with an impressive war record. He had been wounded several times and earned both the Military Cross and Distinguished Service Order.

The Battalion was deployed to Palestine, where it was stationed initially at Sarona Camp on the outskirts of Tel Aviv and soon after at nearby Citrus House. The Battalion's primary objective was to maintain order in an increasingly volatile situation as tensions between Jewish and Arab communities intensified. The 1917 Balfour Declaration, issued by the British government, supported the idea of creating a Jewish homeland in Palestine. This declaration resulted in an increase in the number of Jewish immigrants moving to the region, something the Arab population resisted. After the war and the Holocaust, there was growing international pressure to establish a Jewish state in Palestine.

Nelson faced significant challenges in forging his new command into a Guards battalion, initially having only himself and his adjutant, Captain Michael Jenkins, as guardsmen in the unit. In March 1947, the first reinforcements of guardsmen arrived, and by the end of that year, the Battalion's strength was about 450 guardsmen. By 1948, it was 95 per cent guardsmen.

The Battalion was known for containing many decorated war veterans, including Irish Guards Sergeant John Kenneally, who had won the Victoria Cross in North Africa in 1943. Despite their previous combat experience, all personnel still had to endure the rigorous selection and training of the Parachute Regiment, which included the dreaded 'P' Company and parachute training at RAF Upper Heyford.

Tom Stanley, Coldstream Guards (later Lord Stanley of Alderley) commanded a platoon of Parachute Regiment troops, whom the tall guardsmen rather disparagingly referred to as the 'little men'. Initially, the merging of two very different regimental traditions was a culture shock for all involved. Tom Stanley recalled how the two regimental traditions initially clashed:

> The Parachute Regiment officers no doubt considered us aristocratic and brought up in a protected society. Moreover, we were determined not to give up any of our Regimental customs and etiquette, which were often contrary, indeed anathema, to Parachute Regiment officers, who considered them patronising and indeed insulting. [...] We were, however, led by an exceptional Commanding Officer in Jim Nelson, who managed to inspire us as members of the 1st Battalion rather than as Guardsmen. [...] If he had a fault, it was his ferocious temper, but [...] his outbursts were short, and you were always forgiven.

In Palestine, the Battalion faced the challenging task of maintaining order between the Jewish and Arab communities while also defending themselves against attacks from both sides. As tensions and outbreaks of violence increased between the two sides, the Battalion was repeatedly redeployed to various locations across Palestine, including Citrus House, Camp 260 (near Nahariya), Mount Carmel (near Haifa), Hedera, Rosh Pinna and Samakh (on Lake Tiberias). On 14 May 1948, after the United Nations' Partition Plan failed and with Britain's mandate over Palestine concluded, Jewish leader David Ben-Gurion proclaimed the Declaration of the State of Israel, which immediately sparked the first Arab-Israeli war.[1]

In 1948, the 6th Airborne Division was disbanded, and the 16th Parachute Brigade was formed. The 1st Guards Battalion was able to preserve its identity during this period of reorganisation by forming the Brigade Pathfinder Company. This new formation was initially known as the Guards Pathfinder Company and later as the 16th (Guards) Independent Pathfinder Company. The unit was reduced in size but maintained its distinctive character as 'the only all-Regular unit in the then National Service Army'.[2]

Formation and Early Years (1948–50)

The Pathfinder Company was formed at Pirbright Camp, Surrey, which would remain its home base throughout its 27-year existence. Its first commander was

Major Bobby Steele of the Grenadier Guards, with Captain Stephen Langton of the Irish Guards as second-in-command. The company initially consisted of eight officers and 150 other ranks, all volunteers from the Brigade of Guards who had passed the rigorous P Company selection and completed the six-week parachute course.

According to the book *Guardsmen of the Sky*, the company's primary role was to act as pathfinders to the 16th Parachute Brigade Group. This entailed jumping ahead of the main airborne force to mark out the dropping zone using cloth panels and radar beacons (or flares at night). The pathfinders would then defend the drop zone until the main force arrived. All volunteers had to pass P Company before undertaking parachute training.[3]

The early formation presented challenges in defining the relationship between the company and the Parachute Regiment. The Parachute Regiment, 'the youngest Regiment in the Army with a gallant record and a high *esprit de corps*, expected us [guardsmen] to conform to their ways in most respects'. Eventually, an arrangement was reached where the Parachute Regiment headquarters would be responsible for G (general staff) and Q (quartermaster) matters, while Guards regiments could withdraw officers and NCOs from the company for promotion when necessary.[4]

To emphasise their Guards identity, the company found opportunities to display their ceremonial skills, mounting a King's Guard on 24 August 1948. One onlooker watching the ceremony apparently exclaimed, 'They're as good as the Guards!', not realising they were indeed guardsmen.

Within two months of formation, the company was deployed to Gandersheim in Germany with the army of the Rhine. Located in a modern barracks 40 miles south of Hanover, near the Hartz Mountains, they were stationed close to the 16th Parachute Brigade Group headquarters under Brigadier Walter Kempster. Their operational tasks included patrolling the East/West German border.

During this period, Colonel Ken Darling, commanding the Airborne Forces Depot, visited the company and took issue with the blue-red-blue flash that Major Steele had added to his men's berets and their emphasis on being guardsmen first. This led to a compromise: the Parachute Regiment badge would be worn with the beret, but the Household Brigade flash would remain.[5]

The 1950s: Operations in the Middle East

In June 1951, the company deployed to the Middle East along with the Parachute Brigade following the nationalisation of the Anglo-Iranian Oil Company. They were initially stationed in Cyprus before moving to Egypt when tensions escalated. The book *Guardsmen of the Sky* describes how they were based at

Quinque Camp in the Egyptian desert for approximately twelve months from 1953 to 1954.

A significant development in 1954 was the inclusion of Household Cavalry personnel in the company, starting with troopers from The Blues (Royal Horse Guards). The rather aptly named Trooper Horseman was the first to pass P Company and the parachute course, followed by Corporal-of-Horse Kitney and Corporal Chudleigh. This expansion reflected the king's earlier decision to bring the Household Cavalry under the command of the major general alongside the Brigade of Guards.[6]

The company's most significant operation during this period came during the Suez Crisis. On 4 November 1956, a patrol led by Captain Murray de Klee, Scots Guards, parachuted with French forces into Port Said. This small detachment, consisting of de Klee, Sergeant Longstaff, Coldstream Guards and several others, jumped from a French Nordatlas aircraft at 400 feet. On landing, the patrol immediately met resistance with small arms fire and anti-aircraft shells. One member, Guardsman Murphy, Irish Guards, was wounded in the stomach shortly after landing. Despite this setback, the patrol proceeded with its mission, moving down the Treaty Road and taking several Egyptian prisoners. The company's main body arrived later by sea aboard the LST *Snowden Smith*, landing on 6 November and leading 2 PARA through Port Said before engaging Egyptian forces along the Sweet Water Canal and Treaty Road.[7]

The operation was short-lived. Due to international pressure against the Anglo-French action, a ceasefire was ordered at midnight on 6 November. The company was dug in between the Sweet Water Canal and the Treaty Road, enduring sporadic enemy fire, before being withdrawn back to Cyprus. Captain de Klee was awarded the Croix de Guerre for his actions during this operation, and the detachment received a Mention in Dispatches. The company remained in Cyprus until February 1957.[8]

The 1960s: Modernisation and Deployment to Borneo

By 1960, the company was adapting to new tactical concepts, with reconnaissance becoming its primary role. It was recognised that open-topped Land Rovers equipped with light machine guns would not provide adequate protection during operations; therefore, they were replaced with armoured Ferret scout cars, each carrying a Browning machine gun in its turret. In the autumn of 1960, after extensive trials, the Ferret was successfully parachuted from a Beverley aircraft, and a dozen Ferrets were issued to the company.

This transition to the lightly armoured Ferret scout car required additional training in wireless communication, gunnery and vehicle maintenance, with The

Blues providing valuable instruction for car commanders and drivers. In January 1964, the new vehicles were used for the first time operationally during the company's deployment to Cyprus, when violence broke out between its Greek and Turkish communities.[9]

In February 1964, the company was recalled to Britain for a new assignment. They were selected to form an independent squadron to reinforce the overstretched 21st SAS Regiment, which was combating Indonesian incursions along the Malaysian frontier in Borneo. Major John Head, Irish Guards commanded the company during this period, with Captain Lord Patrick Beresford serving as second-in-command, operations officer and head of the advance party. The company's strength at this time was approximately one hundred and thirty men, with high morale described as 'almost tangible' and a reputation for being 'superbly fit' and 'consciously, though not flamboyantly, tough'.

In May 1964, the company underwent intensive training for the SAS role, first in England and then in Malaya. They learned jungle navigation, survival, tactics and shooting, with additional training in signalling, languages, medicine and demolitions. By June, they were deemed ready for operational deployment and sailed across the South China Sea to Sarawak. Their area of operations encompassed the entire 300-mile border of the Third Division of Sarawak, with much of it being uninhabited for up to 80 miles on the Malaysian side. The company established its base at Bukit Lima near Sibu and deployed sixteen four-man patrols by helicopter across this vast area.

The patrols lived in the jungle for months at a time, clearing landing zones, mapping the terrain, setting ambush positions, and establishing relations with local tribes. Communication was a significant challenge, with Second World War-era radio sets prone to damp and atmospheric interference. Corporal-of-Horse Kersting, Royal Horse Guards managed the vital signals communications, while Company Quartermaster Sergeant (CQMS) Smurthwaite, Coldstream Guards handled the critical re-supply operations.

After completing their initial six-month tour, the company returned to Britain, but most of the unit was returned to Borneo in 1965 for a second tour. During this period, they conducted several missions against Indonesian-dominated areas along the border.[10]

SAS Connection and Later Years

Following the Borneo deployments, a significant development occurred with the formation of a guard squadron within the 22nd SAS Regiment. In 1966, a troop from the company proceeded to Hereford to train and form the nucleus of the squadron. It was duly constituted later in 1966 under the command of Major Murray de Klee.

This connection deepened in the following years. After the company's second Borneo tour, Colonel John Woodhouse of 22nd SAS wrote in the Christmas issue of the SAS Magazine: 'It is to be hoped that the Household Brigade, so prominent in the formation of the 1st SAS, but so scarcely represented since, will continue the good work. It has been a pleasure to be alongside so efficient, well-disciplined and determined a unit. They have won our respect.'[11]

In 1970, the company was deployed to Northern Ireland, based at the Red Hart Bottling Factory in Belfast. Being SAS-trained and reliable, members of the company were often used in covert operations, with the chief intelligence officer finding them a tremendous benefit.[12]

Disbandment and Legacy

On 24 October 1975, after 27 years of service, the Guards Parachute Company was disbanded. Field Marshal Sir Gerald Templer, Colonel of The Blues and Royals, took the farewell parade at Pirbright. He stated:

> The secret of the Company's outstanding success lies, of course, in the fact that all of its members, of whatever rank, brought with them an intense pride in their parent Regiment and in their profession as the Household Troops of the Sovereign.[13]

Almost the entire body of the disbanded company volunteered for G Squadron 22nd SAS and achieved a hundred per cent pass rate on selection. This ensured the Guards Parachute Company's spirit and expertise continued within the special forces community.[14]

The Guards' parachute tradition has persisted in various forms since the disbandment. The 6 (Guards Parachute) Platoon, attached to the 3rd Battalion, The Parachute Regiment (3 PARA), is the surviving link to the former Guards Parachute Battalion, Guards Parachute Coy, and later Pathfinder Platoons. This unit served with distinction alongside 3 PARA in Afghanistan in 2008.[15]

On 14 November 1983, the 5th Infantry Brigade was re-designated the 5th Airborne Brigade, reintroducing an airborne formation into the British Army's order of battle. It came under the command of the 3rd (UK) Division, one of two divisions forming part of the Allied Command Europe (ACE) Rapid Reaction Corps for employment with NATO. The Brigade's secondary role was conducting out-of-area (i.e. outside Europe) operations.

The new brigade fielded two parachute battalions with several parachute arms and services. Two air-mobile (helicopter-borne) infantry battalions were included, and the Household Cavalry provided an armoured reconnaissance regiment, some of which were parachute-trained.

In 1985, the Pathfinder Platoon was established as the Brigade's Advance Force on the lines of the former 16th Brigade Guards Parachute Company. They were trained and equipped for pathfinder skills utilising HALO (high altitude low-opening) tactical free-fall parachute techniques and operated in four-man patrols with all the requisite specialist skills.

In 1994, the Brigade's Logistics Battalion deployed to Rwanda on Operation Gabriel. In 1999, the headquarters were deployed for operational use for the first time in Kosovo. In September 1999, the unit was re-titled 12 Mechanised Brigade, and 1 PARA and 2 PARA, alongside all the brigade's combat and service support units, came under the command of the new 16th Air Assault Brigade that formed up in Colchester.[16]

Today, members of the five Foot Guards and two Horse Guards regiments can request a posting to the Guards Parachute Platoon, which is 6 (Guards) Platoon, B Company, 3 PARA. Guardsmen and troopers wishing to join the Guards Parachute Platoon must pass the selection process and P Company before progressing to parachute training. Just like during the Second World War, one of the benefits of joining the unit is that paratroopers receive jump pay upon qualification.

G Squadron, 22nd Special Air Service Regiment, remains a highly specialised and elite unit known for its diverse operational capabilities, including mobility, mountain, boat and air troop skills. The links between G Squadron and the Household Division remain strong, with past and present members of the Household Division being well represented at the fortieth anniversary of G Squadron in 2006.[17]

In the spring 2009 edition of *The Guards Magazine*, a serving Welsh Guards Lance Corporal described his journey into and experiences with G Squadron, 22nd SAS. At the time of writing, the soldier had served for two years in the SAS and previously worked as a Platoon Sergeant in the Welsh Guards, including deployments in Northern Ireland, with the Close Observation Platoon, and Iraq, with the Brigade Surveillance Company.

His motivation for applying to join the UK Special Forces was straightforward. He explained, 'I wanted to work at the top of my game with highly motivated and positive people and to learn and develop new skills and put them into practice.' His preparation for selection involved intense physical training, including three runs a week of no less than an hour and keeping to a pace of 8 mph, upper body workouts three to four times weekly and swimming twice weekly. He emphasised that 'when thinking about applying for the selection, you have to prepare yourself mentally, as well as physically, and you have to be 100 per cent motivated to train and to pass the course'.

After passing selection, he joined G Squadron and immediately entered an operational phase with high-intensity training. He explained, 'I had to maintain a high level of training, and I learnt new skills, including advanced driving, close-quarter battle, and range work.' He qualified on HGV vehicles and became proficient with heavy weapons like the 50-calibre heavy machine gun (HMG) and general-purpose machine gun (GPMG).

The soldier then deployed with the Squadron on a six-month operational tour, during which he learned a great deal and got to practise the skills he had already mastered. Following this deployment, he took some leave and completed a Category A motorcycle course. He also trained in the USA, where 'the whole Troop hired motorbikes and rode back along the West Coast to San Diego, where still more amusing memories were generated!'

In 2007, he completed a ten-week Arabic language course and deployed to Africa. Throughout his time with the Regiment, he has attended various courses, including demolitions and high-altitude parachuting. The article concludes with the guardsman reflecting on his time in G Squadron, stating, 'I can honestly say that I have thoroughly enjoyed my first couple of years in G Squadron.' He notes that while the hard work he put into passing selection was significant, it was ultimately worth all the effort.[18]

13

The Web of Privilege

The Aristocratic Network in Special Forces Formation

The formation and development of British special forces during the Second World War cannot be properly understood without examining the structural advantages provided by aristocratic networks, particularly those centred on the Brigade of Guards. These connections were not merely incidental but formed a deliberate and effective system that facilitated rapid innovation outside normal military bureaucracy. This chapter examines how the institutional framework of the Guards, combined with established social networks, created unique operational advantages that accelerated the development of special forces precisely when conventional military systems struggled to innovate.

The Institutional Framework of the Guards

The Brigade of Guards functioned effectively as a parallel command structure within the British Army, with its own internal hierarchy, traditions, recruitment and training. This institutional independence provided several critical advantages for special forces development. Guards officers were accustomed to operating with a certain amount of autonomy, a mindset that transferred naturally to special operations. The Brigade maintained its own administrative systems, allowing it to transfer personnel and resources with less bureaucratic friction than standard line regiments experienced. Perhaps most importantly, the Brigade's special status created a buffer zone where experimental units could develop without immediate scrutiny from the wider army establishment.

The Guards' position as the sovereign's personal bodyguard further insulated them, to a degree, from everyday military politics. This institutional protection extended to their experimental formations, offering what might be termed 'aristocratic cover'

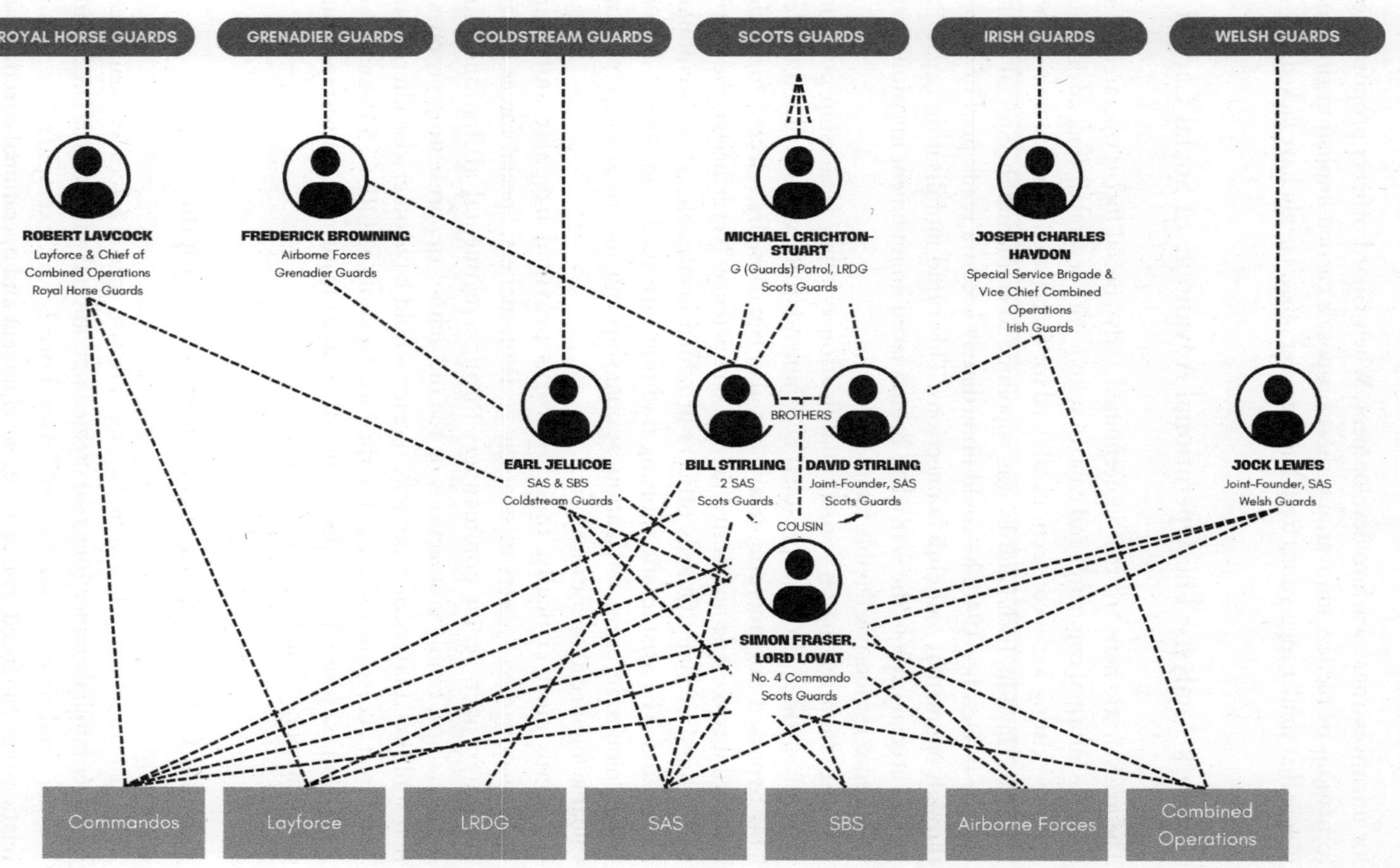

Figure 2. Web of Connections: The Raising of British Special Forces.

for unconventional warfare development. When Guard officers proposed new formations or tactical innovations, these proposals carried implicit institutional weight that similar suggestions from line regiment officers might have lacked.

Network Analysis: The Operational Advantage of Social Capital

The aristocratic network that underpinned early special forces operated as an effective informal command and control system with several distinct advantages. The pre-existing social connections allowed for accelerated unit formation. When Brigadier Haydon, Irish Guards, was appointed to command the Special Service Brigade in October 1940, he could immediately access a ready pool of officers through regimental and club connections. This rapid mobilisation capability proved crucial early in the war when Britain faced an imminent invasion threat and needed responsive, flexible forces.

Rather than relying on formal qualification systems, leadership positions were often filled through personal recommendation within trusted circles. This bypassed bureaucratic delays but also occasionally selected for social compatibility over demonstrated tactical competence. Nevertheless, the shared background of many Guards officers provided invaluable cross-disciplinary integration. The aristocratic sporting tradition furnished ready-made skills in skiing, mountaineering, navigation, seamanship and shooting, which were all valuable for special operations.

Perhaps most critically, these networks provided irregular units with uncommonly direct access to strategic decision-makers. Special forces leaders could approach senior commanders through regimental affiliations, club memberships, family connections or the old school tie, presenting proposals that traditional layers of army bureaucracy would have otherwise filtered out. This direct access proved crucial in the formation of the LRDG, SAS and other special units, where initial proposals often faced institutional resistance that personal connections helped overcome.

Familial Connections in Special Forces Development

The aristocratic network that underpinned British special forces was reinforced by direct familial connections that created operational advantages. The Stirling brothers and their cousin, Simon Fraser, Lord Lovat, exemplify how family relationships enhanced special forces development and operational effectiveness.

Bill and David Stirling, sons of Brigadier General Archibald Stirling of Keir, utilised their complementary skills and shared family background to establish crucial elements of British special forces. Bill Stirling's military experience and connections provided institutional credibility, whilst David Stirling's unconventional thinking generated tactical innovations. Their aristocratic Scottish background offered practical benefits beyond mere social cachet; their ancestral estate at Keir House served as an impromptu operational headquarters for the cancelled Operation Knife team in 1940, demonstrating how private family resources supplemented military infrastructure.

The Stirling-Fraser family connection proved particularly significant. Simon Fraser, 15th Lord Lovat, was a cousin to the Stirlings and, like them, had been educated at Ampleforth College. This familial relationship facilitated operational collaboration that conventional military structures might have impeded. When Bill Stirling and Brian Mayfield established the Special Training Centre at Inverailort, they recruited Lord Lovat as senior fieldcraft instructor, creating a family-connected training pipeline that supplied personnel to multiple special forces units.

The Stirling-Fraser connection allowed informal coordination between the SAS and commandos without bureaucratic friction. The familial network also strengthened resistance to institutional opposition. When David Stirling was captured in January 1943, his brother Bill assumed command of the SAS, thereby maintaining operational continuity that the loss of the founding commander might have disrupted.

Movement Between Special Forces Units

The aristocratic network facilitated significant movement of personnel between various special forces units throughout the war through formal and informal mechanisms. This circulation of experienced officers and men created a continuous exchange of tactical innovations and operational experience that conventional military structures rarely achieved with their rigid regimental affiliations.

The mechanics of this movement operated at several levels. The Guards' administrative autonomy formally allowed officers to be temporarily detached for 'special duties' without permanent transfer from their parent regiments. This maintained their career progression within the Guards while enabling them to serve in specialised formations. Unlike many line regiment officers, who might face career penalties for seeking unconventional assignments, Guards officers could, to a degree, move freely between special forces units with the blessing of their regimental hierarchy.

More significantly, in the early days of British special forces, informal transfers occurred through personal recommendation networks that circumvented normal posting procedures. When a special forces unit needed replacements, commanders typically contacted former colleagues rather than submitting formal requisitions through the personnel system. This practice created direct personnel pipelines between superficially distinct formations. The disbandment of the 5th (Special Reserve) Battalion, Scots Guards in March 1940 provides a clear example: its personnel were dispersed throughout emerging special forces units, creating an informal network of Guards officers across multiple formations.

Similarly, when Layforce dissolved in 1941, its experienced personnel did not return to conventional formations but circulated within the special forces community. David Stirling actively recruited from the remnants of 8 Commando to form his embryonic SAS unit, accessing a pre-vetted pool of volunteers who already possessed the required skills and temperament.

The effectiveness of this movement stemmed from several factors. First, shared social and educational backgrounds created immediate operational trust between officers who might be meeting for the first time but recognised each other as members of the same elite circles. Second, the Guards training system produced soldiers with consistent standards of discipline and physical fitness, allowing rapid integration into new units without extensive retraining. Third, the aristocratic network's emphasis on amateur sporting prowess, such as sailing, mountaineering and skiing, created a pool of transferable skills directly applicable to special operations.

This personnel circulation yielded considerable operational benefits. Tactical innovations spread rapidly between formally distinct units without official doctrine development processes. Officers who had served in the commandos brought amphibious raiding expertise to the SAS, while LRDG veterans contributed desert navigation techniques to other formations. This cross-pollination created an informal body of special operations knowledge that evolved much faster than conventional military doctrine.

Personnel movement also improved administrative efficiency. Special forces units facing disbandment could transfer experienced operators to new formations without losing their specialised training investment. When new units formed, they could rapidly achieve operational capability by incorporating veterans from existing formations rather than starting from scratch.

However, this movement system also carried disadvantages. The continuous circulation of personnel reinforced the socially exclusive nature of special forces, limiting access for qualified candidates without connections to the aristocratic network. Transfers of Guards officers between units likely created resentment among regular army formations, as they saw this as special treatment not extended to line regiment personnel facing disbandment.

Moreover, the informal personnel exchange system occasionally prioritised social compatibility over operational skill. Officers might recommend friends or relations for positions regardless of their tactical proficiency, though this tendency diminished as the war progressed and combat experience became more valued than social connections.

Despite some drawbacks, the aristocratic network's facilitation of personnel movement between special forces units created significant operational advantages that outweighed the disadvantages. The system maintained both social exclusivity and combat effectiveness, demonstrating that the seemingly archaic structure of aristocratic privilege could create genuine military innovation when circumstances demanded it.

Evolution Under Operational Pressure

As the war progressed, the nature of special forces networking evolved in response to operational realities. By 1942–43, demonstrated operational effectiveness began to supersede social connections in officer selection and promotion within special forces, though the senior leadership remained predominantly aristocratic. The success of operations required integration of specialist skills from working-class NCOs and other ranks, gradually diluting the purely aristocratic character of special forces leadership.

Alternative pathways to special forces command emerged, with technical specialists and battlefield promotions creating a more diverse leadership profile in units like the SAS by 1944–45. The remarkable adaptability of the aristocratic network proved capable of selectively incorporating outsiders while maintaining its core advantages of privileged access and institutional protection. This pragmatic evolution ensured that special forces remained operationally effective even as their social composition diversified.

Institutional Tensions

The existence of this parallel command structure did not go unchallenged. As special forces expanded and consumed increasingly scarce manpower resources, conventional army formations voiced growing opposition. Field Marshal Bernard Montgomery and General Sir Alan Brooke both expressed reservations about the proliferation of special forces, arguing that they drained regular formations of leadership talent. However, the aristocratic network's connections to Winston Churchill and other senior political figures often protected special forces from these institutional challenges.

The relationship between special forces and conventional military leadership remained complex throughout the war. The privileged access that helped create these units sometimes became a liability as their operational role expanded, creating tensions with theatre commanders who viewed special forces as operating outside proper chains of command. Nevertheless, the demonstrated operational success of units like the LRDG and SAS gradually overcame much of this institutional resistance, proving that the aristocratic network had created genuinely valuable military capabilities despite its unconventional origins.

The aristocratic network thus provided British special forces with structural advantages that competitors lacked: an informal but highly effective system of personnel selection, operational autonomy and strategic access. This system accelerated the development of Britain's unconventional warfare capabilities at a critical juncture in the war, when innovation and adaptation were paramount.

Institutional Problems

While the aristocratic backgrounds of many special forces officers offered advantages, they also came with their own challenges. The most pervasive issue was an attitude of exceptionalism that manifested as disregard for established military protocols and the chain of command.

General Sir Alan Brooke found himself compelled to discipline Frederick Browning for attempting to bypass the proper channels by 'writing to politicians' rather than following army procedures. Robert Laycock found similar behavioural issues with Lord Lovat of 4 Commando. In December 1942, Laycock wrote a stinging rebuke to Lovat concerning his conduct within Combined Operations (a copy of the letter can be found in Appendix C):

> When will you learn some tact? I know that it is uphill work dealing with touchy
> officers who, to put it very snobbishly, do not come from the same social strata
> as those with whom you were used to deal in peacetime in the Brigade—yet,
> nevertheless, you must learn to bear with them.

Laycock criticised Lovat's 'arrogance' in dealings with naval officers from different social backgrounds and specifically condemned an incident in which a letter of appreciation to a naval captain was signed by an adjutant rather than the commanding officer, a breach of inter-service etiquette that reflected Guards officers' limited experience working outside their social circle.

The reprimand continued with remarkable openness:

> To be absolutely frank with you, I think you are inclined to be getting a
> reputation for arrogance which is a pity. Please rectify this... remember that
> sarcasm and arrogance never got anyone anywhere yet.[1]

These incidents reveal how aristocratic officers could struggle to operate effectively within the broader military establishment, particularly when required to collaborate with personnel from different backgrounds.

Internal Divisions

The special forces units themselves were not immune to the negative effects of class-based recruitment. Bill Stirling faced internal opposition within 2SAS from officers who shared his social background but disagreed with his leadership. Roy Farran, who remained loyal to Stirling, identified the principal conspirators as 'Major Oswald Cary-Elwes, Major Peter Miller Mundy, Major Esmond Baring, a member of the banking family, Major Philip Yorke, the ninth Earl of Hardwicke, and Captain Ralph 'Toby' Milbanke'.

Farran offered a damning assessment: 'All those who opposed Bill Stirling weren't real soldiers, weren't real fighting types... they were academic soldiers.' This distinction between 'academic' and 'real' soldiers often split along social rather than competence lines, with some aristocratic officers valuing theoretical knowledge over practical combat experience.

The attempted 'mutiny' against Bill Stirling occurred during a troopship voyage from North Africa to Britain in March 1944. According to Farran, 'the conspirators had little meetings on the ship, talking about getting rid of Bill and complaining to higher command... They used some pretty unfair tactics, too, saying he had not taken part in operations himself.'[2]

This conspiracy reflected a more profound problem within special forces recruitment. When units drew extensively from a single social class, especially one accustomed to privilege and authority, leadership challenges can arise from a sense of entitlement rather than legitimate operational concerns. Many of these officers had secured their positions through connections at White's Club or similar social institutions rather than demonstrating military competence. Farran referred to these malcontents as 'White's Club warriors'.

The Sacking of Bill Stirling

In May 1944, Bill Stirling of 2SAS was sacked by General Browning following a blazing row over the deployment of SAS troops for the Normandy landings. Montgomery's 21st Army Group wanted SAS troops deployed tactically just beyond the Normandy beachhead, which Stirling strongly opposed as a misuse of his men and their capabilities. Instead, he advocated strategic insertion deep behind enemy lines in Brittany, southern Normandy, and areas south of Paris.

The confrontation between the two men fundamentally reflected the clash between aristocratic entitlement and military hierarchy. Stirling, as Laird of Keir and member of the Scottish landed gentry, operated from a position where social rank often transcended professional position. His Guards background reinforced this mindset, with Guards officers frequently viewing themselves as separate from the conventional army structure. It appears highly likely that Stirling mistakenly believed that their shared membership in the Brigade of Guards established a fraternal relationship, allowing him to challenge Browning's judgment directly. This proved a critical miscalculation. While Browning was commissioned into the Grenadier Guards, he operated firmly within institutional structures and expected adherence to military protocol regardless of social background. Paradoxically, as we have seen, Browning was a man happy to bypass the chain of command when it came to furthering his own personal career ambitions.

Their leadership styles likely amplified the conflict. Stirling championed the special forces approach, prioritising the mission over military protocol. Browning represented conventional military leadership, emphasising chains of command and formal structures. When Stirling directly challenged Browning, telling him 'in no uncertain terms' that he had no confidence in him and his plans were wrong, Browning immediately interpreted this as insubordination and sacked him on the spot.

Despite the dismissal causing significant discontent throughout 2SAS, events ultimately justified Stirling's operational assessment. By 28 May, the SAS received instructions to deploy strategically in central France, precisely as Stirling had advised. This incident exemplifies how aristocratic social dynamics occasionally clashed with military hierarchy during wartime, particularly within the emerging special forces community.

Broader Challenges

The pre-war decadent lifestyle of young, entitled Guards officers could have a corrosive effect when not properly channelled. Many Guards officers volunteered for special service assignments to escape the monotony of regimental life, only to find that commando life consisted of a constant cycle of training exercises and cancelled operations. Although not the most reliable witness, novelist Evelyn Waugh offered a damning assessment of 8 Commando's leadership:

> The standard of efficiency and devotion to duty, particularly among the officers, is very much lower than in the Marines. There is no administration or discipline. The men are given 6s a day and told to find their own accommodation. If they behave badly they are simply sent back to their regiments. Officers have no scruples about seeing to their own comfort or getting all the leave they can.[3]

Social homogeneity limits the diversity of thought and experience. In many instances, the recruitment process of early special forces favoured social connections over proven operational abilities, sometimes resulting in unsuitable appointments. As a Welsh Guards Lance Corporal noted, many of his peers viewed General Browning as a martinet who, 'as a result of his Guards background', thought that 'hard-line, mindless, Regular Army techniques should be applied to men who were, at heart, civilians in uniform'.[4]

Systemic Impact

Beyond the internal challenges, the concentration of leadership talent in special forces created significant systemic problems. Critics argued that special forces drained the regular army of leadership talent. Military historian John Peaty concluded that the proliferation of special forces distorted the British Army's manpower distribution and contributed to its manpower problems, particularly by attracting 'warriors': enterprising, physically fit individuals with initiative who would likely have made excellent junior officers or NCOs in regular formations.

Conclusions

The web of aristocratic connections that underpinned British special forces during the Second World War reveals much about the adaptability and rigidity of Britain's military establishment. While this network facilitated rapid innovation during a critical period, it simultaneously perpetuated a class-based approach to warfare that both strengthened and limited these elite units.

The Aristocratic Advantage

The aristocratic connection provided British special forces with distinct advantages. The speed with which units like the commandos, LRDG and SAS formed and deployed reflected the social shortcuts available to their founders. When David Stirling conceived the SAS, his Guards connections, family name and personal relationship with key commanders enabled him to bypass standard military procedures that might have delayed or prevented the unit's creation. Similarly, Bill Stirling could transform a failed plan for a Norwegian operation into the Special Training Centre at Inverailort through social connections rather than formal channels.

The pre-existing social cohesion among officers who had attended the same schools, belonged to the same clubs and served in the same regiments ensured rapid trust-building and operational integration. This established network dramatically accelerated the formation of special units when time was of the essence. These officers brought with them a range of sporting skills, from skiing to climbing to navigation, that proved directly applicable to special operations.

Systemic Limitations

The aristocratic web also created significant limitations. The social homogeneity restricted the diversity of thought and operational approach. Later in the war, the concentration of leadership talent in special forces, to a degree, depleted conventional units of valuable officers and NCOs when the army faced serious manpower shortages. The attitude of exceptionalism fostered by wealth and privilege often manifested as a disregard for military protocol and inter-service cooperation.

The attempted mutiny against Bill Stirling within 2SAS exemplifies how aristocratic entitlement could undermine unit cohesion and effectiveness. Guards culture, emphasising parade-ground discipline and hierarchy, sometimes proved ill-suited to the adaptability required for special operations.

The True Father of Special Forces

Possibly, the title of 'father of special forces' belongs to Lieutenant General Sir Bertram Sergison-Brooke, GOC London District and major general commanding the Brigade of Guards. He significantly influenced special forces appointments through his institutional position and personal connections. His recommendation directly secured Bob Laycock's appointment to command 8 Commando, accelerating Laycock's promotion from captain to lieutenant colonel. Similarly, Sergison-Brooke encouraged his cousin, General Sir Alan Brooke, to appoint Browning as commander of airborne forces, specifically arguing that the Guards regiments required representation among the general officer corps. Sergison-Brooke's dual authority over the London District and the Household Division created a powerful nexus for patronage, enabling him to position Guards officers at the helm of emerging special forces formations despite their lack of prior experience in unconventional warfare. This pattern of aristocratic Guards officers receiving command appointments through personal connections rather than demonstrated expertise became a defining characteristic of early British special forces development.

Leadership Styles: Laycock and Browning

Robert Laycock and Frederick Browning had different approaches to leading special forces, although they both came from privileged backgrounds and used their social connections to advance their careers.

Laycock was described as imaginative but realistic in planning operations. He emphasised rigid discipline, a common trait of Guards officers, but also recognised the need to develop specialised commando operations techniques. Laycock's career path represents the more adaptive model. He initially recruited extensively from his social circle and appeared somewhat blind to the faults of his peers, but he demonstrated an ability to learn from experience. His reprimand to Lord Lovat regarding inter-service etiquette reveals a recognition that aristocratic arrogance could damage operational effectiveness. As Chief of Combined Operations, Laycock developed a more pragmatic approach to working across traditional boundaries. His progression from commanding a socially exclusive commando unit to effectively leading a complex, multi-service organisation demonstrates a capacity for growth beyond his narrow social origins.

Browning's leadership style was more autocratic. According to one subordinate, he exhibited mannered arrogance in command. Like Laycock, Browning was a strict disciplinarian, and likewise had a quick temper. Browning, by contrast, exemplified some of the limitations of autocratic command born of social elitism. His appointment to lead airborne forces stemmed almost entirely from his Guards background and establishment connections rather than relevant experience. He imported Guards practices wholesale into airborne forces, alienating some volunteers who had joined for a different kind of military service. His willingness to circumvent the chain of command when it suited him reflected the sense of entitlement that characterised many Guards officers. Browning's leadership during Operation Market Garden, where he insisted on accompanying the force despite having no practical role, further demonstrates how personal ambition could override operational considerations.

The divergent paths of these two officers illustrate a fundamental tension within British special forces: the need to balance the advantages of aristocratic connections with the limitations they imposed. Laycock ultimately seems to have transcended his privileged origins or learned to temper his behaviour sufficiently to become an effective commander across service boundaries, while Browning remained more constrained by his Guards background and social expectations. He also appears to have been a man blind to his own faults of vanity, arrogance and ambition. Browning successfully antagonised his American allies, who regarded him with suspicion and disdain. Laycock, by contrast, embraced, befriended and willingly collaborated with the newly formed US Ranger battalions. The sacking of Bill Stirling shows Browning to have been self-righteous and hypocritical. He strongly believed in his moral superiority and tended to judge others harshly while failing to apply the same high standards to his own behaviour.

After the war, Laycock remained Chief of Combined Operations until 1947. In 1954, he was appointed governor of Malta and, in 1960, assumed the honorary role of colonel commandant of the SAS, the unit he inadvertently helped to conceive. Browning served as military secretary at the War Office before becoming controller and treasurer to Princess Elizabeth's Household. Regrettably, alcoholism and mental illness plagued the later years of Browning's life. Laycock's legacy remains largely positive, while Browning's reputation never recovered from the Arnhem disaster.

Enduring Legacy

The aristocratic network behind British special forces created a distinctive military culture that persists in modified form today. Modern special forces units like the SAS maintain elite standards and exclusivity while drawing from a broader demographic base. The Guards connection endures through formations like the Guards Parachute Platoon and G Squadron, 22 SAS but no longer dominates as it once did.

The lessons from this period remain relevant. Special forces benefit from strong internal cohesion and distinctive identity but must avoid becoming socially isolated from the broader military. The rapid innovation enabled by informal networks provides significant advantages during crisis periods but requires integration with established structures for long-term effectiveness.

Most importantly, this history demonstrates that military effectiveness depends on balancing social continuity with adaptability. The aristocratic officers who created British special forces succeeded when they could transcend their privileged backgrounds and learn from diverse experiences, as Laycock ultimately did. They failed when, like Browning in his worst moments, remaining constrained by social expectations and class-based assumptions.

The aristocratic web behind British special forces thus represents both the adaptability of Britain's military establishment in crisis and its deeply entrenched class structures. This complex legacy continues to influence special operations doctrine and practice, albeit in increasingly diminished form, as modern special forces units seek to maintain elite standards while drawing strength from greater social diversity than their founders could have imagined.

Postscript: The Guards and British Special Forces

The relationship between the Brigade of Guards and Britain's special forces represents one of the most significant yet understudied aspects of British military development during the Second World War. This connection fundamentally shaped the character, ethos and operational effectiveness of units that continue to serve today.

The Guards supplied the right calibre of recruits for the new special forces during the war and a unique guiding ethos. The discipline, attention to detail and professional standards instilled at Caterham proved ideal foundations for special operations, where independent action required initiative and composure. This paradoxical combination of rigid discipline as a preparation for unconventional warfare became a defining characteristic of British special forces.

With centuries of history behind them, the Guards are a bastion of Britishness, ceremonial pomp and pageantry. They are also a military elite, famed for their steadiness and reliability in battles from Waterloo to the Falklands, Iraq and Afghanistan. However, the Guards have never allowed tradition to stand in the way of progress or military adaptation for too long.

In 1882, the Guards replaced their scarlet tunics with khaki and switched to camels for transport while fighting the Mahdi's army in Sudan. During the Second World War, elements of the Household Division converted from their traditional infantry role to tanks, forming the Guards Armoured Division and the 6th (Guards) Tank Brigade. Besides the commandos, LRDG, SAS and Parachute Regiment, guardsmen served in the Glider Pilot Regiment, the clandestine Special Operations Executive (SOE) and Military Intelligence. Time spent at Little Sparta taught guardsmen more than just parade-ground discipline and standards of dress and deportment: it also developed them into individuals capable of independent thought and action. Perhaps, most importantly, it taught them to believe in themselves and their abilities, not matter what the situation.

As we have already seen, the Guards officers' social connections and influence proved instrumental in establishing special units. Men like Bob Laycock, Bill Stirling, David Stirling and Frederick Browning leveraged their aristocratic backgrounds and connections to bypass military bureaucracy, secure critical resources and win political support to achieve their objectives.

Many special forces units raised during the war never survived it and were disbanded. The Guards' contribution extended beyond the conflict, with the Guards Parachute Company and G Squadron SAS ensuring continuity of this relationship into the modern era.

Historical evidence demonstrates that what might appear contradictory, that the most traditionally minded soldiers pioneered the most unconventional units, is in fact reflective of a logical connection. The Guards emphasised self-discipline, reliability and professional excellence, providing the proper foundation for soldiers tasked with operating independently behind enemy lines under challenging circumstances.

The seeming paradox dissolves upon closer examination of what Guards training actually produced. The relentless emphasis on cleanliness, smartness and attention to detail at Caterham was never an end in itself. As Keith Briant explained, its purpose was to develop soldiers who would 'consider no trifle too unimportant, no trouble too great, however tired he may be'. A guardsman trained to ensure that every part of his rifle was clear of sand specks because this discipline might save his life, was precisely the type of soldier who could be trusted to operate without supervision deep in enemy territory.

Special operations demanded soldiers capable of functioning at peak efficiency when exhausted, isolated and far from the support structures of conventional units. The Guards system, which forced recruits to maintain exacting standards regardless of fatigue, produced exactly this quality. Cyril Feebery's description of commando training, with its endless mountain marches punctuated by seemingly petty sock inspections, echoed the methods he had already encountered in the Brigade. The commandos adopted these techniques because they worked: ensuring soldiers could overcome their own discomfort and continue to perform when it mattered most.

Crucially, the Guards' training system did more than instil obedience. Major Henniker's 1895 lecture notes reveal that discipline was intended to 'increase his powers of initiative, of self-confidence, and self-restraint' and 'to train him to obey orders, or to act in birthe absence of orders'. This capacity to act decisively without direction, developed through the progressive mastery of increasingly complex tasks, was the quality most prized in special forces. The confidence instilled at Caterham, the unshakeable belief that guardsmen could 'beat the world', translated directly into the audacity required for operations behind enemy lines.

The combination proved potent. When L Detachment needed soldiers who could navigate hundreds of miles through the desert, destroy aircraft on enemy airfields and escape undetected, the ideal candidate possessed both the self-discipline to execute meticulous planning and the initiative to adapt when plans failed. The Guards produced such men in abundance.

This relationship continues to influence contemporary British special forces, where the Guards' ethos remains evident in selection, training and operational procedures. The success of this model has informed the development of special forces worldwide, demonstrating the enduring value of combining disciplined professionalism with operational flexibility.

Key Personalities
and What Happened Next

This section gives a brief follow-up on the main characters behind Britain's special forces, summarising their military careers for the rest of the war and their post-war lives and roles.

BRIGADIER DUDLEY CLARKE

Dudley Clarke was born in South Africa and served as a British Army intelligence officer during the Second World War. He established a unit called 'A Force' to conduct deception operations in North Africa and Europe. His mission was to mislead the enemy through trickery, double agents and espionage. Remarkably, he survived being torpedoed during the war.

Clarke played a key role in creating the commandos and the Special Air Service and influenced the naming of the US Rangers. He retired from the army in 1947 with the rank of Brigadier. After the war, he wrote his first book, *Seven Assignments* (1948), detailing his experiences from 1939 to 1940. He also authored several historical works and a thriller titled *Golden Arrow* (1955). Some of his writings were suppressed from publication under the Official Secrets Act.

Later, Clarke worked for the Conservative Party and was the director of one of Britain's largest security firms. He passed away on 7 May 1974. In 2022, actor Dominic West portrayed Dudley Clarke as the charismatic, cross-dressing spymaster in the BBC historical drama series *SAS: Rogue Heroes*. In October 1944, Clarke was mentioned in dispatches for his work to successfully conceal the intentions of the D-Day landings.

ADMIRAL SIR ROGER KEYES

During the early days of the war, Roger Keyes served as liaison officer to King Leopold III of Belgium. In June 1940, he was appointed the first director of Combined Operations but was removed from the post the following year. On Wednesday, 26 November 1941, the *London Daily News* reported Admiral

Sir Roger Keyes' impassioned speech to the House of Commons on Whitehall's bureaucratic interference, having repeatedly strangled proposed commando operations. Two weeks before, the admiral's son, Geoffrey Keyes, was killed during the failed Rommel Raid (Operation Flipper).

In 1943, after the government successfully side-lined him, the admiral was raised to the peerage as Baron Keyes. During a visit to the American amphibious warfare ship USS *Appalachian*, he suffered smoke inhalation following an attack by Japanese aircraft and never fully recovered. He died at his home in Tingewick on 26 December 1945. During the First World War, Keyes had planned the famous Zeebrugge Raid to block the German-held port. The raid caused heavy British casualties but only led to a brief disruption of German U-boat operations; nevertheless, it was considered a propaganda success, and Keyes was appointed a Knight Commander of the Order of the Bath.

Major General Joseph Charles Haydon, Irish Guards

During the Second World War, Charles Haydon led key Allied operations and was the first commander of the Special Service Brigade. He later served as vice Chief of Combined Operations and commanded the 1st Guards Brigade in Italy in 1944. After the war, he worked as the army's director of plans in Washington, D.C., and with the joint chiefs in Australia. He then headed the Intelligence Division for Germany before retiring from the army in 1951 with the rank of major general. He passed on 8 November 1970. Colonel T. H. H. Grayson, Irish Guards remarked of General Haydon, 'Underneath his strong sense of discipline and intolerance of any form of idleness, there was always fairness and kindness and, above all, a wonderful sense of humour which endeared him to all who served with him.'

Lieutenant General Sir Bertram Sergison-Brooke, Grenadier Guards

Sergison-Brooke was recalled from retirement during the Second World War. He served as general officer commanding the London District and led the Brigade of Guards as major general. The general was one of only two men to hold both positions twice (1934–38 and 1939–42). He advocated the raising of the Guards Armoured Division in 1941. He retired from the army again in 1942.

From 1943 to 1945, he was the British Red Cross Commissioner with the Allied Army of Liberation. His cousin, Sir Alan Brooke, became Chief of the Imperial General Staff. He was married and widowed twice. According to his obituary in the summer 1967 edition of *The Guards Magazine*, he resisted the idea of ageing gracefully and disliked the restrictions that came with it. The affection he generated throughout the Brigade of Guards was best seen and felt at dinners over which he presided at the Blue Seal Club (an exclusive club for Grenadier Guards officers).

Major General Robert Laycock, Royal Horse Guards

In 1947, Robert Laycock retired from the military after serving as Chief of Combined Operations. In 1954, he was named governor and commander-in-chief of Malta and served until 1959, with his term extended twice. From 1960, he held honorary posts with the Special Air Service and the Sherwood Rangers Yeomanry, and in 1962, he became lord lieutenant of Nottinghamshire. He was a keen horseman, yachtsman and book collector. Toward the end of his life, he suffered from circulatory problems in one leg, which left him in constant pain. Nevertheless, Laycock managed his duties and interests with a steady resolve. He died on 10 March 1968, in Wiseton, Nottinghamshire. In a fitting and heartfelt tribute to 'Lucky' Laycock, Major General Charles Haydon wrote:

> He was a valiant character and a man born to lead. He was, at once, daring and fearless, imaginative yet practical, and ready always to accept responsibility and take decisions. There was not a trace of pretence or pretension in his character, and he could not in his life ever have done a mean thing. Men followed him with devotion and willingly, with no qualms in their minds or in their hearts, for he inspired utter confidence, and led by the force of his own personality and example. He never sought the limelight; he never sought fame, but both sought him, and no one grudged him either. The honours and awards that became his were no more than the barest recognition of his worth. Thus, he goes, leaving behind him an illustrious record of high endeavour and achievement, and we who knew him and served with him in the Commandos are proud and privileged to have done so.

Brigadier Simon Fraser, 15th Lord Lovat, Scots Guards

On D-Day, Lord Lovat led his commandos at Sword Beach and helped secure Pegasus Bridge. He was seriously wounded a few days later. He was sent as an envoy to Moscow in early 1945. He joined the government as Parliamentary under-secretary of state for foreign affairs, only to resign with Winston Churchill's election defeat. He retired from the army in 1962 with the honorary rank of brigadier. He served in the House of Lords and on the Inverness County Council for forty-two years. He also managed his family estates and participated in cattle breeding and judging. A year before he died in 1995, the family's ancestral home, Beaufort Castle, was sold to pay inheritance taxes. Known to friends and family as Shimi Lovat, he was depicted by Peter Lawford in the 1962 film *The Longest Day*, based on Cornelius Ryan's book about the D-Day landings. In his obituary, Major W. N. Seymour wrote that many people, upon first meeting Lovat, found him arrogant, conceited and opinionated. 'But those fortunate to know him well, quickly found that they had made a loyal, kind and generous friend who possessed a lovely sense of humour.' Seymour concluded his tribute to Lovat: 'Shimi Lovat possessed a rock-like strength of character without a scintilla of pomposity, and this with his sense of fun, enthusiasm for everything and ready laughter made him a marvellous person to be with.'

Lieutenant Colonel William 'Bill' Stirling, Scots Guards

Frederick Browning sacked Bill Stirling from command of 2 SAS two days before D-Day, after clashing over how to deploy his unit. That sacking ended his active military career. In July 1945, King George VI appointed him Forestry Commissioner. He managed his family estate in Scotland and farmed in Tanzania. In 1974, he lost his 4,000-acre estate in Tanzania under a new government policy of Africanisation. In 1975, he controversially sold his ancestral home, Keir House, which had been in the family for nearly 600 years, along with 15,000 acres of land, without consulting other members of the Stirling clan. He died on 1 January 1983 at King Edward VII's Hospital for Officers. Bill Stirling played a crucial role in the early development of British special forces. He founded the original commando training centre at Lochailort and drafted much of the memorandum that outlined the concept for a parachute raiding unit, which later became the SAS. Gwilym Lee portrays Bill in series two (2025) of the television drama *SAS: Rogue Heroes*.

Lieutenant Colonel Sir Archibald David Stirling, Scots Guards

After his capture in January 1943 in Tunisia, David Stirling spent the rest of the war as a prisoner. He made several escape attempts before being sent to Colditz Castle. While in captivity there, he helped set up a British intelligence unit. In 1947, he transferred to the Army Reserve with the honorary rank of lieutenant colonel. In 1949, he founded the Capricorn Africa Society to fight African racial discrimination. He later formed private military companies to supply arms and soldiers to other nations. During the 1970s, he was linked to a failed attempt to overthrow Libyan leader Muammar Gaddafi and plans to undermine trade unionism.

In the mid-1970s, Stirling formed an organisation known as Great Britain 75 because he feared that the democratic order in the UK might break down. Reminiscent of the days of 8 Commando, he recruited ex-military men, mainly former SAS members from elite Mayfair clubs such as White's, to create a private army ready to step in if the government collapsed. David Stirling was knighted in the 1990 New Year's Honours shortly before his death. Stirling has been the subject of several books, such as *The Phantom Major* (1958), *David Stirling: Founder of the SAS* (1992) and *David Stirling: The Phoney Major* (2022). Actor Connor Swindells portrayed him in the historical drama *SAS: Rogue Heroes*.

Wing Commander Louis Strange, Royal Air Force

On 18 April 1940, aged 50, Strange returned to military service as a pilot officer in the Royal Air Force Volunteer Reserve. He served with 24 Squadron and led the Central Landing School at RAF Ringway. He later commanded the Merchant Ship Fighter Unit and helped plan Operation Overlord. He retired from the service in June 1945 after earning recognition with the OBE (Order of the British Empire) and an American Bronze Star. After the war, he returned to farming in Dorset. He stayed close to aviation and flew in several races during the early 1950s. He kept flying regularly until his death in 1966 at age 75. During his military career, he was awarded the Distinguished Service Order, the Military Cross and the Distinguished Flying Cross and Bar.

Major Charles 'Ivor' Jackson, Royal Tank Regiment

Charles 'Ivor' Jackson began his military career in 1925 as a lieutenant in the Royal Tank Corps. In 1927, he received a temporary commission as a Flying Officer with the RAF, attending 2 Flying Training School at Digby before serving with 4 (Army Co-operation) Squadron until 1931. After a brief return to the Tank Corps, he was seconded again to the RAF in 1936 and then returned to the army two years later. His career saw rapid promotions, from captain in 1935 to major in 1940, and briefly to lieutenant colonel when he commanded 2 Commando in 1940. However, he was later reduced back to major in 1941. Ultimately, his service concluded with a dismissal by general court martial in 1948.

Lieutenant General Sir Ernest 'Eric' Edward Down, Dorset Regiment

After taking command of the 11th SAS Battalion from Lieutenant Colonel Jackson, Ernest Down transformed the unit into a parachute infantry force. He quickly earned a reputation as a strict disciplinarian and effective trainer. His men soon dubbed him 'Dracula'. Down then led the 2nd Parachute Brigade and later served as the temporary commander of the 1st Airborne Division. He served as an adviser in India and helped train a new airborne division.

After the war, he commanded British troops in Greece and led the British Military Mission until 1949. Upon his return to England at the end of 1949, he was given command of the Mid-West District of the Western Command and the 53rd (Welsh) Infantry Division (Territorial Army). In 1952, he was promoted to lieutenant general and served as the general officer, commander-in-chief of the Southern Command for three years. After this, he retired from the army to Andover, Hampshire, at age 53. Eric Down later held the position of (honorary) colonel of the King's Shropshire Light Infantry from 1955 to 1957. He passed away in 1980 at the age of 78. A member of the 11th SAS Battalion noted that it took a long time for the men to realise that 'his stern and often uncompromising manner concealed a stout heart and a generous character.'

Lieutenant General Sir Frederick 'Boy' Browning, Grenadier Guards

During Operation Market Garden in 1944, Browning led the 1st Airborne Corps. In December 1944, he became chief of staff at South East Asia Command under Admiral Lord Louis Mountbatten. After the war, he served as military secretary at the War Office from 1946 to 1948. In January 1948, he became controller and treasurer to Princess Elizabeth. When she became queen in 1952, he worked as treasurer in the office of the Duke of Edinburgh. He began drinking heavily during the war, which is believed to have contributed to his nervous breakdown in 1957; he retired in 1959. He died on 14 March 1965 at Menabilly in Cornwall.

Frederick Browning is known as the 'father of the British airborne forces'. He overcame numerous equipment shortages and bureaucratic hurdles to transform a small parachute raiding force into a formidable military asset. The actor Dirk Bogarde portrayed Browning in the 1977 film *A Bridge Too Far*, which was based on the events of Operation Market Garden. The film portrays him as a cold, arrogant automaton, determined to proceed with the operation regardless of the risks. For many, including his widow, the famous novelist Daphne du Maurier, the film forever tarnished Browning's reputation.

Appendix A

The two documents reproduced here illustrate the development of British special forces doctrine during 1940 and 1941. Taken together, they trace the evolution from the early commando training methods established by Robert Laycock to the conceptual framework for parachute raiding operations proposed by David Stirling. Both documents are held in The National Archives and are reproduced with their original formatting and emphasis preserved.

Document 1: Training Instructions, No. 8 Commando

The following document was issued by Lieutenant Colonel Robert Laycock on 12 August 1940, just weeks after the formation of 8 Commando. It represents one of the earliest attempts to codify commando training methods and articulate the qualities required of special service volunteers. The instructions reveal how Laycock sought to balance the rigours of traditional military discipline with the unconventional skills demanded by raiding operations. Notably, the document emphasises that drill was 'merely a means to an end' and would never be employed operationally. The two sub-appendices detail the individual and collective training subjects that would prepare commandos for their hazardous work.

<u>SECRET.</u>

<u>Training Instructions,</u>
<u>No. 8 Commando.</u>

<u>1.   General.</u>
The ability of No. 8 Commando to accomplish successfully any task allotted to it will depend to a great extent on the training carried out by Troop and Section Leaders before an operation.

A rigid discipline is the first essential, followed by the development of a special technique. The attainment of the former is a comparatively easy matter, whilst that of the latter may prove to be more difficult because it differs in many respects from any other form of training to which the British Army has become accustomed.

2.   Discipline.

The most certain way of ensuring rigid discipline is by maintaining a high standard of drill and turnout. Troop Leaders will therefore order at least two drill parades per week and may allot further periods at their discretion. It has been found by experience that irregular units very soon deteriorate into a second rate rabble unless due attention is paid to drill, but, nevertheless, <u>it cannot be too firmly impressed upon all ranks that drill is merely a means to an end and that the movement of men in formed bodies or in regular formation will NEVER be employed by personnel of No. 8 Commando EXCEPT on drill parades which will be regarded as completely separate and distinct from all other forms of training.</u>

3.   Special Technique.

The attainment of the second essential (i.e. the development of a special technique) entails the acquirement, improvement and perfection of various characteristics in the Individual which will best suit him to the peculiar tasks which he may be called upon to carry out.

Those characteristics include:

Physical fitness.

Mental alertness.

The offensive spirit.

Complete disregard of danger.

The instinct of the hunter.

The lightning, destructive and ruthless methods of the gangster.

Absolute self-reliance.

A knowledge of various tricks, ruses, and devices.

And, above all, the ability to move and act at night fearlessly and noiselessly and to regard the blackest darkness as an aid rather than as a hindrance to the attainment of a difficult and hazardous objective.

Troops will soon realize that the raider who has the initiative will find that the advantage which the burglar possesses over the unsuspecting householder is automatically conferred upon himself.

It must however be borne in mind that personnel will not always be given individual tasks but may often operate in sub-units or even as a Commando.

Training may therefore be divided into Individual Training and Collective Training, the various aspects of which are set out in Appendices "A" and "B" attached.

4.   Esprit-de-Corps.

No. 8 Commando is a force of volunteers recruited from the finest Regiments of the British Army, and undoubtedly, more will be expected from us than from other less fortunate units. Every man must be made to feel proud of belonging to No. 8 Commando and must at all times personally ensure that the highest traditions are maintained. Officers and men must get to know each other and must learn to rely on one another.

The Troops within the Commando are more or less organised on the Regimental basis, but, whereas each Troop must strive to prove itself superior to the others, each individual must work for No. 8 Commando as a whole whether he be a Gunner or a Guardsman, a Light Infantryman or a Household Cavalryman, a Rifleman or a Sapper. Petty jealousies will not be tolerated and cases of "scrapping" between soldiers from different Regiments will invariably be dealt with by expulsion from the Commando.

5.   Security.

All ranks must be made to realize that the nature of the employment of a Commando calls for the strictest secrecy. Every individual must learn to be "security-minded", and secrecy must become a fetish.

The British race is notoriously inefficient in this respect, and there have already been indications that matters concerning Commandos have been discussed injudiciously.

All ranks are forbidden to discuss any military matter (however remotely connected with Commandos) with unauthorised persons. This particularly applies to soldiers on leave. The severest possible disciplinary action will be taken in all cases of infringement of this regulation.

6.   P.A.D.

During the time whilst the Commando remains in the Training Area, Troop Leaders are responsible for ensuring that adequate P.A.D. and Anti-gas measures are maintained.

Appendix "A".
Individual Training.
Weapons, etc.

TOET,
Rifle and Bayonet.
Telescopic Rifle.
Pistol.
L.M.G. (incl. A.A. from boats, ships, etc.).
Machine Carbine.
Grenades (incl. stick grenades).

3" Mortar.
Smoke Generators.
Verey Lights.
Rockets.
Incendiary Bombs.
Improvised Bombs.
Optical instruments (telescope, binoculars, stereoscope).
Wire Cutters.
Bangalore Torpedoes.
Prismatic Compass.
Knives and Knob-kerries.
Enemy Weapons.

<u>General Subjects.</u>

P.T. (incl. Boxing and Ju-jitsu).
X Swimming (and life-saving) with and without life-belts and with and without arms.
Marching.
X Running.
X Boat-work (incl. rowing the storage or arms and equipment and the trans-shipment from ships to small boats).
X Climbing (ropes, poles, houses, cliffs).
X Map Reading.
Field sketching.
Reading Air Photographs.
X Way-finding (stars, etc.).
X Inquisitiveness and Observation.
X Concealment and camouflage (incl. disguises and face blacking).
X Scouting and Sniping.
Reports and messages.
X Elementary Signals (incl. improvised, visual code).
X Self-defence (unarmed combat).
X Thuggery.
X Wire-cutting.
X Demolitions.
X Incendiarism.
X Sabotage.
X Knots and lashings (incl. gagging and securing prisoners).
X Methods of dealing with prisoners.
Action on being taken prisoner.

Notes on the enemy.
Foreign words and phrases (verbal impersonation).
Mess tin cooking.
Periods of abstinence from alcohol and tobacco (ordered from time to time by H.Q.)
X First Aid.
Water Chlorination.
X Subjects marked thus will be practiced at night.

Appendix "B".
Collective Training.

(Progressive stages of: Sub-section Training.
Section Training.
Troop Training.
Commando Training).

Working by night and laying-up by day.
Street Fighting (incl storming of Hotels, H.Q.s and billets).
Wood Fighting.
Patrols and Forays.
Securing of Prisoners and Documents.
Combined Operations (Co-operation with the R.N. and operations from ships)
(Co-operation with the R.A.F. and operations from aeroplanes.)
Visit to and schemes connected with the sabotage of:
M.T. Vehicles (incl. A.F.Vs.)
Dumps (incl. oil dumps).
Docks.
Power Houses.
Factories.
Telephone Exchanges and land and air lines.
Wireless Stations.
Railway Installations (incl stations, signals, tracks, etc.)
Aerodromes.
Water Supply.
Locks and Dams.
Laying of booby traps and delayed-action mines.
Avoidance of enemy defensive installations.
All the above will be practised at night.

Document 2: Training of Parachute Troops

This memorandum, submitted by Lieutenant David Stirling in the summer of 1941, outlined the concept for a parachute raiding unit in the Middle East. Written in the aftermath of Layforce's disbandment, the document argued that small parties dropped at night could achieve strategic results that seaborne raids could not. Stirling's proposal drew directly on the training that 8 Commando volunteers had already received, noting that at least fifty guardsmen possessed 'the very especial qualifications required'. The memorandum formed the basis for what became L Detachment, Special Air Service Brigade, and is thus a founding document of the SAS.

<u>SECRET.</u>

<u>TRAINING OF PARACHUTE TROOPS</u>
(Suggestions from Lieut. D.A. Stirling, Scots Guards)

<u>INTRODUCTION.</u>
With the final disbandment of LAYFORCE there is now no organisation left for prosecuting raids on enemy lines of communication, aerodromes, oil dumps and other enemy dispositions on which damage can be inflicted.

This disbandment is taking place at a moment when the enemy have been forced to turn and expose their back on account of their total commitment in Russia—a moment which seems to be especially propitious for these raids.

The inability to take advantage of this situation in the NEAR EAST is probably caused by the difficulties the Navy have in appropriating the ships for these raids and obtaining the necessary R.A.F. protection. But in England there is effective use being made of the opportunity. With the superior resources of the Navy and R.A.F. at home, they have been able to effect several Commando landings on occupied territory.

If, then, in the Near East, raids of this nature cannot be seaborne, I suggest the immediate establishment of a parachute training centre to supply the answer by air.

The operations of this centre would be necessarily of the strategical type. The Germans have demonstrated with huge losses of personnel (in Crete) that the tactical landing of parachutists is not practicable except in the face of wholly unorganised opposition. On the other hand, they have emphasised with many successes (notably in Greece) the results to be gained by small-scale strategical landings, but so far they have only exploited the daylight possibilities of these strategical landings as part of the process of their offensives. A classical example was their landing in Northern Greece behind our lines to prevent the demolition of a Key Bridge in the face of their advance.

While the enemy in Libya and elsewhere labour under the present restriction of reinforcements of material and men, the landings of small parties at night on a wide range of objectives will produce maximum effect. The enemy will be forced to withdraw from the front considerable bodies of men to protect these objectives, and the material successfully sabotaged, he will find harder to replace. Group-Captain Guest of the Western Desert R.A.F., H.Q., has been approached for his advice and he is convinced of the project's soundness. He strongly maintained the practicability of night parachute landings and the results to be obtained from them. Furthermore, he confirmed that personnel and machines are available for training and operations.

It will be necessary to gain the cooperation of the S.N.O., Commanding Submarines. The withdrawal of parties after operations will usually have to be by submarines. Therefore, the operations must always be on a scale to warrant the use of a submarine's time. If the training of Parachutists in the Near East is to be undertaken, the enterprise should be divided into 2 Phases.

The 1st Phase.

The period in which a small training centre is established which will be both instructional and operational. The instruction at this stage will be designed to enable the original personnel to carry out within two weeks of establishment small scale operations at night.

These operations would be both useful in themselves and would provide the Air Force and ourselves the essential experience and information on which to develop the Training Centre and increase the scope of its activities.

The 2nd. Phase.

The expansion of the Training Centre to an establishment which could look after the training of recruits on a scale to make possible the night landing of 15 to 20 parties at the same time.

A proportion of the personnel of the 1st Establishment would become instructors in the 2nd or expanded establishment.

On the final disbandment of No. 8 Commando there will become available at least 50 Guardsmen who will have the very especial qualifications required in the personnel of the original establishment.

These men have for 11 months had a highly individual type of training which has developed their initiative, power of organisation and individual resource to a level which is impossible to achieve in the personnel of an ordinary infantry battalion. Continual night training over this period has accumulated for them a night wiseness and perception and a confidence of movement in the dark. They are thoroughly trained in the use of Tommy Guns and hand grenades and have had a grounding in elementary demolitions and handling of explosives.

In addition these men have the background of a Guardsman's training with the resulting high standard of routine efficiency and discipline.

I suggest the following type of training for the 1st. 50 personnel:

(1) Instructions in the mechanism and packing of parachutes.

(2) Physical training of a type to toughen them and reduce the risk of injury on landing.

(3) Further training in Demolition and Sabotage and the handling of explosives at night.

(4) Identification of different types of enemy aircraft, tanks, and armoured cars and the point at which they are most susceptible to sabotage.

(5) Instruction on any other type of demolition in which they might be engaged—oil dumps, water supplies, communications, etc.

(6) The writing of observation reports on what has been seen in enemy territory (in many operations they will be required to lie up) some days before or after the tackling of the objective.

(7) A refresher course in all types of training already completed during Special Service.

Appendix B

Operation Colossus: The Tragino Raid, 10–11 February 1941
On the night of 10 February 1941, thirty-eight men of X Troop, No. 11 Special Air Service Battalion, parachuted into southern Italy to destroy the Apulian Aqueduct near Tragino. Although the raiders reached their objective and detonated their charges, the damage was repaired within weeks, and all but one of the party were captured. Despite its limited tactical success, the operation was Britain's first airborne raid and provided valuable lessons for future operations. The documents reproduced below include the nominal roll of X Troop, the operational plan submitted for the Prime Minister's approval, Churchill's subsequent correspondence, and the official lessons learned report.

Operation Colossus

X Troop
The men of X Troop, No. 11 SAS Battalion, who dropped into Italy on the night of 10 February 1941.
Major Trevor Allan Gordon 'Tag' Pritchard, Royal Welch Fusiliers
Captain Christopher Gerald Lea, Lancashire Fusiliers
Captain Gerrard Daly, Royal Engineers
Lieutenant Anthony Deane-Drummond, Royal Signals
2nd Lieutenant George Robert Paterson, Royal Engineers
2nd Lieutenant Arthur Geoffrey Jowett, Highland Light Infantry
Pilot Officer Ralph Henry Lucky, Royal Air Force Volunteer Reserve
Warrant Officer II Arthur William Albert 'Taff' Lawley, Royal Army Service Corps
Sergeant Percy Priestly Clements, Leicestershire Regiment
Sergeant Edward William 'Little Jock' Durie, Royal Engineers
Sergeant Joe Shutt, Leicestershire Regiment

Sergeant John 'Big Jock' Walker, Royal Signals

Corporal C. E. McD. 'Derry' Fletcher, Sherwood Foresters (Nottinghamshire and Derbyshire Regiment)

Corporal J. E. Grice, North Staffordshire Regiment

Corporal Philip Julian, Royal Engineers

Corporal Peter O'Brien, Royal Engineers

Lance-Corporal Harry Boulter, North Staffordshire Regiment

Lance-Corporal Douglas 'Flash' Henderson, Coldstream Guards

Lance-Corporal Doug E. Jones, Royal Engineers

Lance-Corporal Jim E. Maher, Royal Engineers

Lance-Corporal Harry Pexton, South Staffordshire Regiment

Lance-Corporal Harry Tomlin, Royal Engineers

Lance-Corporal Robert Brimer 'Mad Bob' Watson, Royal Engineers

Private Ernest Humphrey, Royal East Kent Regiment

Private Nicola Nastri (using the pseudonym John Tristan), Oxfordshire and Buckinghamshire Light Infantry

Private Albert Samuels, East Lancashire Regiment

Sapper 'Jock' W. Crawford, Royal Engineers

Sapper R. Davidson, Royal Engineers

Sapper Alf Parker, Royal Engineers

Sapper James Parker, Royal Engineers

Sapper Owen D. J. Phillips, Royal Engineers

Driver Glyn Pryor, Royal Engineers

Sapper Alan B. Ross, Royal Engineers

Sapper David L. Struthers, Royal Engineers

Fortunato Picchi (using the pseudonym Private Pierre Dupont), Special Operations Executive.

<u>MOST SECRET.</u>

<u>PROJECT "T"</u>

<u>Object</u>

1. To cut off the water supply from the province of APULIA (including TARANTO, BRINDISI, BARI and FOGGIA) for at least one month, by destroying the bridge carrying the Apulian Aqueduct over the stream at TRAGINO, about 38 miles E.N.E. of SALERNO.

Note: Local water supplies are quite inadequate if the aqueduct is cut.

<u>Method</u>

2. It is proposed to drop a demolition party of Special Service Air Battalion troops to carry out the task. An advance party of 2 Italian-speaking men will be dropped either on D minus 1 night or slightly earlier on D1 night to cut the telephone wires. The demolition party will be covered by a small covering force.

3.   After the operation the party will have to make its way 50 miles by road to the GULF OF SALERNO where a submarine will be waiting on D + 8 and again, if necessary, on D + 15, if C. in C. Mediterranean can arrange.

4.   The whole party will operate from MALTA.

<u>Forces Required</u>
5.   <u>Men</u>

(a) <u>Advance Party</u>	2 Italian-speaking men (these are available)
(b) <u>Demolition Party</u>	2 officers, 16 sappers
(c) <u>Covering Party</u>	1 officer, 15 men
Total Operational party	3 officers, 33 men
(d) <u>Maintenance Party</u>	3 Whitley fitters (inc. 1 N.C.O.)
	3 Whitley riggers
	2 parachute packers (inc. 1 N.C.O.)
Total Maintenance party	8
GRAND TOTAL	44 men.

This does <u>not</u> include aircraft crews.

6.   <u>Aircraft</u>
(a) <u>For journey to MALTA</u>

5 Bombays @ 4 men =	20
2 Whitleys @ 5 men =	10

2 "spare" aircraft	
2 Sunderland @ 7	
men + equipment =	14
	44

(b) <u>For Operation</u>

D minus 1 day—	1 Whitley @ 2 Adv. Party =	2
D1 day—	5 Bombays @ 6 men =	30
	1 Whitley @ 4 men =	4
		36

7. <u>Stores</u>

Explosives, etc.—2,100 lbs divided into 3 loads of 700 lbs.

Arms & wood packing—as necessary.

These will be dropped in Supply Dropping Apparatus Mk VI and in the special arms containers.

8. <u>Training</u>

This will he carried out at C.L.E., Ringway, and R.E. School, Christchurch.

9. <u>Command</u>

The system of joint command to be adopted.

<u>MOST SECRET.</u>

<u>PRIME MINISTER.</u>

<u>PROJECT "T".</u>

The Chiefs of Staff have had under consideration a project prepared by the Director of Combined Operations and his Staff, for cutting off the water supply from towns in the heel of Italy by dropping parachutists to destroy the Apulian Aqueduct. Local water supplies are quite inadequate, and the interruption of this source of supply would prove very embarrassing to the Italians. The damage would take 6–12 weeks to repair.

2. I attach a Summary of the proposed Operation (Flag 'A') together with a photograph of the aqueduct (Flag 'B'). Maps and further details can be furnished should you require them.

3. It is proposed to carry out the Operation in the moonlight period of 10th/19th February, which means sending the party out to Malta about the 4th February. It will require over 3 weeks to prepare the necessary aircraft and to carry out rehearsals of the Operation. An early decision is therefore desirable.

4. The Chiefs of Staff have examined the project and consider that there are reasonable chances of success. They therefore recommend that you should approve the Operation. It can, of course, always be cancelled any time up to the 4th February without incurring serious disadvantages, as troops and aircraft specially fitted for a role of this nature may at any time prove very useful to us.

(Signed) H.L. ISMAY.

<u>28th January, 1941.</u>
I approve. [Initialled] W.S.C. 9/1/41.

10 Downing Street, Whitehall

PRIME MINISTER'S PERSONAL MINUTE
SERIAL No. D. 48/1

GENERAL ISMAY.

I do not remember having been consulted in any way upon the proposal to land parachute troops in Italy.

I remember hearing about the project to land men from a submarine to attack bridges from the coast. The use of parachute troops was a serious step to take, in view of the invasion aspect here, and I would rather not have opened this chapter, raising as it does all sorts of questions about the status and uniform of these troops.

Let me have a report as soon as possible upon the preparation and execution of this plan, showing exactly what authorities were consulted. Make sure that for the future my initial is obtained to all projects of this character.

WSC
15.2.41

OFFICE OF THE MINISTER OF DEFENCE

<u>SECRET</u>

<u>PRIME MINISTER.</u>
With reference to your Minute No. D.48/1 (Flag "A").
2.   I attach a Minute (Flag "B") which was submitted to you outlining the Operation. In paragraph 1 of the Minute, reference was made to the proposal to land parachutists. You will see that you approved the Operation on 9th February.
3.   I attach (Flag "C") a further Minute submitted to you prior to the Operation, and at (Flag "D") a Minute suggesting one possible reason for its failure.
4.   The Operation was conceived and prepared by the Director of Combined Operations and was approved by the Chiefs of Staff for submission for your approval. No other authorities were consulted, nor were any others cognisant of the plan, except the local Commanders who were required to give certain facilities to the troops taking part.
5.   If further information concerning the actual Operation should come to light, it will be submitted to you.

<u>15 February 1941.</u>

Most Secret

Offices of the War Cabinet
Richmond Terrace
Whitehall, S.W.1.
13th February, 1941.

Prime Minister

The Secretary to the Chiefs of Staff Committee has just informed me that a decision has been taken this afternoon by the Chiefs of Staff to cancel the arrangements which had been made to attempt to rescue by submarine the thirty-six parachutist troops who volunteered for a hazardous enterprise. I understand that this decision has been arrived at on the suspicion that the point of withdrawal may have been compromised by a code signal made by one of the aircraft which was employed in a diversion prior to making a forced landing.

In view of the fact that there is 100 fathoms of water within seven miles of the rescue position, the orders given by the Vice-Admiral Malta to the Submarine Commander, and the arrangements made with A.O.C. Mediterranean to give warning to the submarine in the event of enemy patrol activity, I consider our failure to make any effort to carry out the salvage arrangements, promised to the parachutists, amounts to a clear breach of faith.

I do beg of you to instruct that the decision as to whether the rescue is to be attempted or not be left to the Vice Admiral Malta who, under the C. in C. Mediterranean, is the authority on the spot.

[Handwritten signature] Roger Keyes

A section of a report on the lessons learned during the Tragino Raid, 13 February 1941.

5. Conclusion.

The failure of the operation cannot yet be explained. Although the order and times of dropping were not exactly as planned, the whole of the 'X' troop force was dropped, apparently under good conditions, in the vicinity of the objective. The charges, ladders, and equipment dropped were the full amount required for execution of the complete demolition plan. The arms containers dropped contained 2 Bren Guns and 7 Tommy Guns and ammunition. While the lack of 7 further Tommy Guns may have been serious, nevertheless the Force could probably give a good account of itself with the arms available and their personal weapons—and, in any case, no sign of opposition was observed from the air. The late arrival of Captain Daly was no doubt a serious handicap, but every member of the demolition party was familiar with the objective as it was thought to exist, if it was in fact the western bridge and not that on the main stream, the party Could not have failed to recognise it, since in attacking the adjacent farm, many must have passed close to it, and their rendezvous was in fact within 100 yards of it. It seems impossible that some vital piece of equipment necessary for the demolition was lost or not taken on the operation. The only possibilities that seem to remain are that:

The details of the operation were known to the enemy, and the party was captured immediately upon making the ground.

That the objective was entirely different in construction from the anticipated design, and the equipment available was insufficient for its destruction.

It is a significant fact that up to 1930 hours on the night prior to the operation no one concerned had any knowledge of a second bridge within about 230 yards of that over the Tragino.

A number of points have emerged having a bearing upon any future operations of a similar nature.

1. It is clear that up to date intelligence supported by air photographs is absolutely essential at the time of planning the operation, and that the parachute party and the Captains and crews of aircraft must have ample time to study and memorise the details of the terrain.

2. The time required for dropping at night on an objective not previously known, even in ideal conditions, is much longer than was thought necessary. After arrival at the rendezvous, the Air Attack Commander requires 10 minutes for reconnaissance and to confirm the arrival of other aircraft. Each aircraft should be allowed at least 10 minutes for general reconnaissance of the area before dropping. Approximately 10 minutes is required from giving Zero until dropping begins. 5 minutes must be allowed to each aircraft for making runs over the target. In these circumstances, considerable disturbance in the target area seems unavoidable when parachute troops are employed at night.

3. For the actual dropping, all available eyes must be employed. In a Whitley, it is desirable that the navigator, in the front turret, should direct the run-up. The second pilot, looking downwards, should work the red and green signal lights, the Captain should concern himself primarily with the flying of the aircraft, and the rear gunner must observe the dropping and report to the Captain immediately the last man has gone, so that he can put on engine and get clear, and if necessary, make a second run to release containers that have not fallen. Moreover, up to the time of the first drop, it is essential that the Attack Commander Ground and the Attack Commander Air be in personal contact so that decisions regarding the sufficiency of the available force, the timing of the operation and details of the attack can be taken together. It is thought that the Attack Commander Ground should not be a Section Commander but should drop separately on a second run.

4. The present arrangement for container release is not satisfactory. The five-pin plug should be put in and fixed before the flight begins. The container cells should be selected, the distributor timing set and the distributor then set to "safe". When "prepare for action" is given, the navigator will then turn the distributor to "Distributor" and confirm that the Section Commander has the tell-tale light in the fuselage on. Alternatively, it is thought that when containers are dropped last, the navigator could very well release them on a signal from the rear gunner that the last man has gone.

5. The present design of the container must be entirely revised, and the bomb release gear must be studied to ascertain that it will function properly with large containers. The new design should incorporate a rigid harness that can be fixed to the bomb rack and firmly stabilised before the container is raised into position. A mechanical means of raising the container to the harness should be provided so that one or two men can fix or lower containers.

The dimensions of the container must be such that there is no possibility of jamming in the bomb cell.

6. Army personnel should be given opportunities to become completely familiar with the aircraft use and their bomb release equipment and should have more air experience under operational conditions than was possible in the case of the present operation.

Signed for Wing Commander Sir Nigel Norman Bt. (Absent on duty)

13th February 1941.

Appendix C

This letter from Robert Laycock to Lord Lovat, dated 3 December 1942, offers a candid insight into the tensions that could arise between Guards officers and their counterparts from other services and social backgrounds.

<u>COPY</u>
Ref: SS/151/G.1.
3rd December, 1942.
My dear Shimi,
When will you learn some tact? I know that it is uphill work dealing with touchy officers who, to put it very snobbishly, do not come from the same social strata as those with whom you were used to deal in peacetime in the Brigade—yet, nevertheless, you <u>must</u> learn to bear with them.

A little forethought on your part will often make for a better feeling between the Services, which is so frightfully important in Combined Ops.

As an example, I was horrified to hear the other day (though I admit that it is now past history) that the Captain of, I think, the Prince Charles? had received a letter of appreciation after Dieppe from No. 4 Commando—a gesture in the right direction—but one which was entirely ruined because it started: "I am directed by my Commanding Officer" and finished up by being signed by the <u>Adjutant</u>.

The Navy, especially the R.N.R. and R.N.V.R. , are really touchy about this sort of thing which I should have thought you would have known by now. Commanding Officers of H.M. Ships expect letters to them from Army Units signed by the Colonel and NOT by the Adjutant.

If you are too busy to write your letters yourself by all means get someone to draft them for you, but for God's sake sign them yourself.

To be absolutely frank with you I think you are inclined to be getting a reputation for arrogance, which is a pity. Please rectify this.

You know me well enough to realise that I do not mean by any of the foregoing that I wish you to take a tolerant view of inefficiency or complacency which you may meet in officers either in the Army or in the other Services. But do for goodness sake <u>think</u> before you commit yourself and remember that sarcasm and arrogance never got anyone anywhere yet!!

It ought to be quite unnecessary for me to have to waste time writing you this sort of letter. I trust that you will not give me cause to do so again.

Yours,

BOB.

Appendix D

In November 1948, Colonel David Stirling prepared this memorandum for the Staff College at Camberley, setting out his account of the origins of the Special Air Service Regiment.

STAFF COLLEGE CAMBERLEY 1948 COURSE: HISTORY OF S.A.S.

<u>MEMORANDUM BY COL. DAVID STIRLING, DSO, OBE.</u>
<u>ON THE ORIGINS OF THE SPECIAL AIR SERVICE REGT.</u>
CONFIDENTIAL
PRELIMINARY
I came out to the Middle East with the Guards Commando in January 1941, which formed part of Layforce.

The particular purpose for which Layforce had been brought out was a combined operation on the island of Rhodes. The success of the Germans in the Western Desert and in Greece, developments which took place after the arrival of Layforce in Africa, had rendered this objective abortive.

Layforce in the succeeding period up to about July was split up and used independently in a variety of roles, including the holding of a small section of the Tobruk perimeter; the covering of the evacuation of Crete, an opposed landing off the coast of Syria, and in various raids on the Cyrenaica coastline.

No. 8 Commando, to which I was attached, was at this time based at Mersa Matruh and had been engaged in three raids on objectives along the Cyrenaica coast—two against coastal communications in the Gazala area and one against an aerodrome near Bomba. All three raids were planned on the same pattern— approach by either Gun Boat or Destroyer, so timed that the landing on the coast took place as early as possible in the night to allow the greatest possible period of darkness for the carrying out of the operation. In each case, about 20 Officers and men took part. The raids failed in the case of the Destroyer due to rough weather and in the case of the Gun Boats, due to being spotted by enemy reconnaissance aircraft, which was followed by intense bombing which resulted in damage and, more importantly, loss of surprise.

In the meantime, the C.G.S. had decided to disband Layforce. The reasons for his decision were presumed to be:

(a) The Commandos had been brought out from England at a time when it appeared that the M.E.F. had only Italians to contend with and when it appeared that the Italians were beaten. It was believed, therefore, that a small, well-planned combined operation on Rhodes, carried out by well-equipped Commando Units, would enable such a force to occupy the island. However, as already indicated, the situation had entirely altered with the appearance of the Germans in Greece, Crete, and the Desert.

(b) The Commando training establishment and equipment were not adjusted to defensive tactical operations, and the necessary facilities, such as Naval Units, could not be spared for offensive raids because the general situation was too grave to be able to afford them.

(c) The greatest shortage of reinforcements due to losses in Greece, Crete, and the Desert caused the A.G. Branch of M.E.H.Q. to look upon Layforce as a heaven-sent reservoir of bodies which could be allocated to formations requiring reinforcements.

During the last period before the disbandment of Layforce, Brigadier Laycock had authorised Jock Lewes (of the Welsh Guards), myself, and six Other Ranks to experiment with some parachutes we heard had arrived in the Middle East (by error—they had been intended for India). This was on Lewes' initiative. We succeeded in borrowing an old Valencia aircraft for an afternoon and each of us did a jump. The static lines were secured to the aircraft seat legs. I was unlucky and landed on rocky ground and severely injured my back. This resulted in two months in hospital, which gave an ideal opportunity to evaluate the factors which would justify the creation of a special service unit, to carry on the Commando role, and amass a case to present to the C-in-C in favour of such a Unit.

My written appreciation to the C-in-C (which led to the formation of "L" Detachment) was on these lines:

(a) I pointed out that the Enemy was exceedingly vulnerable to attack along the line of his coastal communications and on his various transport parks, aerodromes, and other targets strung out along the coast, and that the role of No 8 Commando, which had attempted raids on these targets, was a most valuable one.

(b) I submitted that the scale on which the Commando raids had been planned, i.e., the number of bodies employed on the one hand and the scale of equipment and facilities on the other, prejudiced surprise beyond all possible compensating advantage in respect of the defensive and aggressive striking power afforded; and that, moreover, the facilities that the Navy had to provide to lift the Force resulted in the risking of Naval Units valuable out of all proportion to the maximum possible success of the raid.

(c) I argued the advantages of establishing a Unit based on the principle of the fullest exploitation of surprise and of making the minimum demands on manpower and equipment. I argued that the application of this principle would mean in effect the employment of a sub-unit of five men to cover a target previously requiring four troops of a Commando, i.e., about 200 men. I sought to prove that, if an aerodrome or transport park was the objective of an operation, then the destruction of 50 aircraft or units of transport was more easily accomplished by a sub-unit of five men than by a force of 200 men. I further concluded that 200 properly selected, trained, and equipped men, organised into sub-units of five should be able to attack at least thirty different objectives at the same time on the same night as compared to only one objective using the Commando technique; and that only 25% success in the former was equivalent to many times the maximum possible result in the latter.

(d) I insisted with the C-in-C that the Unit must be responsible for its own training and operational planning and that, therefore, the Commander of the Unit must come directly under the C-in-C. I emphasised how fatal it would be for the proposed unit to be put under any existing Branch or formation for administration. (I was determined to combat in advance any risk of being taken over by G(R), the Middle East equivalent of S.O.(E), which was already showing signs of being the monstrous and inefficient octopus it later became; or coming under the control of the Director of Combined Operations.) I pointed out that the Head of any such Branch or Formation would have less experience than myself or my successor in the medium in which we proposed to operate.

(e) In order to help sell the proposition, I put forward a detailed plan for the employment of the Unit in the approaching offensive (November 1941), the preparation for which was no secret.

The proposed operation (which was in fact undertaken) was, in brief, to drop by parachute five parties on the night of D minus 2 to attack the five main forward Fighter and Bomber Enemy landing grounds, at Timini and Gazala. The DZs of these sub-units were to be some 12 miles south into the Desert from their objectives, and they were to be dropped at night without moon, thus preserving surprise to the utmost. A heavy raid on the Gazala and Timini areas, with the dropping of many flares, was to be laid on in order to assist the aircraft carrying out the lift to establish a point on the coastline from which the navigators could have fixed line bearings for the DZ. After re-assembling on the DZs, each party was to spend the balance of that night getting to the pre-arranged lying up place from which, the next day, they could observe their target. The following night (D minus 1 to D), each party was to carry out its raid so as to arrive on the landing grounds at the same time. Each party was to carry a total of about 60 incendiary cum explosive bombs equipped with two-hour, half-hour, ten-minute time pencils and also a twelve-second time fuse. (Thus, in the early stages of the raid, a two-hour time pencil was used, followed later on by the one-hour and the half-hour, thereby reducing the risk of the enemy removing the bombs after the warning given by the first explosion.)

After the raid, the Sections were to retire into the Desert to a pre-arranged meeting place south of the Trig el Abd, where a patrol of the L.R.D.G. would pick them up.

Having submitted these proposals to the C-in-C, I was three days later summoned to the D.C.G.S., Maj-Gen Neil Ritchie. He took me along to the C-in-C and OGS, and after some discussion, they agreed that the Unit should be formed forthwith and that I should continue to plan the operation proposed in conjunction with the DMO. Being at that time only a Subaltern, they promoted me to Captain and gave me authority to recruit the Unit from Layforce, and if this did not provide the number required, from certain forward formations in the Desert.

ORIGIN OF THE S.A.S. NAME

At the time of the Unit's formation, about the end of July 1941, Brigadier Dudley Clarke (later of "A" force) was responsible for a Branch in the Middle East which dealt, among other things, with enemy deception. One of his objectives was to persuade the enemy that there was a fully equipped parachute and glider brigade in the Middle East. To help delude the enemy, he used to drop dummy parachutists to simulate training exercises near POW cages, and he also parked bogus gliders in the Desert, hoping for photographic reconnaissance by the enemy. He called this phantom brigade the first S.A.S. Brigade.

Dudley Clarke welcomed the creation of a flesh-and-blood parachute unit, which greatly assisted him in his game with the enemy. To humour him, we agreed to name our unit "L" Detachment, S.A.S. Brigade. This was the origin of the name Special Air Service. Having helped him on this, Dudley Clarke gave constant assistance and help in the early days of the establishment of "L" Detachment.

RECRUITMENT

The original establishment passed by the War Establishment Committee for "L" Detachment was 7 Officers and about 60 ORs with a very high proportion of NCOs. The Unit was divided down into 5 troops, each of which had two Sections of 10 men and an NCO or Officer in command—the balance was made of HQ and camp Staff.

I recruited the bulk of the Unit from Layforce, which had by this time been largely disbanded. They were first-class material and all of them had already had considerable operational experience and had done a good deal of night training. I also got a few men from my own Regiment, the Scots Guards, who had a Battalion in the Desert.

I found, during this and subsequent stages, that the A.G. Branch was unfailingly obstructive and uncooperative. Most Branches of the Middle East HQ were helpful at the top level, but astonishingly tiresome at the middle or lower levels. The A.G. Branch was unfortunately obstructive right up to the top, and it was only by appealing to the DCGS that I could ever have made my way. You will appreciate that it was essential for me to get the right Officers, and I had a great struggle to get them. In particular, I wanted Jock Lewes, who I reckoned would be the ideal Officer for the Unit's training programme. I finally extricated him, and he arrived a week after the Unit's formation at Kabrit.

TRAINING

The formation of the Unit was completed at Kabrit in early August 1941, thus allowing a period of about three months to train for the Gazala/Timini operation. The Unit, during this period, had also to be trained to operate on the general lines indicated in Paragraph 7. Jock Lewes, who was in full charge of the training, was the best training officer I have ever associated with or heard of in the War. (He was also brilliant operationally.)

We had to devise parachute training methods from scratch. Repeated requests to Ringway produced no assistance whatsoever. Finally, after we had lost two men in our only fatal accident throughout training, I sent a final appeal to Ringway, and they sent some training notes and general information, which arrived at the end of October after the completion of our parachute training course. Included in this information, we discovered that Ringway had had a fatal accident caused by exactly the same effect as in our case. Therefore, if they had sent the information earlier, we would have undoubtedly avoided this accident. (Mention of this episode and other rather derogatory remarks in these notes are for your own information, obviously not for publication.) In favour of Ringway, I must add that they sent us out Captain Peter Waugh, who arrived three days before the Gazala operation, and he was most useful in the final preparations. Waugh stayed with us and later joined the SAS.

In our training programme, the principle on which we worked was entirely different from that of the Commandos. A Commando unit, having once been selected from a batch of volunteers, was committed to those men and had to nurse them up to the required standard. "L" Detachment, on the other hand, had set a minimum standard to which all ranks had to attain and we had to be most firm in returning to their units those who were unable to reach that standard.

I might also add that we insisted on the Brigade of Guards' standard of discipline and smartness of turnout. There had grown up in the Commandos a tradition that to be a tough Regiment, it was necessary to act tough all the time in the Barracks and on leave and they were liable to be badly dressed, ill-disciplined, and noisy in the streets and restaurants of Cairo. We insisted with "L" Detachment that toughness should be reserved entirely for the benefit of the enemy.

FIRST PARACHUTE OPERATION S.A.S. NOVEMBER 1941

This operation was undertaken without any modification as planned and put forward to the C-in-C in Paragraph 7. Unfortunately, the night on which it took place was almost unbelievably unsuitable for a parachute operation. There was no moon, and the wind was so strong that on arriving in our Bombay aircraft over the Gazala coastline, the flares dropped by the Wellington bombers were quite insufficient for our navigators to pick up any fixed point on the coast because the Desert sand and dust were obscuring the whole coastline. Therefore, in effect, the navigators had to take potluck in their dead reckoning, and as far as I know, no party was dropped within 10 miles of the selected DZs. One of the five Bombays never dropped its stick of parachutists at all but landed the next morning on the Gazala landing ground with the whole unit still on board. This fantastic affair was brought about by a chain of mischance. The Captain of the aircraft had decided that conditions were too bad to drop his party and was, therefore, returning to his base when engine trouble occurred. He had to make a forced landing in the Desert. After the engine was repaired, he radioed for a direction beam, which was promptly provided by the German staff on one of the Gazala landing grounds. Unsuspecting, the Captain accepted the course and a little later discovered that his Bombay was being escorted by German fighters, which forced him to put down on the main Fighter landing ground at Gazala. The fate of the four other parties was a mixed one. Two men were killed on landing, owing to the severity of conditions, and of the rest only 18 ORs and 4 Officers (Paddy Mayne, who later commanded the 1st SAS Regiment, Bill Fraser, Jock Lewes, and myself) got to the LRDG rendezvous. Thus, the operation was a complete failure.

SUBSEQUENT OPERATIONS

December 1941/March 1942

During these four months, we carried out about 20 actual raids against various targets, mostly enemy landing grounds, which the C-in-C had laid down should be top priority. These raids included targets at Nofilia, Agheila, Buerat, Sirte (twice), Tamet (twice), Berce, Berka, and Benina (twice). We destroyed about 115 aircraft and also a considerable number of enemy road transport units—we concentrated particularly on heavy diesel and petrol-carrying vehicles. All these raids were carried out in conjunction with the LRDG, who were able to drop us more comfortably and more accurately within striking distance of the target area than was possible from the air. Our casualties were very light but unfortunately included Jock Lewes, who was killed by enemy bombing while returning from a raid on the Marble Arch aerodrome.

Our method of operation, apart from the means of arrival, was very much as planned for the Gazala/Timini raids.

April, May, and June

About April, the Unit had been increased in size. "L" Detachment was recruited back to its old strength, and the recruits were undergoing training. I had taken on a Unit of 60 Free French parachutists under Captain Berget, all of whom had been parachute trained at Ringway. On arriving at Kabrit, they were given six weeks of intensive training in SAS methods. They were first-class operatives. In addition, Captain Buck with his German-speaking Unit had joined "L" Detachment. His Unit of a dozen men consisted mostly of ex-German regular soldiers who had got out of Germany before the war for political and other reasons.

Sometime in April or May 1942, an important convoy had assembled in Alexandria. Its safe arrival in Malta was vital. "L" Detachment offered to attack on the same night the main landing grounds from which the Intelligence Branch reckoned the enemy would conduct their main efforts at strafing the convoy. The operation went reasonably well. We attacked nine landing grounds, two of which were in Crete and seven in Cyrenaica, destroying a total of about 75 aircraft and grounding a good many more over the vital period. The two sub-units covering Crete were landed by submarine and folboat, whereas those in Cyrenaica were dropped by LRDG and picked up by them after the operation—that is, all except one party of French which arrived at their aerodrome as a party of POWs under German escort, the German escort being made up of Buck's Germans.

By the end of June, "L" Detachment had raided all the more important German and Italian aerodromes within 300 miles of the forward area at least once or twice and a few of them, even three or four times. Methods of defence were beginning to improve, and although the advantage still lay with "L" Detachment, the time had come to alter our own methods. Therefore, we developed the jeep with two sets of twin Vickers K guns or alternatively, one set of Vickers K guns and one Browning point 5. The astonishing agility of the jeep enabled us to approach a target at night over almost any country. The technique turned out to be most successful and enabled the Unit to be very much more flexible in its methods of operation.

By the end of July, the Unit was entirely motorized—our transport consisting of jeeps and four-wheeled drive 3-tonners. The LRDG had given us tremendous assistance in training a cadre of navigators and in many other ways and we were now self-supporting.

July to October

During the period which the 8th Army stood at El Alamein, we maintained almost continuously a base between Siwa and Mersa Matruh. Originally we had established this base and supplied it by infiltrating through the El Alamein position. When this became too much of an organised line, we established a route through the Quattara Depression. Later still, when our route across the Depression was mined and patrolled by the enemy at the Cara end, we had to divert our supplies and reinforcements along the Nile and across the Desert via El Kharga to the Kufra Oasis and North through the Great Sand Sea at Howards Cairn to our forward base near Siwa. Thus patrols had to cover nearly 1,800 miles to deal with an objective that might be only 40 miles from the 8th Army's forward positions.

The most important and least successful operation undertaken in this period was a large-scale raid on the harbour installations and shipping at Benghazi, which took place late in September. You can envisage the difficulties of supply in operating against a target as far away as Benghazi on a scale of a battalion. I lost about 50 three-tonners and about 40 jeeps on this raid, but fortunately not very many personnel. I had become committed to this Benghazi operation before I fully understood its implications and it was a sharp lesson which confirmed my previous views on the error of attacking strategic targets on a tactical scale. Prior to and subsequent to the Benghazi operation, our main efforts from our base near Siwa had been directed against enemy landing grounds and a variety of other targets, such as dumps of materials, wireless stations, coastal rest camps, transport parks, etc. We also frequently mined the main coastal road and left booby traps wherever opportunity offered. In early October, we abandoned the attacking of enemy landing grounds and concentrated on interrupting the enemy supply system, particularly their Desert railway line.

Mid-October to January 1943

After Rommel's rout at El Alamein, General Montgomery instructed us to continue our concentration exclusively on the enemy's communications. During late November, when Rommel was making an apparently determined effort to stabilise his position in the Agheila area, we were able to contribute quite importantly to Rommel's difficulties. On previous campaigns, it had been at Agheila that the supply position usually began to swing in favour of the enemy. We undertook at this stage to maintain continuously a patrol covering off over a 40-mile section of the enemy's coastal communications from Tripoli to Marble Arch. This required the establishment and supplying of 16 sub-bases from which 16 patrols could operate against the coastal communications at least twice or three times a week, each within their own allocated 40-mile sectors. This meant a minimum of about three to four raids every night somewhere on the enemy's main coastal communication between Tripoli and Agheila. In practice, the operation went very successfully east of and including the Buerat area. North of Wadi Zem Zem the country was very much more difficult for operations due to its dense population, and the SAS patrols, although very successful to start off with, were mostly driven off or rounded up after three weeks. However, we certainly succeeded in stopping enemy transport movement by night for a considerable period, thus forcing transport movement by day, which provided the RAF with good strafing targets. By the middle of January, we had shifted our activities westwards and were mounting patrols and continued raiding on enemy communications as far north as Sfax in Tunisia (incidentally, this is where I was captured by a German Reconnaissance Unit).

Endnotes

FOREWORD

1. Charles Messenger, *Commandos: The Definitive History of Commando Operations in the Second World War*, Kindle edition (London: William Collins, 2015), pp. 331–57.
2. The National Archives, Kew, London (TNA), CAB 106/3, History of the Combined Operations Organisation 1940–1945 (London, 1956), p. 108.
3. Richard Mead, *Commando General: The Life of Major-General Sir Robert Laycock KCMG, CB, DSO* (Barnsley: Pen & Sword Military, 2016), p. 87.
4. Peter Young, *Commando: A History of the Elite British Military Force and Its Operations in World War Two* (Bradford: Sapere Books, 1969 [2024]), p. 13.

CHAPTER 1

1. TNA, CAB 106/3, History of the Combined Operations Organisation 1940–1945, p. 11.
2. Hilary St George Saunders, *The Green Beret: The Story of the Commandos 1940–1945* (London: Michael Joseph Ltd, 1949), p. 21.
3. TNA, CAB 120/414, Office of the Minister of Defence, Subject: Strategy and Operations. Combined Operations—Organisation, etc. (3.6.1940–10.11.1943).
4. TNA, CAB 106/3, History of the Combined Operations Organisation 1940–1945, p. 83.
5. Messenger, *Commandos*, eBook location 228–54.
6. Messenger, *Commandos*, eBook location 331–57.
7. TNA, CAB 106/7, Combined Operations, The Commando Group, p. 21.

8. TNA, CAB 106/3, History of the Combined Operations Organisation 1940–1945, p. 12.

9. TNA, CAB 106/3, History of the Combined Operations Organisation 1940–1945, pp. 204–05.

10. TNA, CAB 106/3, History of the Combined Operations Organisation 1940–1945, pp. 108–09.

11. TNA, CAB 106/3, History of the Combined Operations Organisation 1940–1945, pp. 13–14.

12. Robin Neillands, *The Raiders: The Army Commandos, 1940–1946* (London: Weidenfeld and Nicolson, 1989), p. 25.

13. TNA, CAB 106/3, History of the Combined Operations Organisation 1940–1945, pp. 92–93.

14. TNA, CAB 106/7, Combined Operations, Development of Combined Operations Part 1. Historical Summary, p. 3.

15. TNA, CAB 106/7, Combined Operations, Development of Combined Operations Part 1. Historical Summary, pp. 4–5.

16. TNA, CAB 106/3, History of the Combined Operations Organisation 1940–1945, p. 93.

17. Saunders, *The Green Beret*, pp. 64–81.

18. TNA, CAB 120/414, Office of the Minister of Defence, Subject: Strategy and Operations. Combined Operations—Organisation, Etc. (3.6.1940–10.11.1943), Prime Minister's Personal Minutes.

19. Neillands, *The Raiders*, pp. 27–42.

CHAPTER 2

1. Captain J. A. Speares, 'Recollections of the 5th Special Reserve Battalion Scots Guards', *The Guards Magazine*, 1999, pp. 59–61; David Erskine, *The Scots Guards, 1919–1955* (London: William Clowes and Sons Ltd, 1956), pp. 21–26.

2. Alan Hoe, *David Stirling: The Authorised Biography of the Creator of the SAS* (London: Warner Books, 1992 [1994]), pp. 26–45; Gavin Mortimer, *David Stirling The Phoney Major: The Life, Times and Truth about the Founder of the SAS* (London: Constable, 2022 [2023]), pp. 9–43.

3. IWM Sound Archive, Interview with David Carol Mather, Catalogue No. 19629, reel 1, 1999.

4. Carol Mather, *With Stirling's SAS in the Desert* (Barnsley: Pen & Sword Military, 1997 [2021]), p. 16.

5. Erskine, *The Scots Guards*, p. 26.

6. Peter Kemp, 'Chapter Two: Operation "Knife"', in *No Colours or Crest: The Secret Struggle for Europe*, Kindle eBook, 1958, pp. 11–17.

7. Lord Lovat, *March Past: A Memoir By Lord Lovat* (London: Weidenfeld and Nicolson, 1978), pp. 175–180.

CHAPTER 3

1. TNA, WO 218/8, War Diary, No. 8 Commando, July–November 1940.
2. Mead, *Commando General*, pp. 73–84.
3. David Niven, *The Moon's a Balloon: The Guardian's Number One Hollywood Autobiography* (London: Penguin, 1984 [2005]), Kindle eBook, p. 284.
4. TNA, WO 218/8, War Diary, No. 8 Commando, July–November 1940.
5. Liddell Hart Centre for Military Archives (LHCMA), King's College London, Series LAYCOCK 1/1—Papers Relating to Volunteers for Special Service Brigade, 1940.
6. IWM Sound Archive, Interview with George Patrick John Rushworth Jellicoe, Later Lord Jellicoe, Catalogue No. 13039, reel 1.
7. Mortimer, *David Stirling*, p. 57.
8. 'Https://Theguardsdepot.Co.Uk/Shining-Parades-Swabbing-and-Losing-Your-Name/', *The Guards Depot*.
9. IWM Sound Archive, Interview with David Carol Mather, Catalogue No. 19629, reel 1.
10. John Lewes, *Jock Lewes: Co-Founder of the SAS*, Kindle edn (Barnsley: Pen & Sword Military, 2000 [2016]), pp. 131–58.
11. TNA, WO 199/1849, Formation of Irregular Commandos, June 1940– September 1942, Memorandum on the Selection of Volunteers for Special Service Units, 23 April 1941.
12. David Feebery, *Guardsman & Commando: The War Memoirs of RSM Cyril Feebery DCM* (Barnsley: Pen & Sword Military, 2008).
13. IWM Sound Archive, Interview with James Barlow Brooks Sherwood, British NCO Who Served with No. 8 Troop, No. 8 Commando, Catalogue No. 9783, Produced 1987, REEL 1.
14. LHCMA, Laycock 1/3, Engagement of Volunteers, Conditions of Service for All Personnel of Commandos, 1940.
15. IWM Sound Archive, Interview with James Barlow Brooks Sherwood, British NCO Who Served with No. 8 Troop, No. 8 Commando, Catalogue No. 9783, Produced 1987, REEL 1.
16. Saunders, *The Green Beret*, pp. 36–47.
17. Keith Briant, *Fighting with the Guards* (London: Evans Bros. Ltd, 1958), pp. 15–18.
18. Feebery, *Guardsman & Commando*, p. 29.
19. T. G. Lea, 'The Employment and Development of Britain's Second World War Commando, 1940–1941' MA diss. (University of Chester, 2010), pp. 34–36

20. Michael Davie (ed.), *The Diaries of Evelyn Waugh* (London: Phoenix, 1976 [1995]), p. 491.
21. IWM Sound Archive, Interview with James Barlow Brooks Sherwood, British NCO Who Served with No. 8 Troop, No. 8 Commando, Catalogue No. 9783, Produced 1987, REEL 1.
22. Mortimer, *David Stirling*, p. 58.
23. TNA, DEFE 2/54, Commando War Diaries. SS Brigade Vol. I. 1st Oct 1940–31st Aug 1941, Appendix II, Ref. BM. 2/4, Notes on the Re-Organisation of Special Service Units.
24. TNA, DEFE 2/54, Commando War Diaries. SS Brigade Vol. I. 1st Oct 1940–31st Aug 1941, SPECIAL SERVICE BRIGADE, Training Instructions, BM.17/2., Sheet 8, Certain difficulties which face Battalion Commanders.
25. TNA, DEFE 2/54, Commando War Diaries. SS Brigade Vol. I. 1st Oct 1940–31st Aug 1941, POINTS OF DISCIPLINE AND TRAINING LECTURE GIVEN TO OFFICERS OF EACH BATTALION DURING DECEMBER 1940, p. 3.

CHAPTER 4

1. Joll and Weldon, *The Drum Horse in the Fountain*, p. xiii.
2. Christopher Joll and Anthony Weldon, *The Drum Horse in the Fountain & Other Tales of Heroes and Rogues in the Guards* (London: Nine Elms Publishing, 2018), p. xiii.
3. Part 3: Col. E. R. Hill Part 1: Col. R. J. Marker, DSO, Part 2: Maj. Gen. A. G. C. Dawnay, CBE, DSO, *The Record of the Coldstream Guards 1650–1950* (London: Williams Clowes and Sons Ltd, 1950), pp. 1–3.
4. Ian F. Beckett, 'Household Cavalry and Foot Guards', in *Discovering British Regimental Traditions*, 2nd edn (Princes Risborough: Shire Publications Ltd, 2007), pp. 24–27.
5. Major Sir Henry Legge-Bourke, *The Queen's Guards: Horse and Foot* (London: Macdonald & Co. (Publishers) Ltd., 1952 [1965]), p. 13.
6. Briant, *Fighting with the Guards*, p. 13.
7. Ronald Melvin, *The Guards and Caterham: The Soldier's Story* (Old Coulsdon: Guardroom Publications, 1999), pp. 13–17.
8. Melvin, *The Guards and Caterham*, pp. 60–61.
9. Briant, *Fighting with the Guards*, pp. 13–22.
10. Melvin, *The Guards and Caterham*, pp. 110–11.
11. Melvin, *The Guards and Caterham*, p. 2.
12. Russell Braddon, *All the Queen's Men: The Household Cavalry and the Brigade of Guards* (London: Hamish Hamilton, 1977), pp. 149–66.
13. Alan Allport, *Browned Off and Bloody-Minded: The British Soldier Goes to War, 1939–1945* (New Haven: Yale University Press, 2015), pp. 21–22.

14. Anthony Clayton, *The British Officer: Leading the Army from 1660 to the Present* (Harlow: Pearson Education Limited, 2006 [2007]), pp. 121–22.

15. Allport, *Browned Off and Bloody-Minded*, pp. 111–113.

16. Christopher Bulteel, *Something About a Soldier: The Wartime Memoirs of Christopher Bulteel, MC* (Shrewesbury: Airlife Publishing Ltd, 2000), pp. 16–32.

17. Michael Eliot Howard, *Captain Professor: A Life in War and Peace* (London: Continuum UK, 2006), pp. 53–58.

18. Peter Alexander Rupert Carrington, *Reflect on Things Past: The Memoirs of Lord Carrington* (Glasgow: Collins, 1988).

19. Carrington, *Reflect on Things Past*, p. 31.

20. TNA, CAB 120/414, Office of the Minister of Defence, Subject: Strategy and Operations. Combined Operations—Organisation, Etc. (3.6.1940–10.11.1943), 3 June 1940, Note from Churchill to General Ismay.

21. 'TNA, CAB 120/414, Office of the Minister of Defence, Subject: Strategy and Operations. Combined Operations—Organisation, Etc. (3.6.1940–10.11.1943), Notes on Raiding Operations, p. 1.'

22. TNA, CAB 120/414, Office of the Minister of Defence, Subject: Strategy and Operations. Combined Operations—Organisation, Etc. (3.6.1940–10.11.1943).

23. David Cannadine, *The Decline and Fall of the British Aristocracy* (London: Penguin Books Ltd, 2005), pp. 606–08.

24. Braddon, *All the Queen's Men*, pp. 163–64.

25. TNA, CAB 120/414, Office of the Minister of Defence, Subject: Strategy and Operations. Combined Operations—Organisation, Etc. (3.6.1940–10.11.1943), 23 July 1941, Prime Minister's Personal Minute, Serial No. D222/1, To General Ismay for C.O.S. Committee.

26. Patrick Forbes, *6th Guards Tank Brigade: The Story of Guardsmen in Churchill Tanks* (London: Sampson, Low, Marston & Co., 1946), pp. 8–12.

27. Howard, *Captain Professor*, pp. 53–58.

28. '"Scott's Last Expedition", First Published in 1913', *National Library of Scotland*, https://www.nls.uk/learning-zone/geography-and-exploration/scotts-last-expedition/published-account/ (accessed 17 October 2024).

29. TNA, PREM 3/103/1, Commandos and Special Companies 1940, Prime Minister's Personal Minutes, Note from Secretary of State for War, Anthony Eden to the Prime Minister, 26 August 1940.

30. *War Diaries, 1939–1945: Field Marshal Lord Alanbrooke, ed. by Alex Danchev and Daniel Todman* (London: Weidenfeld & Nicolson, 2001), p. 185.

CHAPTER 5

1. TNA, WO 218/166, War Diary, (Z Force) HQ Layforce, January–June 1941.
2. TNA, WO 218/166, War Diary, (Z Force) HQ Layforce, January–June 1941.
3. Antony Beevor, *Crete: The Battle and the Resistance* (London: John Murray (Publishers), 1991 [2005]), pp. 218–21.
4. Philip Eade, *Evelyn Waugh: A Life Revisited*, Kindle edn (London: Weidenfeld & Nicolson, 2016).
5. Robin Neillands, 'Layforce, 1941', in *The Raiders: The Army Commandos 1940–46* (London: Weidenfeld and Nicolson, 1989); Charles Messenger, 'Layforce and After', in *Commandos: The Definitive History of Commando Operations in the Second World War*, Kindle edn (London: HarperCollins Publishers, 2016).
6. IWM Sound Archive, Interview with George Patrick John Rushworth Jellicoe, Later Lord Jellicoe, Catalogue No. 13039, Produced: 1993, reel 2.
7. Mather, *With Stirling's SAS in the Desert*, pp. 49–53.

CHAPTER 6

1. The British Newspaper Archive (TBNA), 'Commando, Aged 36, Becomes Chief of Combined Operations', *News Chronicle* (London, 23 October 1943).
2. TBNA, 'Men Who Shape Our Destinies: No. 20 Major General Robert Edward Laycock, D.S.O., Chief of Combined Operations Since October 1943.', *The Illustrated London News* (London, 20 May 1944), p. 599.
3. Mead, *Commando General*, pp. 170–90.
4. Messenger, *Commandos*, pp. 267–93.
5. Mead, *Commando General*, pp. 197–15.
6. TNA, DEFE 2/1066, Major General R. E. Laycock, Biography and Other Papers Connected with Commando and Chief of Combined Operations Activities, an Article Written by Stuart Scheftel, p. 8.
7. Mead, *Commando General*, pp. 227–8.

CHAPTER 7

1. Churchill Archives Centre (CAC), The Papers of Brigadier Ralph Alger Bagnold, Press-Cuttings, 1939–1941, GBR/0014/BGND C.11., 1941.
2. Colin Smith, 'NASA Studies Martian Sand Dunes Named in Honour of Imperial Leading Light', *https://www.imperial.ac.uk/news/173278/nasa-studies-martian-sand-dunes-named/* (accessed 1 July 2016).

3. IWM Sound Archive, Interview with Ralph Bagnold, Catalogue No. 9862, Produced: 1997, reel 1.

4. Mike Morgan, *Sting of the Scorpion: The Inside Story of The Long Range Desert Group*, Kindle edn (Sutton Publishing, The History Press, 2000 [2011]), pp. 40–42.

5. Erskine, *Scots Guards*, p. 74.

6. 'Desert Innovator: Bagnold's Sun-Compass', Gunner Jimmy Patch The National Army Museum Https://Www.Nam.Ac.Uk/Explore/Sun-Compass.

7. IWM Sound Archive, Interview with Spencer William Seadon, 3rd Battalion Coldstream Guards, 1st Guards Brigade, Catalogue No. 19044, Produced: 1999, reel 1.

8. Michael Eliot Howard and John Hanbury Angus Sparrow, *The Coldstream Guards: 1920–1946* (Oxford: Oxford University Press, 1951), p. 561.

9. Michael Crichton-Stuart, *G Patrol* (William Kimber and Co. Limited, 1958 [1959]), pp. 22–26.

10 W. B. Kennedy Shaw, *Long Range Desert Group: Behind Enemy Lines in North Africa*, Kindle edn (Frontline Books, 1945 [2015]), pp. 23–26.

11. TNA, WO 201/716, ME, Layforce, A.G.—Questions, February–July 1941.

12. TNA, WO 201/717, Personal Papers Layforce Commander June–July 1941.

13. TNA, WO 201/716, ME, Layforce, A.G.—Questions, February–July 1941.

14. Mortimer, *David Stirling*, pp. 81–87.

15. IWM, Private Papers of Sir Carol Mather MC, Catalogue No. Documents.17403, Box No. 11/28/1, CM 4—Papers Relating to Lieutenant Jock Lewes and SAS Raids. 1941–1942., Training of Parachute Troops, Suggestions from Lieut. D. A. Stirling, Scots Guards.

16. Harvey Grenville, 'EXTENDED HISTORY OF 11 SPECIAL AIR SERVICE (SAS) BATTALION', *ParaData*, https://www.paradata.org.uk/article/extended-history-11-special-air-service-sas-battalion (accessed 4 August 2024).

17. TBNA, THEY WERE OURS! British Parachute Troops' Daring Drop into Italy, *Sunday Pictorial* (16 February 1941), p. 1.

18. IWM Sound Archive, Interview with George Patrick John Rushworth Jellicoe, Later Lord Jellicoe, Catalogue No. 13039, reel 2–3.

19. TNA, WO 201/716, Layforce—A.G. Questions, Feb/July 1941, Volunteers for Special S.S. Unit (GHQ MEF, CRME/1668/AG1), 8 August 1941, OC, "C" Bn LAYFORCE, 1941.

20. TNA, WO 201/721, History of SAS. 1941–42, Brief History of "L" Det. S.A.S. Brigade & 1st S.A.S. Regiment.; TNA, WO 201/785, S.A.S History of Parachute Det, June 1943.

21. IWM, Private Papers of Sir Carol Mather MC, Catalogue No. Documents.17403, Box No. 11/28/1, CM 4—PAPERS RELATING to LIEUTENANT JOCK LEWES AND SAS RAIDS. 1941–1942., Letter of Condolence from David Stirling to Mr Lewis [sic], 20 November 1942.

22. IWM, Private Papers, Misc: TVS (Television Scotland) SAS Interviews, Catalogue No. 21759, Box No. 62/137/1, David Stirling, Side 1, pp. 1–5.

23. IWM Sound Archive, Interview with David Carol Mather, Catalogue No. 19629, reel 4–5.

CHAPTER 8

1. Gilberto N. Villahermosa, 'THE SPEARHEAD SHATTERED', in *Hitler's Paratrooper: The Life and Battles of Rudolf Witzig* (Frontline Books, 2010).

2. TNA, PREM 3/32/1, Airborne Troops 1941, 22 June 1940, Churchill Writes Memo to General Ismay Requesting a Corps of at Least 5,000 Parachute Troops.

3. TNA, CAB 106/3, History of the Combined Operations Organisation 1940–1945.

4. 'No 1 PTS RAF Ringway, 1940–1946', *ParaData*, https://www.paradata. org.uk/unit/no-1-pts-raf-ringway, (accessed 27 December 2024).

5. Niall Cherry, *Striking Back: Britain's Airborne and Commando Raids 1940–1942* Kindle edn (Warwick: Helion & Company Ltd, 2009 [2010]), pp. 65–67.

6. Max Arthur, *Men of the Red Beret: Airborne Forces 1940–1990* (London: Hutchinson, 1990), p. xiv.

7. Cherry, *Striking Back*, pp. 76–82.

8. Arthur, *Men of the Red Beret*, pp. xiii-xvi.

9. Harvey Grenville, 'Extended History of 11 Special Air Service (SAS) Battalion', *ParaData*, https://www.paradata.org.uk/article/extended-history-11-special-air-service-sas-battalion (accessed 30 January 2025).

10. Alan Ogden, '"A DAMNED GOOD LOT" Major Peter Bromley-Martin, the Formation of the Parachute Regiment and the Valiant Death of Captain Michael Bolitho', *The Guards Magazine*, 2022, pp. 54–55.

11. Arthur, *Men of the Red Beret*, p. 3.

12. Reg Curtis, *The Memory Endures: The Story of a Grenadier Guardsman and Pioneer of the Parachute Regiment 1937–1945* (Pilots Publishing, 2014), pp. 43–44.

13. Hilary St George Saunders, *The Red Beret* (London: New English Library, 1971), p. 42.

14. LHCMA, Laycock 1/3 2/1-3, MAY/224/A Engagement of Volunteers, 19 July 1940.

15. TNA, WO 166/4107, War Diary, 1st Battalion, Scots Guards, 24th Guards Brigade, September 1939–December 1941.

16. Curtis, *The Memory Endures*, pp. 21–34.

17. IWM Sound Archive, Interview with John Morgan-Griffiths, Guardsman, Headquarters Company, 2nd Battalion Irish Guards, 20th Guards Brigade, Catalogue No: 15478, Produced: 1995, reel 1.

18. N. Cherry, 'Tragino (Operation Colossus)', *ParaData*, https://www.paradata.org.uk/event/tragino-operation-colossus (accessed 2 March 2025).

19. Arthur, *Men of the Red Beret*, p. 8.

20. Raymond Foxall, *The Guinea-Pigs: Britain's First Paratroop Raid* (London: Robert Hale, 1983), p. 17.

21. Foxall, *The Guinea-Pigs*, pp. 58–59.

22. 'Major-General Deane-Drummond on Blowing the Tragino Aqueduct', *ParaData*, https://www.paradata.org.uk/media/69 (accessed 2 March 2025).

23. Foxall, *The Guinea-Pigs*, pp. 77–78.

24. Foxall, *The Guinea-Pigs*, p. 81.

25. Lawrence Paterson, *Operation Colossus: The First British Airborne Raid of World War II* Kindle edn (London: Greenhill Books, 2020), pp. 200–02.

26. 'Major-General Deane-Drummond on the Tragino Raid: Ex-Filtration to Submarine', *ParaData*, https://www.paradata.org.uk/media/70 (accessed 2 March 2025).

27. TNA, PREM 3/100, 1941, Colossus Operation in Italy, January–February 1941.

28. TBNA, 'THEY WERE OURS—Official!', *Sunday Pictorial*, 16 February 1941.

29. '1941: British Parachutists Invade Italy', *International Herald Tribune*, https://archive.nytimes.com/iht-retrospective.blogs.nytimes.com/2016/02/15/1941-british-parachutists-invade-italy/ (accessed 2 March 2025).

30. Tragino (Operation Colossus), Official Accounts 2, *ParaData* (accessed 2 March 2025).

31. St George Saunders, *The Red Beret*, pp. 17–18.

CHAPTER 9

1. William F. Buckingham, *Paras: The Birth of British Airborne Forces from Churchill's Raiders to 1st Parachute Brigade* (Stroud: Tempus Publishing Ltd, 2005), pp. 69–71.

2. John Greenacre, *Churchill's Spearhead: The Development of Britain's Airborne Forces in World War II*, Kindle edn (Barnsley: Pen & Sword Aviation, 2010), pp. 64–66.
3. TNA, AIR 2/7239, Air Ministry or Royal Air Force, Airborne Forces Organisation, Parachute Troops Corps, 10 June 1940.
4. *By Air to Battle: The Official History of the British Paratroops in World War II*, ed. by Bob Carruthers (Barnsley: Pen & Sword Aviation, 1945 [2012]), pp. 10–12.
5. TNA, CAB/80/57/04, Appendix to Enclosure 5., Air Staff Note., Present Situation in Respect to the Development of Parachute Training, Plans, 12 August 1940, p. 8.
6. Carruthers, *By Air to Battle*, pp. 23–25.
7. TNA, AIR 2/7239, Air Ministry or Royal Air Force, Airborne Forces Organisation, Minutes of a Meeting Held on Wednesday 11th December 1940, at the Air Ministry to Recommend Action and Formulate Air Ministry Policy Regarding the Raising and Training of Airborne Forces.
8. Greenacre, *Churchill's Spearhead*, p. 75.
9. TNA, CAB/80/57/04, War Cabinet, Chiefs of Staff Committee, Parachute Troops and Gliders, 26 May 1941. Prime Minister's Personal Minute Serial No. D. 169/1.
10. Buckingham, *Paras*, pp. 173–76.
11. TNA, AIR 2/7574, Ministry of Defence, Parachute Troops, Training of., a Letter from Major General F. A. M. Browning, Commander, The Airborne Division, to GHQ Home Forces on the Subject of Accommodation for the 1st Parachute Brigade, 2 December 1941.
12. Buckingham, *Paras*, pp. 176–77.
13. TNA, WO 32/4723, The War Office, Parachute Badge 1940, Urgent Postal Telegram, from the Director of Recruiting and Organisation to the GOCs of All UK Army Districts, Volunteers for Special Service (Physical Standards for Parachute Units), 30 June 1940.
14. TNA, WO 166/1151, War Diary, Headquarters, 1st Parachute Brigade, 1941. Report on Medical Fitness of Parachute Troops.
15. TNA, AIR 2/7574, Ministry of Defence, Parachute Troops, Training of., Conclusions of a Conference Held in Room 414 Bush House on the 21st of November 1941. Formation of New Units for the Airborne Forces Establishment, Air Ministry, Director of Organisation, 22 November 1941.
16. TNA, AIR 2/7574, Ministry of Defence, Parachute Troops, Training of., War Office Memorandum 0164/6437(S.D.4.) on "the Policy to Be Adopted for the Composition of Airborne Forces Which Are to Be Formed in the United Kingdom and Overseas", 29 October 1941.

CHAPTER 10

1. Richard Mead, *General 'BOY', The Life of Lieutenant General Sir Frederick Browning* (Barnsley: Pen & Sword Military, 2010), pp. 5–10.
2. Mark Urban, *Red Devils: The Trailblazers of the Parachute Regiment in World War Two: An Authorised History* (London: Viking, 2022), p. 30.
3. Mead, *General 'BOY'*, pp. 11–30.
4. Major P A J Wright OBE, 'The Capture of Gauche Wood—1st December 1917', *The Grenadier Guards Gazette*, Issue No. 40, 2017, pp. 32–34.
5. Mead, *General 'BOY'*, pp. 31–39.
6. Mead, *General 'BOY'*, pp. 45–50.
7. William F. Buckingham, *Arnhem 1944* (Stroud: Tempus Publishing Ltd, 2002 [2004]), p. 15.
8. Urban, *Red Devils*, p. 30.
9. Charles Richard Trumpess, *A History of the Guards Armoured Formations 1941–1945* (Barnsley: Pen & Sword Military, 2025), pp. 7–8.
10. Danchev and Todman, *War Diaries, 1939–1945: Field Marshal Lord Alanbrooke*, p. 193.
11. Mead, *General 'BOY'*, p. 69.
12. David Fraser, *Alanbrooke* (London: HarperCollins Publishers, 1982 [1997]), p. 187.
13. Buckingham, *Arnhem 1944*, pp. 14–15.
14. Mead, *General 'BOY'*, p. 70.
15. Urban, *Red Devils*, pp. 31–41.
16. Buckingham, *Arnhem 1944*, p. 17.
17. Buckingham, *Arnhem 1944*, p. 16.
18. TBNA, 'Our Parachute Regiment', *Daily Herald* (London, 9 December 1942).
19. Buckingham, *Arnhem 1944*, pp. 17–18.
20. Lewis Sorley (ed.), *Gavin at War: The World War II Diary of Lieutenant General James M. Gavin* (Havertown: Casemate Publishers, 2022), pp. 59–60.
21. Gavin Mortimer, *2SAS: Bill Stirling and the Forgotten Special Forces Unit of World War II*, Kindle edn (Oxford: Osprey Publishing, 2023), pp. 242–44.
22. IWM, Private Papers, Documents.21759, Box No 62-137-1, Misc: TVS, SAS Interviews, Transcript, Subject: Pat Hart.
23. Buckingham, *Arnhem 1944*, p. 9.
24. Buckingham, *Arnhem 1944*, pp. 229–30.

CHAPTER 11

1. Andrew Lennox Hargreaves, 'An Analysis of the Rise, Use, Evolution and Value of Anglo-American Commando and Special Forces Formations, 1939–1945', PhD thesis (King's College London, 2008), pp. 177–90.
2. John Robert Peaty, 'British Army Manpower Crisis 1944', PhD thesis (King's College London, 2000), pp. 107–11.
3. Hargreaves, 'An Analysis of the Rise, Use, Evolution and Value of Anglo-American Commando and Special Forces Formations, 1939–1945', pp. 205–07.
4. Hargreaves, 'An Analysis of the Rise, Use, Evolution and Value of Anglo-American Commando and Special Forces Formations, 1939–1945', pp. 221–27.
5. William Frederick Buckingham, 'The Establishment and Initial Development of a British Airborne Force, June 1940–January 1942', PhD Thesis (University of Glasgow, 2001), p. 288.
6. Hargreaves, 'An Analysis of the Rise, Use, Evolution and Value of Anglo-American Commando and Special Forces Formations, 1939–1945', pp. 228–30.
7. Greenacre, *Churchill's Spearhead*, pp. 179–93.
8. Hargreaves, 'An Analysis of the Rise, Use, Evolution and Value of Anglo-American Commando and Special Forces Formations, 1939–1945', pp. 236–38.
9. Greenacre, *Churchill's Spearhead*, pp. 179–193.
10. Hargreaves, 'An Analysis of the Rise, Use, Evolution and Value of Anglo-American Commando and Special Forces Formations, 1939–1945', pp. 243–47.
11. Hargreaves, 'An Analysis of the Rise, Use, Evolution and Value of Anglo-American Commando and Special Forces Formations, 1939–1945', p. 182.
12. Hargreaves, 'An Analysis of the Rise, Use, Evolution and Value of Anglo-American Commando and Special Forces Formations, 1939–1945'.
13. Peter R. Mansoor and Williamson Murray (eds), *The Culture of Military Organizations* (Cambridge University Press, 2019 [2021]), pp. 201–02.
14. Hargreaves, 'An Analysis of the Rise, Use, Evolution and Value of Anglo-American Commando and Special Forces Formations, 1939–1945', pp. 231–55.
15. Allport, *Browned Off and Bloody-Minded*, pp. 217–20.
16. Buckingham, 'The Establishment and Initial Development of a British Airborne Force, June 1940–January 1942', pp. 289–90.

CHAPTER 12

1. J. N. P. Watson, *Guardsmen of the Sky: An Account of the Involvement of Household Troops in the Airborne Forces* (Wilby: Michael Russell (Publishing) Ltd, 1997), pp. 37–43.
2. 'No. 1 (GUARDS) INDEPENDENT COMPANY, THE PARACHUTE REGIMENT', *The Guards Magazine*, Autumn, 1975, p. 110.
3. Watson, *Guardsmen of the Sky*, p. 50.
4. 'No. 1 (GUARDS) INDEPENDENT COMPANY, THE PARACHUTE REGIMENT', p. 111.
5. Watson, *Guardsmen of the Sky*, pp. 50–51.
6. Watson, *Guardsmen of the Sky*, pp. 59–73.
7. 'No. 1 (GUARDS) INDEPENDENT COMPANY, THE PARACHUTE REGIMENT', pp. 112–115.
8. Watson, *Guardsmen of the Sky*, pp. 80–84.
9. Watson, *Guardsmen of the Sky*, pp. 91–106.
10. 'No. 1 (GUARDS) INDEPENDENT COMPANY, THE PARACHUTE REGIMENT', pp. 116–119.
11. 'No. 1 (GUARDS) INDEPENDENT COMPANY, THE PARACHUTE REGIMENT', p. 118.
12. Watson, *Guardsmen of the Sky*, p. 133.
13. 'No. 1 (GUARDS) INDEPENDENT COMPANY, THE PARACHUTE REGIMENT', p. 119.
14. Watson, *Guardsmen of the Sky*, p. 149.
15. 'Guards Parachute Platoon, 3 PARA', *ParaData*, https://www.paradata.org.uk/unit/guards-parachute-platoon-3-para (accessed 21 March 2025).
16. 'Formation of 5 Airborne Brigade', *ParaData*, https://www.paradata.org.uk/article/formation-5-airborne-brigade (accessed 21 March 2025).
17. Officer Commanding G Squadron SAS, 'The Guards and the SAS', *The Guards Magazine*, 2008, p. 242.
18. A Welsh Guards Lance Corporal G Squadron 22 SAS, 'A SOLDIER'S VIEW OF G SQUADRON', *The Guards Magazine*, Spring, 2009, pp. 68–69.

CHAPTER 13

1. LHCMA, Laycock Personal Papers, King's College London KCL 6-15-16 Correspondence 1942, Letter from Robert Laycock to Shimi Lovat, No 4. Commando, 3 December 1942.
2. Mortimer, *2SAS*, p. 248.
3. *The Diaries of Evelyn Waugh*, p. 488.
4. Urban, *Red Devils*, pp. 31–41.

Bibliography

Archives (primary sources, unpublished)

CHURCHILL ARCHIVES CENTRE
'Churchill Archives Centre, The Papers of Brigadier Ralph Alger Bagnold, Press-
    Cuttings, 1939–1941, GBR/0014/BGND C.11.', 1941

IMPERIAL WAR MUSEUM (IWM)
IWM, Private Papers, Documents.21759, Box No 62-137-1, Misc: TVS, SAS
    Interviews, Transcript, Subject: Pat Hart.
IWM, Private Papers, Misc: TVS (Television Scotland) SAS Interviews, Catalogue
    No. 21759, Box No. 62/137/1, David Stirling, Side 1, Pages 1–5.
IWM, Private Papers of Sir Carol Mather MC, Catalogue No.
    Documents.17403, Box No. 11/28/1, CM 4—PAPERS RELATING to
    LIEUTENANT JOCK LEWES AND SAS RAIDS. 1941–1942., Letter of
    Condolence from David Stirling to Mr Lewis [sic], 20 November 1942.
IWM, Private Papers of Sir Carol Mather MC, Catalogue No.
    Documents.17403, Box No. 11/28/1, CM 4—Papers Relating to Lieutenant
    Jock Lewes and SAS Raids. 1941–1942., Training of Parachute Troops,
    Suggestions from Lieut. D. A. Stirling, Scots Guards.
IWM Sound Archive, Interview with David Carol Mather, Catalogue No. 19629,
    reel 1, 1999
IWM Sound Archive, Interview with George Patrick John Rushworth Jellicoe,
    Later Lord Jellicoe, Catalogue No. 13039, reel 1, 1993
IWM Sound Archive, Interview with James Barlow Brooks Sherwood, British
    NCO Who Served with No. 8 Troop, No. 8 Commando, Catalogue No. 9783,
    Produced 1987, reel 1, 1987

IWM Sound Archive, Interview with John Morgan-Griffiths, Guardsman, Headquarters Company, 2nd Battalion Irish Guards, 20th Guards Brigade, Catalogue No: 15478, reel 1, 1995

IWM Sound Archive, Interview with Ralph Bagnold, Catalogue No. 9862, reel 1, 1997

IWM Sound Archive, Interview with Spencer William Seadon, 3rd Battalion Coldstream Guards, 1st Guards Brigade, Catalogue No. 19044, reel 1, 1999

THE LIDDELL HART CENTRE FOR MILITARY ARCHIVES (LHCMA), KING'S COLLEGE LONDON

Laycock 1/3 2/1-3, MAY/224/A Engagement of Volunteers, 19 July 1940.

Laycock 1/3, Engagement of Volunteers, Conditions of Service for All Personnel of Commandos, 1940.

Laycock Personal Papers, King's College London KCL 6-15-16 Correspondence 1942, Letter from Robert Laycock to Shimi Lovat, No 4. Commando, 3 December 1942.

Laycock 1/1—Papers Relating to Volunteers for Special Service Brigade, 1940.

THE NATIONAL ARCHIVES (TNA), LONDON

AIR 2/7239, Air Ministry or Royal Air Force, Airborne Forces Organisation, Minutes of a Meeting Held on Wednesday 11th December 1940, at the Air Ministry to Recommend Action and Formulate Air Ministry Policy Regarding the Raising and Training of Airborne Forces.

AIR 2/7239, Air Ministry or Royal Air Force, Airborne Forces Organisation, Parachute Troops Corps, 10 June 1940

AIR 2/7574, Ministry of Defence, Parachute Troops, Training of., a Letter from Major General F. A. M. Browning, Commander, The Airborne Division, to GHQ Home Forces on the Subject of Accommodation for the 1st Parachute Brigade, 2 December 1941

AIR 2/7574, Ministry of Defence, Parachute Troops, Training of., Conclusions of a Conference Held in Room 414 Bush House on the 21st of November 1941. Formation of New Units for the Airborne Forces Establishment, Air Ministry, Director of Organisation, 22 November 1941

AIR 2/7574, Ministry of Defence, Parachute Troops, Training of., War Office Memorandum 0164/6437(S.D.4.) on 'the Policy to Be Adopted for the Composition of Airborne Forces Which Are to Be Formed in the United Kingdom and Overseas', 29 October 1941

CAB 106/3, *History of the Combined Operations Organisation 1940–1945* (London, 1956)

CAB 106/7, Combined Operations

CAB 106/7, *Combined Operations, Development of Combined Operations Part 1. Historical Summary*

CAB 120/414, Office of the Minister of Defence, Subject: Strategy and Operations. Combined Operations—Organisation, Etc. (3.6.1940–10.11.1943).

CAB/80/57/04, Appendix to Enclosure 5., Air Staff Note., Present Situation in Respect to the Development of Parachute Training, Plans, 12 August 1940, p. 8.

CAB/80/57/04, War Cabinet, Chiefs of Staff Committee, Parachute Troops and Gliders, 26 May 1941. Prime Minister's Personal Minute Serial No. D. 169/1.

DEFE 2/54, Commando War Diaries. SS Brigade Vol. I. 1st Oct 1940–31st Aug 1941

DEFE 2/1066, Major General R. E. Laycock, Biography and Other Papers Connected with Commando and Chief of Combined Operations Activities, an Article Written by Stuart Scheftel, p. 8.

PREM 3/32/1, Airborne Troops 1941, 22 June 1940, Churchill Writes Memo to General Ismay Requesting a Corps of at Least 5,000 Parachute Troops

PREM 3/100, 1941, Colossus Operation in Italy, January to February 1941

PREM 3/103/1, Commandos and Special Companies 1940, Prime Minister's Personal Minutes, Note from Secretary of State for War, Anthony Eden to the Prime Minister, 26 August 1940

WO 32/4723, The War Office, Parachute Badge 1940, Urgent Postal Telegram, from the Director of Recruiting and Organisation to the GOCs of All UK Army Districts, Volunteers for Special Service (Physical Standards for Parachute Units), 30 June 1940

WO 166/1151, War Diary, Headquarters, 1st Parachute Brigade, 1941. Report on Medical Fitness of Parachute Troops

WO 166/4107, War Diary, 1st Battalion, Scots Guards, 24th Guards Brigade, September 1939–December 1941

WO 199/1849, Formation of Irregular Commandos, June 1940–September 1942, Memorandum on the Selection of Volunteers for Special Service Units, 23 April 1941

WO 201/716, Layforce—A.G. Questions, Feb/July 1941, Volunteers for Special S.S. Unit (GHQ MEF, CRME/1668/AG1), 8 August 1941, OC, "C" Bn LAYFORCE

WO 201/716, ME, Layforce, A.G. —Questions, February–July 1941

WO 201/717, Personal Papers Layforce Commander June–July 1941

WO 201/721, History of SAS. 1941–42, Brief History of "L" Det. S.A.S. Brigade & 1st S.A.S. Regiment

WO 201/785, S.A.S History of Parachute Det, June 1943

WO 218/8, War Diary, No. 8 Commando, July–November 1940
WO 218/166, War Diary, (Z Force) HQ Layforce, January–June 1941

PRIMARY SOURCES, PUBLISHED

Bulteel, Christopher, *Something About a Soldier: The Wartime Memoirs of Christopher Bulteel, MC* (Airlife Publishing Ltd, 2000)

Carrington, Peter Alexander Rupert, *Reflect on Things Past: The Memoirs of Lord Carrington* (Collins, 1988)

Crichton-Stuart, Michael, *G Patrol* (William Kimber and Co. Limited, 1959)

Curtis, Reg, *The Memory Endures: The Story of a Grenadier Guardsman and Pioneer of the Parachute Regiment 1937–1945* (Pilots Publishing, 2014)

Danchev, Alex, and Daniel Todman (eds), *War Diaries, 1939–1945: Field Marshal Lord Alanbrooke* (Weidenfeld & Nicolson, 2001)

Davie, Michael (ed.), *The Diaries of Evelyn Waugh* (Phoenix, 1995)

Feebery, David, *Guardsman & Commando: The War Memoirs of RSM Cyril Feebery DCM* (Pen & Sword Military, 2008)

Howard, Michael Eliot, *Captain Professor: A Life in War and Peace* (Continuum UK, 2006)

Kemp, Peter, 'Chapter Two: Operation "Knife"', in *No Colours or Crest: The Secret Struggle for Europe*, Kindle edn, 1958, pp. 11–17

Kennedy Shaw, W. B., *Long Range Desert Group: Behind Enemy Lines in North Africa*, Kindle edn (Frontline Books, 1945)

Lovat, Lord, *March Past: A Memoir By Lord Lovat* (Weidenfeld and Nicolson, 1978)

Mather, Carol, *With Stirling's SAS in the Desert* (Pen & Sword Military, 1997)

Niven, David, *The Moon's a Balloon: The Guardian's Number One Hollywood Autobiography*, Kindle edn (Penguin, 2005)

Sorley, Lewis, ed., *Gavin at War: The World War II Diary of Lieutenant General James M. Gavin* (Casemate Publishers, 2022)

Secondary Sources

BOOKS

Allport, Alan, *Browned Off and Bloody-Minded: The British Soldier Goes to War, 1939–1945* (Yale University Press, 2015)

Arthur, Max, *Men of the Red Beret: Airborne Forces 1940–1990* (Hutchinson, 1990)

Beckett, Ian F., 'Household Cavalry and Foot Guards', in *Discovering British Regimental Traditions*, 2nd edn (Shire Publications Ltd, 2007)

Beevor, Antony, *Crete: The Battle and the Resistance* (John Murray (Publishers), 2005)

Braddon, Russell, *All the Queen's Men: The Household Cavalry and the Brigade of Guards* (Hamish Hamilton, 1977)

Briant, Keith, *Fighting with the Guards* (Evans Bros. Ltd, 1958)

Buckingham, William F., *Arnhem 1944* (Tempus Publishing Ltd, 2004)

Buckingham, William F., *Paras The Birth of British Airborne Forces from Churchill's Raiders to 1st Parachute Brigade* (Tempus Publishing Ltd, 2005)

Cannadine, David, *The Decline and Fall of the British Aristocracy* (Penguin Books Ltd, 2005)

Carruthers, Bob, ed., *By Air to Battle: The Official History of the British Paratroops in World War II* (Pen & Sword Aviation, 2012)

Cherry, Niall, *Striking Back: Britain's Airborne and Commando Raids 1940–1942*, Kindle edn (Helion & Company Ltd, 2009)

Clayton, Anthony, *The British Officer: Leading the Army from 1660 to the Present* (Pearson Education Limited, 2007)

Eade, Philip, *Evelyn Waugh: A Life Revisited*, Kindle edn (Weidenfeld & Nicolson, 2016)

Erskine, David, *The Scots Guards, 1919–1955* (William Clowes and Sons Ltd, 1956)

Foxall, Raymond, *The Guinea-Pigs: Britain's First Paratroop Raid* (Robert Hale, 1983)

Fraser, David, *Alanbrooke* (HarperCollins Publishers, 1997)

St George Saunders, Hilary, *The Red Beret* (New English Library, 1971)

Greenacre, John, *Churchill's Spearhead: The Development of Britain's Airborne Forces in World War II*, Kindle edn (Pen & Sword Aviation, 2010)

Forbes, Patrick, *6th Guards Tank Brigade: The Story of Guardsmen in Churchill Tanks*, The Naval (Sampson, Low, Marston & Co, 1946)

Hoe, Alan, *David Stirling: The Authorised Biography of the Creator of the SAS* (Warner Books, 1992)

Howard, Michael Eliot, and John Hanbury Angus Sparrow, *The Coldstream Guards: 1920–1946* (Oxford University Press, 1951)

Joll, Christopher, and Anthony Weldon, *The Drum Horse in the Fountain & Other Tales of Heroes and Rogues in the Guards* (Nine Elms Publishing, 2018)

Legge-Bourke, Major Sir Henry, *The Queen's Guards: Horse and Foot* (Macdonald & Co. (Publishers) Ltd., 1965)

Lewes, John, *Jock Lewes: Co-Founder of the SAS*, Kindle (Pen & Sword Military, 2000)

Mansoor, Peter R., and Williamson Murray (eds.), *The Culture of Military Organizations* (Cambridge University Press, 2021)

Mead, Richard, *Commando General: The Life of Major General Sir Robert Laycock KCMG, CB, DSO* (Pen & Sword Military, 2016)

Mead, Richard, *General 'BOY', The Life of Lieutenant General Sir Frederick Browning* (Pen & Sword Military, 2010)

Melvin, Ronald, *The Guards and Caterham: The Soldier's Story* (Guardroom Publications, 1999)

Messenger, Charles, *Commandos: The Definitive History of Commando Operations in the Second World War*, paperback edn (William Collins, 2015)

Messenger, Charles, 'Layforce and After', in *Commandos: The Definitive History of Commando Operations in the Second World War*, Kindle edn (HarperCollins Publishers, 2016)

Morgan, Mike, *Sting of the Scorpion: The Inside Story of The Long Range Desert Group* , Kindle edn (Sutton Publishing, The History Press , 2011)

Mortimer, Gavin, *2SAS: Bill Stirling and the Forgotten Special Forces Unit of World War II*, Kindle (Osprey Publishing, 2023)

Mortimer, Gavin, *David Stirling The Phoney Major: The Life, Times and Truth about the Founder of the SAS* (Constable, 2022)

Neillands, Robin, 'Layforce, 1941', in *The Raiders: The Army Commandos 1940–46* (Weidenfeld and Nicolson, 1989)

Neillands, Robin, *The Raiders: The Army Commandos, 1940–1946* (Weidenfeld and Nicolson, 1989)

Part 1: Col. R. J. Marker, DSO, Part 2: Maj. Gen. A. G. C. Dawnay, CBE, DSO, Part 3: Col. E. R. Hill, *The Record of the Coldstream Guards 1650–1950* (London: Williams Clowes and Sons Ltd, 1950)

Paterson, Lawrence, *Operation Colossus: The First British Airborne Raid of World War II*, Kindle edn (Greenhill Books, 2020)

Saunders, Hilary St George, *The Green Beret: The Story of the Commandos 1940–1945* (Michael Joseph Ltd, 1949)

Trumpess, Charles Richard, *A History of the Guards Armoured Formations 1941–1945* (Pen & Sword Military, 2025)

Urban, Mark, *Red Devils: The Trailblazers of the Parachute Regiment in World War Two: An Authorized History* (Viking, 2022)

Villahermosa, Gilberto N., 'THE SPEARHEAD SHATTERED', in *Hitler's Paratrooper: The Life and Battles of Rudolf Witzig* (Frontline Books, 2010)

Watson, J. N. P., *Guardsmen of the Sky: An Account of the Involvement of Household Troops in the Airborne Forces* (Michael Russell (Publishing) Ltd, 1997)

Young, Peter, *Commando: A History of the Elite British Military Force and Its Operations in World War Two* (Sapere Books, 1969)

Journals and Newspapers

A Welsh Guards Lance Corporal G Squadron 22 SAS, 'A SOLDIER'S VIEW OF
G SQUADRON', *The Guards Magazine*, 2009, pp. 68–69

'No. 1 (GUARDS) INDEPENDENT COMPANY, THE PARACHUTE
REGIMENT', *The Guards Magazine*, 1975, pp. 110–110

Officer Commanding G Squadron SAS, 'The Guards and the SAS', *The Guards
Magazine*, 2008, p. 242

Ogden, Alan, '"A DAMNED GOOD LOT" Major Peter Bromley-Martin, the
Formation of the Parachute Regiment and the Valiant Death of Captain
Michael Bolitho', *The Guards Magazine*, 2022, pp. 54–55

Speares, Captain J. A., 'Recollections of the 5th Special Reserve Battalion Scots
Guards', *The Guards Magazine*, 1999, pp. 59–61

Commando, Aged 36, Becomes Chief of Combined Operations, *News Chronicle*
(London, 23 October 1943)

Men Who Shape Our Destinies: No. 20 Major General Robert Edward Laycock,
D.S.O., Chief of Combined Operations Since October 1943., *The Illustrated
London News* (London, 20 May 1944), p. 599

Our Parachute Regiment, *Daily Herald* (London, 9 December 1942)

THEY WERE OURS! British Parachute Troops' Daring Drop into Italy, *Sunday
Pictorial* (London, 16 February 1941), p. 1

Wright OBE, Major P A J, 'The Capture of Gauche Wood -- 1st December 1917',
The Grenadier Guards Gazette, 2017, pp. 32–34

Academic Papers

Buckingham, William Frederick, 'The Establishment and Initial Development of
a British Airborne Force, June 1940–January 1942', PhD thesis (University of
Glasgow, 2001)

Hargreaves, Andrew Lennox, 'An Analysis of the Rise, Use, Evolution and Value
of Anglo-American Commando and Special Forces Formations, 1939–1945',
PhD thesis (King's College London, 2008)

Lea, T. G., 'The employment and development of Britain's Second World War
commando, 1940–1941', MA diss. (University of Chester, United Kingdom,
2010)

Peaty, John Robert, 'British Army manpower crisis 1944', PhD thesis (King's
College London, 2000)

Websites

'1941: British Parachutists Invade Italy', *International Herald Tribune*, https://archive.nytimes.com/iht-retrospective.blogs.nytimes.com/2016/02/15/1941-british-parachutists-invade-italy/ (accessed 2 March 2025)

Cherry, N, 'Tragino (Operation Colossus)', *ParaData*, https://www.paradata.org.uk/event/tragino-operation-colossus (accessed 2 March 2025)

'Desert Innovator: Bagnold's Sun-Compass', *The National Army Museum*, https://www.nam.ac.uk/explore/sun-compass

'Formation of 5 Airborne Brigade', *ParaData*, https://www.paradata.org.uk/article/formation-5-airborne-brigade (accessed 21 March 2025)

Grenville, Harvey, 'EXTENDED HISTORY OF 11 SPECIAL AIR SERVICE (SAS) BATTALION', *ParaData*, https://www.paradata.org.uk/article/extended-history-11-special-air-service-sas-battalion (accessed 4 August 2024)

'Guards Parachute Platoon, 3 PARA', *ParaData*, https://www.paradata.org.uk/unit/guards-parachute-platoon-3-para (accessed 21 March 2025)

'Https://Theguardsdepot.Co.Uk/Shining-Parades-Swabbing-and-Losing-Your-Name/', *The Guards Depot*

'Major-General Deane-Drummond on Blowing the Tragino Aqueduct', *ParaData*, https://www.paradata.org.uk/media/69 (accessed 2 March 2025)

'Major-General Deane-Drummond on the Tragino Raid: Ex-Filtration to Submarine', *ParaData*, https://www.paradata.org.uk/media/70 (accessed 2 March 2025)

'No 1 PTS RAF Ringway, 1940–1946', *ParaData*, https://www.paradata.org.uk/unit/no-1-pts-raf-ringway (accessed 27 December 2024)

'"Scott's Last Expedition", First Published in 1913', *National Library of Scotland*, https://www.nls.uk/learning-zone/geography-and-exploration/scotts-last-expedition/published-account/ (accessed 17 October 2024)

Smith, Colin, 'NASA Studies Martian Sand Dunes Named in Honour of Imperial Leading Light', *https://www.imperial.ac.uk/news/173278/nasa-studies-martian-sand-dunes-named/* (accessed 1 July 2016)

'Tragino (Operation Colossus), Official Accounts 2', *ParaData*, https://www.paradata.org.uk/event/tragino-operation-colossus (accessed 2 March 2025)